REG EVERETT

From Rocker to RACER

Dedication

Several people could qualify for the dedication of this book, none more so than my dear wife Ronnie who has been through a really trying period, coping with many losses and also my serious illness.

The main instigator, though, in inciting me to put pen to paper was my close long-time friend Mike Balls, who first put the idea into my mind late one evening. We were together on the river bank eeling after a session in the local pub. We talked and reminisced, and he said then that I must write my story, as what happened was a passage in our history which will never be repeated.

Sadly, Mike is no longer with us as he was seriously ill at the same time as I, and he finally succumbed. Both of us were writing at the time and it helped with the situation as there was little else we could do.

So, Mike, this book is for you with my gratitude and thanks for so many good times and happy memories.

Reg Everett

REG EVERETT
From Rocker to
RACER

REG EVERETT with Mick Walker

breedon **books**
PUBLISHING

First published in Great Britain in 2009 by
The Breedon Books Publishing Company Limited
Breedon House, 3 The Parker Centre,
Derby, DE21 4SZ.

ISBN 978-1-85983-679-8

Printed and bound Gutenberg Press Ltd, Malta.

Contents

Every so often a unique snapshot of times gone by is discovered in a dusty vault or in shoeboxes in an attic by an enthusiastic amateur photographer. They are living history. Each and every one of us cannot resist the temptation as we marvel at the quality of the images, to let our mind drift back to the good old days and wonder what it was really like.

We at Mortons Motorcycle Media, market-leading publishers of classic and vintage titles, own one of the largest photographic archives of its kind in the world. It is a treasure trove of millions of motorcycle and related images, many of which have never seen the light of day since they were filed away in the dark-room almost 100 years ago.

Perhaps the biggest gem of all is our collection of glass plates – almost two tons of them to be precise! They represent a largely hitherto unseen look into our motorcycling heritage from the turn of the century. Many of the plates are priceless and capture an era long gone when the pace of life was much slower and traffic jams were unheard of.

We are delighted to be associated with well known author Mick Walker in the production of this book and hope you enjoy the images from our archive.

Terry Clark,
Managing Director,
Mortons Media Group Ltd

Acknowledgements

I really must say that I just did not realise the amount of investigative work a book of this nature would involve. Trying to obtain all the programmes and official results was a most daunting task – helped, fortunately, by all my original photos and records made at the time. Without the help of Joe Iszard, Dick Standing and Martin Hayward, who had boxes of their own collections of results and programmes, it would have been impossible and with the exception of just one or two we together managed to make a complete set.

Stuart Hull, my long-serving mechanic/assistant and friend, came up with many reminiscences and photographs to jog my memory. Bob Baxter (one of the original members of the Blue Star gang) helped in this area, especially with a great photograph of us all – priceless. John Parry and Malcolm Hasler (Derek's younger brother) from Greenways assisted in the Early Day's memories, Ron Freeman with the Southend boys, and Bunny Dowsett with the Gold Star rockers.

Sponsors Derek Cornell, Brian Woolley, Pat Onions, Geoff Dodkin and Vic Camp were inspirational, and my unconditional gratitude goes to them for what they did for me during my racing days. I must also mention Bob Mills of Greeves, the only one there who really helped (with the backing of Derry Preston-Cobb) and who gave me his full support. Without this, the Greeves road racer would never have been a reality.

Very special thanks go to Ted Broad for providing me with not only the machines to do the job, but also his total commitment to me and my racing career.

Additionally, to all the other racers, bikers, mechanics, fans, spectators, The St Johns Ambulance who picked me up, friends and Val Seller who kindly typed the manuscript.

Finally, the indebted acknowledgement to Mick Walker, without whose help, guidance and expertise this book would never have materialised.

Reg Everett

Foreword

I have written well over 100 books during the last 25 years or so, and I have been sent several manuscripts throughout that time from other, prospective authors. Sadly, the vast majority of these have not been of sufficient quality and I have been faced with the unenviable task of telling the person concerned. Although it is always best to be entirely truthful in these matters, it is nonetheless still difficult to tell someone this fact.

I have known Reg Everett for many, many years. First, when as an enthusiastic spectator I watched his early racing career, then, from the mid-1960s as a fellow

21.	S. P. Hitchcock	...	Bultaco	59.	G. A. Kennedy	...	Greeves
23.	L. C. Harfield	...	LCH Honda	61.	M. Ing	...	D.M.W.
25.	E. G. Kismul	...	D.M.W.	63.	R. A. Holmes	...	Aer Macchi
27.	M. J. Edland	...	Ducati	65.	A. Plumridge	...	Greeves
29.	J. D. Aldworth	...	Greeves	67.	R. Scivyer	...	F.H.S.
31.	M. Baker	...	Greeves	69.	D. T. Page	...	Bultaco
33.	D. Starkey	...	Honda	**71.**	**M. Walker**	...	**Ducati**
35.	A. E. Dawson	...	N.S.U.	73.	R. D. Rippingdale		Greeves
37.	P. H. Gardner	...	Greeves	**75.**	**R. Everett**	...	**Yamaha**
39.	A. E. Blain	...	Yamaha	109.	G. Lane	...	Greeves

competitor. The example given here is an extract from a Castle Combe programme. Then later, when compiling *Greeves* with Rob Carrick (first published by Osprey in 1987), I re-engaged with Reg to tell the true story about the birth of the Silverstone road racer.

We kept in touch, and when Reg was taken ill in the autumn of 2004 he rang me up and asked if I would visit him at his home in Gallywood, Chelmsford, Essex. This I did and one day in November 2004 we spent several hours talking about many things – including Reg's idea of writing his life story. At this time I explained what I thought was the best way to go about it, but I also advised him that it could end in disappointment if the completed manuscript failed to be good enough. But, sensibly, Reg said that if this happened he would simply 'put a rubber band round it' and put it away in his filing cabinet. For my part I said I would be happy to give him as much assistance as I could to make his job as easy as possible, and so he began.

Rather than write the complete story, Reg began by doing what he considered to be 'the first chapter'. He duly finished this on 9 December 2004. When I received this my advice was to continue and see what I thought of the story as a whole.

This was finally finished on 11 May 2007, and the completed draft dropped through my letterbox a few days later and I set about reading it. My impressions were generally much more favourable than they had been in the other cases mentioned earlier. In particular the chapter containing the 1968 Barcelona 24 Hours was, as I said to Reg at the time, brilliant. Now, at least, there was a landmark of the quality needed. I also knew how to bring the rest of the text up to the same standard.

It is important that already I could see 'real potential'. So the next task was improving the small percentage I had deemed as 'needing extra work'. As for my own assistance going forward, this was mainly in the areas such as added detail, general editing, creating sub-headings, finding enough illustrations of the right quality and diversification, captioning, generally tidying things up and coming up what I considered an appropriate title,. Only then could we approach a publisher. Strangely, this was in exactly the reverse of how my own writing career has progressed. This is because, strange as it may seem, I have never actually approached a publisher – they have always approached me.

Anyway, after careful consideration, I decided to offer the now 'finely tuned' work to Breedon Books of Derby. And, yes, they accepted *From Rocker to Racer* for publication.

So here you have it – with my seal of approval – something I have never done before! As I have told Reg, this is not simply his own life story, but one of much wider significance; one that charts the era, the social change and the honest fun that a generation of youngsters experienced growing up in post-war Britain, without all the hi-tech advantages of today.

Rocker to Racer is something special, I am sure reading it will make you appreciate just why I so enthusiastically embraced the project. It will also, I am sure, make you laugh on several occasions – no bad thing!

Happy Reading.

Mick Walker
Wisbech, Cambridgeshire

Chapter 1

Early Days

13 August 1940: The Germans called it *Adler Tag*, 'Eagle Day', the launch of the biggest bomber invasion ever, aimed at the British Isles. It also happened to be my birthday, which was at St John's Hospital, Wood Street, Chelmsford, Essex – the birth by all accounts being relatively straightforward.

The Battle of Britain

Raging over us during this period was the Battle of Britain. Chelmsford was a very strategic target for our adversaries being the home of Radar and Wireless with the Marconi company. Hoffmans was one of our biggest producers of ball and roller bearings and Cromptons was an electric motor manufacturer, all on a direct route from the east coast to London. We had our fair share of bombs; one landed near the ward in the hospital where I was born – fortunately it did not go off, otherwise I might not be writing this story!

The period was very austere, and I wish to try and convey a flavour of it as a complete contrast to the latter years of comparable luxury. We lived in a rented house in Greenways, Chelmsford. My father Les was a maintenance electrician at Hoffmans and during the war my mother Birdie, who was born in Canada, looked after me. Obviously my memories are very few from this time, but a few things stick in my

Reg, aged six months – then with four wheels instead of two.

mind: Being carried by my mother to our neighbour's shelter, which was small and underground, when the air-raid warning sounded, where we all sat huddled up until the planes had passed overhead and the siren sounded the 'all clear'. An alternative to this was a metal cage which was supplied by the government and put up in our front room. Sometimes we slept in this. My father belonged to the Hoffmans fire brigade and had to deal with the aftermath of bombing and the chaos caused by bombs exploding in the large drums containing steel balls used for bearings.

Reg's parents Leslie and Birdie in 1950, when the family was on holiday in Shanklin, Isle of Wright.

Towards the end of the war my memories include the unmistakeable sound of 'doodlebugs' – V1 rockets – which flew over on their way to London, and watching and waiting for the pulse-jet engine to stop, then the silence and the inevitable explosion. Sometimes they did not go off, and one 'dud' landed within a mile of our house and was put on display after the war. I remember climbing over it and playing around it with other children. One day we had a barrage balloon land in our road. It was huge, like a grey elephant with big ears. One day an RAF lorry came and took it away.

Boreham

My father used to take me on his bicycle to a USAF airfield to watch the twin-engined Marauders leaving and returning (with luck) at Boreham. Post-war the disused airfield was turned into a car and motorcycle racing circuit, and it staged meetings during the late 1940s and early 1950s.

Victory in Europe (VE) Day was celebrated on Tuesday 8 May 1945 and was followed by huge celebrations. Our local highlight was a street party where the road was closed and all the children were seated and given jelly and sandwiches. Entertainment included fancy dress and singing competitions with everyone having a great time. Particularly the children, as in our street there were a large number (all born within about four years of each other), in total there were about 49 to 26 boys and 23 girls living in 46 houses, all semi-detached.

There were no cars, motorcycles, telephones or television. In fact, with rationing still severely in force there was not much of anything, but we all played well together and generally had a nice time without getting bored.

Starting school

During 1945, in September to be precise, I started school at Kings Road Juniors. I really was not at all sure what school was all about, and I went there mainly because my mother took me by way of a seat mounted on the rear of her bicycle (this being the only type of transport apart from buses or trains that my parents were ever to have).

School was of little interest, but I had developed a real liking for model aircraft. I spent hour-upon-hour attempting to construct elementary 'chuck' gliders made from bits of balsa wood given to me by an older boy from my road, Derek Hasler, who was making really good models at that time. Another love, though, which was a gift from my parents, was a small, red, two-wheeled bicycle – on which my need for speed was born! Using this to ride up and down our local hill at the fastest possible rate then skidding to a halt gave me the first worn-out tyre, the first puncture and the first good hiding (of several!) I was to receive from my father. To add to this, one day I was riding up the road as fast as I could go, with my head down, and I collided with a parked car. It not only really hurt my head, on which a huge bump developed, but also hurt my pride! It shook me as there were never any parked cars in our road with the exception of one neighbour, a baker, who had a small green van in which he delivered his wares. To this day, I can still remember the smell of freshly-baked bread when he opened the doors at the back. The van, however, was usually empty but we kids hoped for a roll or other morsel to come out as we were always hungry.

By the age of six or seven we were all getting about more; having long walks in the summer, swimming in the local River Chelmer, playing cricket, football and rounders in the road or nearby fields (without any fear of molestation), these were fun times.

Geoff Hurst

One day a new seven-year-old boy moved into Greenways and, unbeknown to us, was to become one of the most famous footballers of our time, now known as Sir Geoffrey Hurst, the 1966 World Cup-winning goalscorer. To all of us at that time he was just Geoff and we all played football together, usually with a tennis ball as an actual football was very hard to find. In fact, no one nearby owned one. One day the local policeman, who was on his bike, saw us playing football in the road. Whether he had had a complaint from someone we do not know, but he took our names and addresses and shortly after, to our utter disbelief, we were summoned to court where we were each made to pay 7s 6d (35p) costs – including Geoff Hurst! It was obvious then that Geoff was a good player – we could all tell – and he played for his school before moving away back to West Ham at about 13 or 14 years old to become one of their stars, and thereafter a legend.

The winter of 1947–48 was particularly severe, with snow on the ground from December through to the end of February. We had to walk to school, about two miles, as my mum's bike could not negotiate the ice or frozen slush.

Austere times

Times were still austere, food was on ration and coal for the fire was difficult to get. In our house we only had one coal fire which was restricted to being alight from 5.30pm until 10pm; causing the house to be exceedingly cold when waking in the mornings – when ice on the inside of the windows was the norm! I often wondered how my poor grandmother, Agnes, survived as her husband had been killed during World War One. She augmented her very modest war widow's pension by letting out two rooms to two other 'old' ladies, but her house only had a coal fire for cooking in the kitchen range in the scullery and no electricity, the house being lit by candles and oil lamps. She had an outside toilet – but no bath. We cannot imagine this in these affluent times, but it was all we knew and was therefore accepted.

Part of Greenways Boys football team. Back row left to right: John Parry, Malcolm Lee and Colin Bridge; front row Reg and Colin Edwards. Missing is Geoff Hurst (now Sir Geoff Hurst, the 1966 England World Cup goalscorer).

For us boys in the street our quest for action and speed took us into the realms of 'trolleys', basically a plank of wood with a rudimentary seat at the back, the two rear wheels being a fixture and the front two on a pivoted crossmember allowing the contraption to be steered. As our road was built on a hill it was simply a matter of pulling it up and going down as fast as possible. These trolleys were made in all designs to fit the materials which were freely available – nothing was ever bought so imagination was allowed to run riot! The favoured wheels came from prams or old pedal cars, but as my father worked in Hoffmans mine sported four-inch diameter ball bearing assemblies! The trolley, needless to say, had a good turn of speed and won many of the races down that hill.

The only drawback (not to me!) was the noise of these wheels on the concrete path or road. Apparently the noise disturbed the local policeman who was on nights and trying to get his sleep. He came out of his house in a truly foul mood, but looking exceedingly comical in his pyjamas and dressing gown, and confiscated my trolley. On coming home from work my father inquired as to the whereabouts of the trolley as he had some grease and wanted to ensure the Hoffman bearings did a good job. When I told him the policeman had taken it he was very upset and left immediately to visit the said person. Very shortly after my trolley was returned, I was given a clip round the ear and the whole incident was over!

Fireworks

Fireworks slowly became available and my father managed to get hold of a few 'pre-war' items, which were spectacular but very unpredictable. Father, being a man of many facets, decided it was not beyond the realms of possibility to make his own! So we looked in the dictionary for gunpowder and found it was made from sulphur, saltpetre and charcoal. We duly visited the local chemist where we bought the first two ingredients and made the charcoal ourselves. These we mixed on the dining room table and the resulting powder was tested for its ability to burn quickly by throwing a teaspoonful on the fire. This later became the best way of cleaning the chimney cheaply! However, the fireworks made from these materials were never really successful, as unfortunately we never got a bang even though we mixed in shavings from a magnesium incendiary bomb which my father had found at Hoffmans – would you believe that in my workshop I still have the remains of that bomb!

Holidays were taken mainly with my mother, and for one week during the school summer holidays she bought a railway runabout ticket. This gave unlimited travel within a certain area and generally took us to Walton-on-the-Naze or Clacton. It also generated an interest of steam trains, and I spent most of the holidays going backwards and forwards getting off at many of the stations on the way and even hitching rides on the footplate of the locomotives, which was a great thrill. So already, at that young age, I was interested in bikes, aircraft, trolleys, football, gunpowder and steam engines. Life seemed limitless. However, school was still a mystery.

Fishing with my father was yet another outlet for my search for the mysteries of life and, as with everything, it became another passion. There were just not enough hours in the day in which to do it all.

Model aircraft

My interest in model aircraft was progressing and my father took me to Gamages, a huge East London department store in Holborn where we bought my first diesel engine for model aircraft, a lcc E.D. Bee. I soon built a simple control-line aircraft for it with a kit from our new model shop in Chelmsford owned by Michael Kemp's father – Michael allowed me to pay for it on instalments of 2s 6d per week as this was my pocket money at the time, and the kit cost 14s 7d. I soon learnt to work the engine; the way to start it was to flick the propeller with your finger and adjust the compression and control the fuel needle valve. The only thing you had to do was to get your finger out of the way as it started, otherwise a severely damaged digit was the result!

Control line flying was a lot of fun and we went to aerodromes and fêtes displaying these aircraft by team racing and combat. The tails had streamers attached. We performed with two, three or four people in a circle at the same time, trying to cut each other's streamers. This was a recipe for disaster, of course, and many crashes ensued.

An introduction to powered two-wheelers

My friend who had introduced me to aeromodelling, Derek Hasler, had now invested in a better means of transport than bicycling (only just!). It was his, and my, first introduction to motorcycling – a Cyclemaster. This was a 25cc auxiliary engine which was mounted into the rear wheel of a conventional bicycle and generally did away with the need to pedal except for going up steep hills, and it would achieve a maximum speed of 25mph on the flat. It was controlled by a simple paddle lever on the handlebars to the carburettor as a throttle and a clutch so you could disengage and ride as a normal bicycle – generally it was OK. Other variants existed, one of which was called a Powerpak (again 25cc), but this one fitted on top of the rear wheel and featured a serrated roller which was lifted on and off the wheel via a clutch – again controlled by a paddle lever. This was not so good in the wet as the serrated drive slipped on the tyre more quickly, and if you stopped and did not declutch in time the roller rubbed through the tyre, then it went bang and you were stranded. Motorised transport thus entered my imagination.

Although I was only 10 years old, it was time to take the 11-plus examination (I was always the youngest in the class as the intake date was 1 September, therefore many people were nearly a year older). I failed this ignominiously and was sent to Rainsford Secondary Modern. It was a much more severe and rebellious regime, and I entered another phase of my life. Soon finding out that it was better to be strong than weak I took an interest in gymnastics and running. On the academic front I only followed engineering enthusiastically. Our master for this was Albert Wiffen, a former RAF pilot; he had an open Austin Seven and was building a Rudge to take part in motorcycle racing events. He was not only our metalwork master

1951, Rainsford Secondary Modern School gymnastic team. Reg is on the bottom row, second from the right.

but he also took us for woodwork. We enjoyed this because we were making small Fleetwind yachts, and it was also a good way for Albert to go sailing for free! His pretext for making these was to take us boys sailing when the yachts were completed, but apart from one or two 'favourite' pupils (I was not one of them) they were used at the Maldon Littleship Club for races instead.

During the winters, though, the sledges we made were put to good use by Albert, towing us in his Austin Seven around the playing field. In metalwork I learned the art of elementary blacksmithing, casting, riveting, soldering and brazing, and the general use of small hand tools, drills and an introduction to the lathe, all of which were to hold me in good stead in later years. The two years I spent at Rainsford were good and at 12 years old I became captain of our gymnastics team and began to know the meaning of fitness; although I was still very small and light even for my age. This did not deter me, however; in fact, in those days I did not even think about it. Running long distances also became a habit and I would run on the playing field track every lunchtime, very often completing 3–4 miles each time, which built up my stamina.

Roller skating

I started to develop a new activity which aided my fitness, roller skating. A building in the centre of Chelmsford called the Corn Exchange (which was built for the farmers to sell their corn in) had a new maple floor fitted, mainly for dancing, but was also used for wrestling and roller skating. I had, in the past, owned a pair of metal skates which clipped to my shoes and were used on the pavement outdoors, but this was different. All kinds of boys and girls went here, young and old, but every Saturday morning during general skating they had a slot for racing – boys up to 15, then 15 and over! Well, I could not resist this and my first real competitive spirit was born for real racing as it was me, at 12, up against 15-year-olds! Usually about 10 competed in each race. I soon learnt the tricks and at my third attempt, I won. The prize for winning was free entry and free skates for the following Saturday, which made me determined never to pay to go in again, and I never did!

Cycling was a necessity to get backwards and forwards to school, and by then the little red bike had given way to a slightly larger model. Using this to go to aeromodelling days at Debden about 15 miles away, and to go to any other activity I wished to take part in, helped me to get fit as well.

A real adventure

Holidays were now taken with both parents and we ventured further afield, namely to the Isle of Wight. Travelling there was a real adventure as we had to get to Portsmouth via Waterloo Station on the Southern railway (I still enjoyed the steam engines) and thence by boat on the crossing to Ryde, followed by another small steam train to our final destination, Shanklin. These holidays were really enjoyable and I learnt to canoe, but the great thrill for my 12th birthday was a flight in an Auster from Sandown grass airfield, cementing forever my love of anything to do with aircraft and a will to become a fighter pilot! Great ambitions!

A second chance of a better education was given to us in the form of the 13-plus examination. This time, to everyone's surprise, I gained an oral interview at my local technical school. As it was summer I went casually dressed (I was still in short trousers and was to remain so until my 14th birthday – it was not out of place in those days) carrying my towel and swimming costume under my arm as I intended to go to the local outside swimming pool that afternoon. Well, I obviously answered all the questions to the required standard as I was granted a place, and I later found out that one of the interviewers was the sports master and he had liked my approach.

A uniform then had to be purchased; cap, tie and a blazer with school badges (something very new and extreme), which was joined by a new bicycle – a Raleigh Lenton in metallic red, as a present from my parents for passing the exam. It was about this time, 1953, when I ate my first banana and saw my first television which was showing the Queen's Coronation. The television was owned by the local baker who invited the children who lived nearby around his house to watch the boat race and Cup Final as well. It was a real treat for all trying to see the nine-inch screen – black and white only of course.

The bicycle was soon stripped and lightened with alloy wheels and crank, bought or exchanged with another boy at the technical school who seemed to have an endless supply of new parts. It was many years later that I found out that these parts were 'borrowed' from a local cycle shop!

Reg, aged 13, with his Raleigh Lenton Sports cycle, c.1953.

A 1956 photograph of No. 64 Greenways, Chelmsford, the Everett family home at the time.

Evenings after school were spent in training for 25-mile cycling time trials, going from Chelmsford to Brentwood, Billericay and back to my home, and these usually took about an hour and 10 minutes.

During this period at my new school my ability to absorb knowledge took a very positive turn. Finally I was able to learn, and I finished my first year in first place in my class, which was mixed 50-50 boys and girls, and I certainly started to change my outlook on life.

Air Training Corps

My love of aircraft took me into joining the ATC (Air Training Corps) as I had plans to join the RAF, and I also studied hard there. On summer camps I visited a couple of RAF stations (Shawbury in Shropshire and Wittering near Peterborough) where I had the opportunity to go for flights in Avro Ansons and an English Electric Canberra, which was a huge, never-to-be-forgotten thrill. My studies took me further into engineering and technical drawing. Physics was also teaching me the theory of the workings of many items, and I became enthralled by all of this. So much so that at the end of my fifth year when I was 15 I passed the GCE in six subjects.

My cycling friends at school, with whom I travelled as far afield as Portsmouth, were a little older than me and Stan Vanhinsbergh (whose father owned a garage in Billericay) was by now 16. One day he turned up at school on a 350 Matchless and my eyes opened wide. This meant my chums were moving on, and as much as I visited the garage on my bicycle it was obvious that my cycling days were numbered.

What to do?

What was I to do? I had already decided to continue my education, staying on at school to do my A levels in mathematics and physics to help my entry into the RAF. Before this, though, was the long school summer holiday and my chance to earn some money. What for? A motorcycle of course, so I could keep up with my friends!

A job was obtained at the local swimming baths as an attendant giving out the clothes baskets. I should have been 16 years old but never mind, I was 15 and 11 months. This job proved boring as the summer was miserable and we only had a crowd on two days, but I could swim as much as I liked in the 15°C water! However, I was earning, and by September (two weeks after my 16th birthday) I had managed to save £35 – a

Aged 15, now a keen aero modeller.

princely sum for seven weeks' work. A friend of mine from Rainsford school, Clifford Foster, was a year older than me and was doing a job as a plumber (most people were leaving school at 14–15 years old). He owned a motorcycle, to be exact an ex-WD 3HW Triumph single cylinder 350cc with rigid rear end but the front had a pair of AJS telescopic forks grafted on it; to me a great bike. Wanting to sell this to buy a 500, Cliff was only too willing to help me part with my money, and so a meeting was arranged.

Early motorcycling experiences

My motorcycling experience up to that point had been limited to a single ride on the pillion of my friend Stan's 350 Matchless (which had already been replaced by a new Douglas Dragonfly in black and silver, a most handsome machine). Cliff, however, did not see this as a drawback and at the appointed time and place we met. I jumped on the back and off we went to the nearby country lanes in the Chignals. Of course, needless to say, we had no helmets or gloves or any special clothing at all. Certainly I had no licence or any form of insurance, although Cliff was legal.

This did not deter us, and at a suitable spot he stopped and explained the controls briefly to me. The clutch, he said, should be let out slowly, the throttle should be turned slowly, and to change gear pull in the clutch, lift up the lever with the right foot, let out the clutch and off you go. Of course, my first couple of attempts led to stalling and as he was foolhardy enough to be sitting on the pillion he was shouting 'slower with the clutch – faster with the throttle!' and at the third attempt with a great lurch we were off.

Into second and even third went relatively well and I was enjoying the experience with the wind rushing by my ears and my eyes watering so much I could hardly see. The country lanes were full of bends and Cliff was saying 'slow down and change down a gear, we are coming to a sharp one!' Unfortunately, my instructor had forgotten to explain how to change down and by now was screaming the instructions to me as I began to panic. The corner loomed, the grass verge was encountered and crossed, the front wheel subsequently dropped into a ditch and Cliff and I ended up in a hedge. More accurately, I was in the hedge and Cliff was over it, and by the time I had extracted myself and found him, he was moaning and groaning and holding his right arm. His language, to say the least, was colourful – he was not happy with me or my ability to ever ride a motorcycle properly. This, however, did not help our existing situation. It was obvious he could not ride the motorcycle because of his arm.

Fortunately, on examination, after I had pulled the machine from the ditch it seemed relatively unscathed apart from a few minor scratches and bent levers which were soon straightened.

Cliff was now in some pain, and the only way to get him to hospital was on the back of the bike! Needless to say he was less than enthusiastic, but there was no alternative. He made me swear I would not attempt to even change gear either up or down and to promise to stop when he shouted at me (he also gave me lengthy instruction on the braking system). Getting back on must have been a lesson in fear for him, but the journey to the hospital went by with relatively little incident. When we arrived he was white and asked me to lean the bike exactly where it had stopped and leave it alone.

Thus my introduction to motorcycling had begun, I had no negative thoughts but realised my journey was to be more filled with obstacles than I originally had anticipated.

Purchasing the ex-WD Triumph

When I next saw Cliff one week had passed, and he had been diagnosed as having a broken wrist and his arm was in plaster. Unable to work, he was not best happy with me and I felt guilty in causing him so much pain and problems. I offered him £37.10s for his machine which he quickly accepted. We met at his house the next day, I handed over the money and he gave me his crash helmet – a high crown ACU model in brown! This, he said, I would surely need and should wear it at all times (I do not remember any occasion, after this, riding a motorcycle without one).

Very slowly riding the bike home, I came down our road and the other kids cheered, and for that moment I was proud – until my parents saw the bike. They had no idea it was even in my thoughts. To say they were not happy was an understatement; my mother burst into tears announcing my death knell and my father exploded with rage and told me to take it back. I parked it on its side stand outside the house and went in. It was days before we talked, but by then at least I had got it taxed and insured and had purchased gloves and a plastic jacket. For sure I could not afford a leather one and with winter coming it needed to be waterproof.

My motorcycling for a while was a very lonely affair, being a learner with 'L' plates and trying very hard to learn how to ride without help of any description. During the next few months I had many mishaps, including a crash on the same bend as the first one with Cliff but in the opposite direction! I locked up the rear wheel and skidded all over the place before learning that it was the front brake that stopped the bike, and I also learnt that wet roads are horrible! The roads back then had surfaces that could only be described as 'various'. The dreaded cobblestones, the very worst tarred wooden blocks, stones in tar of various grades, etc. All had to be mastered. Well, my mastery was very slow and sometimes I came home nearly in tears believing that I would never manage the art of motorcycling.

Still, my love of aircraft, flying and the RAF beckoned and I applied to Hornchurch for the possibility of joining for aircrew training. This was a three-day initial aptitude interview and we were given many written and pictorial tests for hand and eye co-ordination, leadership possibilities and, of course, a very strict medical examination and eye test.

There were 12 of us at this particular intake and I passed the medical A1G1 with excellent eyesight and an aptitude for flying. So, I thought, I had passed, and it would be only time before I received a posting to Canada for aircrew training – my dream was coming to fruition. This dream, however, was to be short-lived – I received a letter within a few weeks saying 'Sorry, but due to cutbacks within the whole of the RAF your services will not be needed, and do not re-apply for five years'.

The Blue Star Gang

With my rejection from the RAF, together with the poor standard of my motorcycling, this was to be a very tough time for me as now I had to rethink what I was going to do. My education was not going too well either as I found pure mathematics virtually incomprehensible – my engineering logic did not comply with the theoretical nature of mathematics, which did not seem to have a practical application. By now, however, I had met up with a group of motorcyclists in my area, who called themselves 'The Blue Star gang'. Most were a year or two older than me and had a real variety of machines – a Matchless G9, Velocette 350 MAC, Vincent 500 Comet, AJS 350, Scott Squirrel 600cc, Triumph Tiger Cub and a Douglas Plus 80.

We travelled all over and had good times together but one day, coming back through London in the dark and wet, the dreaded cobbles, traffic lights and too much back brake again caught me out and I hit my pal John Houghton on his Velocette MAC up the back. It did no damage to the bikes, but his rear brake connecting rod protruded beyond the adjusting nut by about four inches, and I had to pull my foot off this as it had gone through my boot and my foot!

The Blue Star gang, with their respective motorcycles in 1957. Left to right: Mick Carr (1947 350cc Matchless), Bob Baxter (1950 500cc Vincent Comet), Philip Lenoir (1938 500cc HRD), Keith Cranness (1955 350cc Matchless), John Houghton (1948 350cc Velocette), Bonk Turner (1955 200cc Triumph), Dick Hart (1951 125 BSA Bantam), Reg (1947 350cc Triumph 3HW).

We rode to Bethnal Green hospital where I was stitched up, but this accident was to have many repercussions. For a while I could not go to school. I also had further problems with the foot, as there was still a lot of pain after the stitches were removed and I could not get my shoe on. I returned to my local hospital and the resulting X-rays revealed broken bones, so my foot and lower leg were put in plaster. I reverted back to my bicycle which had a fixed wheel for transport, as I could pedal with one leg which was OK for a while. Once the plaster was removed I thought all would be OK, but a few weeks after I knew it was not, as I had protrusions and still could not get my shoe on. Another visit to the hospital and yet another X-ray showed that the bones had not joined properly and splinters of

Members of the Blue Star gang in 1957.

these were sticking up. The specialist (he was known as Dr Butcher Bones!) said I would either have to put up with it or I would have to have an operation. Opening up my foot, they filed all the rough ends of bone down and sewed it all back together again. I was in hospital for two weeks.

Problems

Missing so much school effectively eliminated any chance of getting A levels, and a decision had to be made as far as work was concerned. After my failure to get selected for RAF aircrew my next choice was to work on aircraft, so I applied for an apprenticeship with several aircraft manufacturers and BOAC at Heathrow. All letters were returned saying 'Sorry, but our next intake is already full'. Options were becoming few, and although our local factories – Hoffmans and Marconi – were interviewing for apprentices, my father intervened by saying his father had worked at Hoffmans for 51 years and he (my father) was to do 50 and he was sure I would not! So, with no other real option available, Marconi was chosen.

While these major decisions were being forced on me, we were experiencing a phenomenon known as 'petrol rationing' due to the Suez Crisis. Great Britain was attacking Egypt to keep open the Suez Canal, to stop them from nationalising it, during October to December 1956. Because of the fuel shortage it was decided by the government to put petrol on ration from 17 December 1956 to 17 April 1957, but it continued until 14 May 1957. Following the announcement during November 1956 panic buying ensued (my father bought five gallons in a jerry can!) and the price went up to six shillings a gallon – about £7.50 in today's money.

We motorcyclists were allowed one gallon per week or about 50 miles' worth, which for social riding was just about adequate. Of course, coupons became a source of currency to be traded, sold or bartered, and generally our Blue Star gang got adequate supplies.

Visiting Brands Hatch

Early in 1957, during Easter, I went to watch my first-ever road race at Brands Hatch. We went in convoy with our various bikes. It was quite a journey for us in those days, going into London and through the Blackwall Tunnel, Kidbrook, Sidcup and Swanley on back roads to get there, and it took two to two and half hours in all.

My first glimpse of motorcycle racing was during practice, seeing the 50cc bikes going round Paddock Bend. I thought they were fast, but when the 500s came I was amazed and became smitten by it all, and the likes of Derek Minter, Bob McIntyre, Ginger Payne and Alan Trow were to become my heros. This day lives in my memory: the speed, the smell of burnt Castrol R, the black faces, black leathers and, above all, the racing – with its man and machine combination being the perfect blend of excitement coupled with engineering excellence. To me the sound of a 500 Manx Norton with an open 'megga' was the sound of music to be played over and over.

The ride home was now something else, we were all so hyped up that we were all aces and it was nothing less than a race! Returning via the Blackwall Tunnel we saw our first real traffic jam, but this only added to the excitement. In the tunnel we were all revving our bikes to the full just to hear the noise reverberating off the walls, trying to re-create the sound we had just heard. My joy was short-lived because of severe inexperience – my revving was done in gear with the clutch pulled in. Needless to say, the clutch had started to slip and got progressively worse until I had no drive left at all. I just made it to the exit. The Blue Star gang, however, soon had the chain case off and one by one we all 'pee'd' over the (too hot to handle) clutch so we could work on it. Once it had cooled down we soon had it apart only to confirm a completely useless burned out set of cork clutch plates! What to do now? Well, necessity is the mother of invention! We all emptied our pockets and found as many halfpennies as we could. We placed these in between all the plates so that, when it was all reassembled, it would not slip. Obviously the downside was that also it would not disengage, so a new rapid learning curve was about to take place!

Starting was the biggest problem, which was achieved by the lads pushing until at a suitable speed I banged it into gear. Generally I did OK and got home without mishap, but jumping a few red lights caused some anxiety trying not to come to a standstill and having the inevitable problem of restarting. Taking more time than I would ever have thought was the replacing of all the individual corks into their plates (about 20 per plate and five plates – 100 in all) but the result was OK and it worked well with no further trouble – it was a real lesson in putting the bike into neutral as soon as possible when stopping and keeping the brain engaged.

I passed my interview to get into Marconi and had been advised of a starting date – 16 September 1957, so as I had left school in April I had a few months to fill.

The blow-up

My riding skills had continued to be honed and I was using the 3HW as often as I could. With my new-found love of motorcycle racing I attempted to break all records on the road wherever possible, it made me push my bike to the limit, not only cornering but by my total lack of understanding of the properties of metal and the engine. Winding the throttle to the stop, letting the engine revs go up until there was a noticeable dying off in acceleration before changing gear (now knowing, reaching the valve spring bounce limit). This inevitably led to disaster, and one day while pulling out of my road I accelerated until the valves bounced in first gear, then did the same in second, at which point there was an almighty bang; then silence as I coasted to a standstill. Looking beneath the tank I beheld a sight that nearly made me cry, my beloved bike had disintegrated and there was a vital piece missing – the cylinder! The cylinder head was being supported by the exhaust pipe; the barrel, piston and top half of the con-rod (which had cried enough) had gone.

Mournfully I pushed it home realising that now I had no bike and no money to repair it or in fact to do anything else, so out came the bicycle. A job had to be found quickly, anything would do as the summer was coming, I had race meetings to go to, and no bike.

I got a job at McPhersons (a local soft drink manufacturer) on the production line, it was quite well paid but very boring. My first activity for eight-and-a-half hours a day was putting plastic screw caps on top of lemonade bottles and making sure they were tight with a kind of electric drill with a cup on the end. I pressed the button and it rotated and tightened the cap. These bottles passed me at about 30 per minute so I had two seconds to pick up the cap, put it on the bottle and tighten it. In eight hours (two 15 minutes breaks) I had to do about 14,000 bottles! This was not for me.

Cliff, from whom I had purchased the Triumph, was also working there and was about to leave for pastures new. He had had a job as a truck driver's mate which seemed a lot better. This entailed loading the truck in the morning, delivering soft drinks to pubs in the area all day and returning in the evening.

The next evening I waited until they returned and introduced myself to the driver who tested my suitability for the job by asking me to hold a crate of lemonade bottles in each hand and swing them in place on the top of the truck. I passed this test OK and he recommended me as Cliff's replacement. I started the following Monday. Fresh air, a pub every half hour or so, a free pub lunch and £8 per week.

Pride & Clarke

Now to repair the bike. The parts, new barrel, piston, con-rod, crankpin assembly and a set of gaskets were duly ordered by mail-order from that prolific London-based company Pride and Clarke of 158 Stockwell Road, Brixton, who seemed to have everything including a lot of ex-WD items. You could even buy complete engines, for example 1948 Ariel 350 for £5 (the 1945 version was only £3). So the £3 10s I had paid for my parts seemed quite expensive! The parts soon arrived and my friend Stan at the garage in Billericay offered to help me rebuild the bike. Duly he came over to my house on his Douglas Dragonfly with a piece of rope, the idea being to tow me on the bike from Chelmsford to Billericay with me hanging on to the rope and with the parts in a box on the pillion seat. Eventually we made it. I thought my arm would be pulled out of its socket even with the rope looped once around the steering damper. We had thought it too dangerous to tie the rope on securely, to this day I really do not know why!

We removed the crankcase, split it, removed the flywheels and split those, and rebuilt the whole crankshaft assembly and then attached the new piston and cylinder, etc. The head was refurbished by grinding in the valves, then fitted – the whole assembly was then placed once more into the frame. I learnt the intricacies of retiming the magneto so the points opened ³⁄₁₆ BTDC (Before Top Dead Centre)

Later Reg gave his ancient Triumph the cafe racer treatment, with flyscreen, clip-ons, a home-made racing seat and even a Burgess silencer.

with the aid of a Rizla Red cigarette paper, and she was now ready to run again. It was great to hear her, and I was proud to have to 'run in' the new cylinder and took it steady for the obligatory 500 miles, which was the prescribed distance in those days.

The Suez Crisis

Strangely enough I had not yet passed my test, one of the reasons being that during the Suez Crisis I was not allowed to take it. There was a concession, however, that after having a bike for five months you were allowed a pillion passenger. Only a few weeks passed before my test was arranged and I passed OK, but the examiner said I rode much too fast (the examiner stood in one place while we negotiated a 1.2 mile course, so they could only see you once a lap – they probably timed it, hence the remark on speed). My friend Ted (Mason) Merrick in the Blue Star gang, with the 500 Vincent Comet, took his test the same day but decided it would be easier to pass on a Cyclemaster engined bicycle. It was a really bad decision because when the examiner appeared from behind a parked car and held his hand up for the emergency stop, Ted's Cyclemaster's brakes were useless in the wet and poor Ted knocked over the surprised examiner. Needless to say – he failed. Merrick went on to not only sprint a Vincent V-twin but also race on the grass with a 500cc JAP.

I enjoyed my job and did a lot of riding on the bike that summer and became proficient and confident. I really began to enjoy my motorcycling.

Shortly afterwards I had to start my apprenticeship with Marconi. 16 September 1957 duly arrived and I was informed that for my first year I would attend Bocking (Braintree) College of Further Education where I was to take the City & Guilds' Intermediate in Machine Shop Engineering along with S2 (Second Year) National Certificate. I was then getting the princely sum of £3 17s per week and using the Triumph every day – a round trip of 22 miles. This obviously entailed riding in all conditions, ice, snow, wet, dry and everything in between. It soon became a 'beat the clock' time trial, which was great.

The college was blessed with good tutors and my engineering knowledge expanded and included engineering drawing which I readily took to. As my riding experience grew my thoughts started wandering into the realms of changing the Triumph – maybe just for something different.

The first bike I looked at was a pre-war Rudge Ulster with girder forks, which I liked, but I really wanted something more modern and faster – but of course I was on a very limited budget. Then one day I bumped into my cousin John who also rode bikes, but, as he was some five years older than me, our paths rarely crossed. What was he riding? Well, it was a 500 Clubmans BSA Gold Star – and somehow I just had to have one myself!

Chapter 2

The Gold Star

Since meeting my cousin John there was only one machine that I wanted, and that was the (big fin motor, swept back exhaust, clip-on bars) BSA Gold Star. With spring and summer approaching in 1958, owning such a machine was uppermost in my mind but two things were the overriding implication, to sell my trusty Triumph and to find enough money to purchase such an exotic bike. A new machine was totally out of the question as, even in those far off days, it cost a huge £310 12 7d. When you realise I was only earning about £5 per week as an apprentice, it was over a year's income and even most used machines would cost more than £200 – so to realise my dream was not going to be easy. Locally, there did not seem to be any choice at all, although there were one or two riding about in our town. Every time I heard one with the distinctive 'twitter' on the overrun of the exhaust I became more and more anxious to be an owner.

Monty & Ward

Scouring the motor cycle magazines of the time, the 'Blue Un' (*The Motor Cycle*) and the 'Green Un' (*Motor Cycling*) made me aware of a particular motorcycle shop which specialised in road racing and sports machines. The name was also known to me; from my visits to Brands Hatch, by their racing exploits and construction of specials. This was Messrs Geoff Monty and Dudley Ward, i.e. Monty & Ward, 47 Hampton Road, Twickenham, tel 5040 – unfortunately one of the most difficult places to get to from Chelmsford either by road or public transport.

Reg, the budding rocker, c.1958.

This was a small deterrent, however, so I first collected some pennies together and walked up the road to my local telephone box, put in some of the coins and dialled. The response of Monty and Ward came quickly so I pushed button 'A' and we were connected. I was totally unused to the telephone and said nervously that I was looking for a very cheap Gold Star for not more than £150. 'We have the very thing in stock, sir – a 1954 model, first of the big fin motors, priced at £154. Perhaps you would like to see it?' I replied that I most certainly would. The thought of how I would pay for it came to me and I asked if I could have £100 on Hire Purchase and they assured me it could be arranged, so I agreed to go up to the shop the following weekend.

This still left me with the problem of getting the deposit and I frantically passed around that the Triumph was up for sale. At the Braintree College I was attending, furthering my education for my Marconi apprenticeship, were several people who admired my (by now) sporty Triumph. Dropped handlebars with a fly-screen, a bucket seat of red leather and with the megaphone exhaust all nicely cleaned and polished, it really looked the part. One lad, who had taken a real interest in it, had a 125cc four-stroke 1933 hand-change BSA and had suddenly become desperate to own my bike. His friends were also giving him a lot of encouragement to replace his ancient girder-forked machine.

A great deal was made as far as I was concerned and this lad acquired my Triumph for the princely sum of £50 plus his ancient BSA. The following day the paperwork was handed over along with the cash and I rode home on the old BSA, having to get used to the three-speed hand-change, which I found extremely slow and cumbersome along with the performance, but I knew it would not have to last for long.

Saturday arrived and my long journey to Twickenham began. My £50 was secure in my pocket and with my crash hat over my arm I boarded the bus, then a steam train from Chelmsford to Liverpool Street – followed by the underground to Waterloo (changing at Bank) for the special Waterloo line train and thence by British Rail to Twickenham. From the main line station it was a walk of about 1¼ miles on unknown territory – constantly asking the way, until in a leafy road on my left, set back, lay the red painted shop of Monty and Ward. Even in those days it looked a little old fashioned with small windows, but behind the glass what treasures! My eyes popped out of my head to see Manx Nortons, AJS 7R's and various other racing machinery, a real sight, which even made that journey worthwhile.

I went in and a dapperly dressed moustachioed gentleman greeted me with a smile – I could also feel his the expectation of parting me with my money! It was Geoff Monty (I never met or saw Allan Dudley Ward). There was another much younger salesman there at the time, probably in his 20s – I got to know Cyril Bennett well. Only a few years later, maybe two or three, he won the 'football pools' to the tune of £75,000 which probably equates to about £1–1.5 million these days. He actually moved to Chelmsford and became an owner/shareholder in an Esso Garage in the town centre. We kept in touch at the time but business deteriorated and he moved away.

The Gold Star

He took me over to a corner of the shop and showed me the Gold Star he had for sale at £154. It looked in a sad state – not damaged but unloved, it did not have the tapered Goldie silencer but a rather standard Burgess looking type, and it had no

With the five-hundred BSA Gold Star Clubman purchased from Monty and Ward in early 1958.

rear set of footrests, but again the standard roadster ones. We took it outside to get a better look and leaned it on its side stand (it had no centre stand).

This bike (engine number 54GS CB114) did, though, have a huge air scoop on the 8in front brake and a large bore exhaust pipe which expanded to 1⅞in after exiting the manifold. Generally it still really appealed to me and Geoff kicked it over and it started OK. I took it for a run up the road and enjoyed the huge amount of power it had over the Triumph – I was sold. The gearbox was not the RRT2 of close ratio type, but a more usable lower first gear STD (Standard) box (I knew nothing of these details at the time), which was really good for roadwork. On returning to the shop the paperwork was drawn up and I was the very proud owner of SKP 647, a 500cc Gold Star.

Now I had to negotiate the London traffic and find my way home over the Thames at Richmond. Again at Kew to the Chiswick Flyover, round the North Circular past the now legendary Ace café, Hendon, Finchley, Wood Green, Tottenham, Waltham Forest then up through Woodford High Beach (the old speedway track), Epping to North Weald (still then an operational aerodrome) where I decided to stop for petrol. Pulling into the National Benzole garage I bought two gallons, 10s worth (50p), more than enough to do the remaining 15 miles home.

Unknown to Reg at the time, but his Gold Star was the actual bike upon which Derek Minter had begun his own racing career – Derek is seen here on the machine at Brands Hatch in 1956.

If you have ever seen anyone start a Gold Star you will know that it is vital to do this on the centre stand so one can get maximum leverage and swing to help the starting technique. As I mentioned, my 'new' bike only had a side stand and now I had to restart it. Well, of course, I kicked and kicked it but it would not go. I checked the plug, spark, fuel flow, all were OK but it just would not start. After 20 minutes, on the point of exhaustion (even though I had well maintained my fitness level, mainly by regularly swimming and gymnastics), for no apparent reason it restarted and I was on my way again. This in no way reduced my enthusiasm for my new machine and instead made me more determined to ensure reliability and knowledge of the Gold Star.

The ride home, with about 100 traffic lights and having most types of road conditions over the 60 miles, gave me good feelings for the ability of the bike and rider. The STD gearbox helped the tractability considerably, and I really enjoyed having such fantastic acceleration over what I was used to with the old Triumph.

Ex-Minter

When I finally sat down that evening I had a chance to examine the paperwork and, especially, the log book. The Goldie had two previous owners – my predecessor lived in Sidcup, Kent – but owner number one was to be a huge surprise (and subsequent influence). It was none other than the famous 'King of Brands' Derek Minter, and the address was Hallets of Canterbury (the motorcycle shop which assisted Derek in his early days).

Wow, I owned a bike which at one time was raced by my hero, this was real elation! The STD (wide ratio, roadster) gearbox threw me a bit but other signs were really there, such as the large air scoop on the front brake and extended brake arm (later recognised by me on Derek's Gold Star racing photographs), the worn out Avon racing tyres, the Armstrong shock absorbers, modified damping of the front forks, large-bore exhaust (scraped badly underneath the side through exuberant cornering) and the gear change which as the reverse plate had been fitted and the foot rests had been put back to standard the gear lever pointed forward, making the gear change up for 'up' and down for 'down', the same as the Triumph – very convenient. Other such mods were also discovered, making this machine a little unique.

First, however, I was absolutely determined to make it more reliable on starting, and the first job was to strip the 1⁹⁄₃₂in GP carburettor (later DB & DBD models had 1½in giving better top-end performance but losing out on bottom and mid-range acceleration). Imagine my surprise when I initially removed the top to reveal the slide which was worn through completely with holes on both sides! I replaced this, checking all the jets, replacing the worn needle and needle jet, the aluminium needle on top of the float in the float chamber and, most importantly, adjusted the height of the float chamber so the petrol level inside coincided with the top of the main jet.

Next, the ignition system was thoroughly checked, the points replaced as well as the HT lead and plug (a much too hard racing Lodge RL46), and then it was retimed – again with a Red Rizla, but I was about to buy a set of feeler gauges for the tappets. The primary chain case had been removed to allow me to fit the cardboard Castrol Degree disc so as to set the timing correctly at 39 degrees BTDC (Before Top Dead Centre).

While taking this opportunity to adjust the chains, it also revealed something else. The engine sprocket was just 18 teeth (I had been told that, as standard, they came with a 23-tooth item to give the highest possible top speed for the Clubman's TT in the Isle of Man).

Brands gearing

Well, what mine had (as I later became only too aware of) was the correct sprocket for Brands Hatch short circuit which gave fantastic acceleration. Back to the tappets, and referring to the workshop manual the clearances for inlet and exhaust were both .006in – to be measured when cold by removing the cover from the push rod tunnel and inserting the feeler gauge between the two flat portions on the cam follower and the pushrod. This was puzzling as – poke as I might – the feeler would not go in even though the engine was at the correct position and the pushrod free to rotate with clearance I could feel. Well, these pushrods in my engine had cup ends with domed cam followers so there was no way the feelers would go in here! On examining the rocker box covers, it was soon obvious that a mod had been made, as strategically placed holes had been drilled and tapped into the alloy cover to take ½in allen headed screws. Remove these and you could get the feeler in to measure the valve clearance in the actual place it was needed, between the top of the valve and the rocker arm.

When this was completed to my satisfaction I was eager to try it out – it started second kick (and I never had any trouble starting it again), and the road test also went well. I came home and gave it a good clean and was ready to show it off to the Blue Star gang and the other 'rockers' (as we had become known) at the newly opened Long Bar Coffee Shop in the centre of Chelmsford.

My full-time year at Braintree College finished in July 1958 and I was transferred to the main Marconi works in New Street, Chelmsford, to continue my apprenticeship in the radio transmitter department, assembling cabinets. This was interspersed with weeks spent in the Apprentice Training Centre where we made our own toolboxes, screwdrivers, box spanners, etc. It also gave me the opportunity to make parts for the Goldie.

The first piece I made was for an adaptor between the 1⅞ exhaust pipe and the new 1¾ tapered-style Gold Star silencer – the bike really looked the part. Alloy covers were made to go between the rear mudguard and its support brackets filling in the void and making the bike look very distinctive. Going to the Long Bar I soon made friends with another Gold Star owner, Ron Fisher. His bike was a new DBD 34 with a five gallon alloy tank painted red. He had a red beard and was known locally as 'The Flying Postman', although he worked as a bricklayer.

Bunny (Bernard) Dowsett had a beautiful Norton Dominator five-hundred 88. He worked as a fireman on steam railway engines and appeared at the Chelmsford Corn Exchange in boxing and wrestling bouts. Another guy, Don Smith, also had a Norton Dommie but his was a 600 99 model – he was a roofing contractor/tiler.

We all spent the rest of the summer along with some of the members of the Blue Star gang going to the seaside, Walton-on-the-Naze and Clacton, in convoy when there were no race meetings on at either Brands or Snetterton. We were avid fans of the likes of Minter, McIntyre, Hailwood, Alastair King, John Hartle, Alan Shepherd, Alan Trow, Ginger Payne, Tony Godfrey, Paddy Driver, John Surtees, Dickie Dale, Dave Chadwick, Bob Anderson, Bruce Daniels and Lewis Young, just to mention a few of those who entertained us, demonstrating their undoubted skill of man over machine that was just terrific to watch.

D.A. Cornell Motorcycles

A new motorcycle shop opened locally on our parade not far from my home, known as D.A. Cornell Motorcycles. It immediately attracted my attention as it had

two used Gold Stars in the window, so I called straight in to make myself known and look at the Goldies.

Derek Cornell was a nicely rounded man and we got on well. I, of course, introduced all of my friends to him and his business got off to a good start. He soon became the local Greeves agent and was very interested in scrambles (Moto Cross), sponsoring Pete Smith who was a very good local rider in these events. Autumn soon followed and the racing finished, as did the trips to the seaside. One day per week I still had to go to the Braintree College on Day Release taking my ONC (Ordinary National Certificate) in Mechanical Engineering, plus endorsements, which required me to attend the college one evening and not on the same day.

I covered the 12 miles to college (each way) throughout the winter twice a week. This truly became a time trial and the Goldie was the right bike to do it on, enjoying every mile whatever the conditions. I had only one mishap, which occurred on a very frosty, icy road on an early morning start to Braintree. On reaching Broomfield (a small village about 1½ miles from my home where my mother and grandmother grew up) one of the local coal merchant Mr Moy's trucks made a sudden stop in front of me. I braked hard and lost the front end, the bike went on its side under the truck and I struck my shoulder on the tailgate. Fortunately, no harm was done to bike or rider and so, without the knowledge of Mr Moy, I extracted the bike and went on my way!

That winter I had little spare time as I was trying to augment my wages by working overtime on transmitter cabinets' production most Saturdays and Sundays and also evenings until 8.30pm. This made a considerable difference in boosting my income from £5 to £7 per week and feeling 'in the money'! The rest of my time was taken up studying and completing tasks for the ONC, plus one evening for swimming, with any spare time spent playing with the Goldie.

Spring 1959

Thankfully, the spring of 1959 soon arrived and brought with it the start of the road racing season. Having made and fitted the same side plates to the rear guards of Ron's Gold Star as mine, our bikes looked similar. Bunny had also part exchanged his Dommie for a new DBD model from Don Hunt's shop in Witham, Essex. Don was a real Goldie fan and had finished 10th in the 1955 Senior Clubman's TT on one of the BSAs. Bunny wanted side plates as well and personalised his bike with a superb black leather tank cover.

Together our three Goldies looked great and were admired everywhere we went, especially at race meetings when we lined them up. Brands Hatch and Snetterton were joined with other circuits further afield and that year we went to our first Thruxton 500 – a production bike race at that circuit near Andover in Hampshire which covered 500 miles. It was terrific to see Gold Stars battling with Triumphs, Velocettes, AJS, Matchless and one or two BMWs in a race on the rough former airfield circuit with straw bale chicanes.

Vibration seemed to be the killer, with petrol and oil tanks splitting, mudguards and stays fracturing and falling off, and even sheer fatigue – the two riders on the

A trio of Gold Stars at Brands Hatch during Spring 1959, the Everett/Minter bike is on the far left. The middle one is Ron Fisher's, 'the Flying Postman', and the third is 'Bunny' Dowsett's.

bikes for about four and a half hours each in roughly two-hour stints. A real test of man and machine, but to me it looked real fun and I wished I could take part.

After the Thruxton meeting we were all 'revved' up and did not want to go home, so we went on to Stonehenge and camped among the stones for the night. A camp fire, a few beers and a singsong made the perfect end to a long day of racing, but we were up with the Druids to see the sun rise – unfortunately it never really did, though, as it was too cloudy!

Never mind, we had a 100 mile (approximately) ride home to look forward to. We stopped for lunch at the Ace café in Hendon on the North Circular to look at all the other bikes. There were usually between 50 and 100 riders who congregated, and it was the Rockers' Mecca (and has since been resurrected as a monument to the time). Riding was great but the Rockers were attracting the attention of the police as speeds were ever increasing, and there was no overall speed limit on any road where the de-restricted sign was shown. This meant that 100mph was common but generally a maximum was 110 as very few bikes could do more, although some owners said they could get 125 (no chance, even a Vincent Black Shadow 1000cc had a job to do that on the road!).

Falling foul of the law

I certainly fell foul of the law and got fined for speeding in Stratford, East London, and on 6 July 1959 I was fined two pounds there by the Court for excess speed in a built-up area and my licence was endorsed. Generally the police showed some tolerance providing you were not too cheeky. On one instance late at night in a built-up area, four of us – Ron, Bunny, myself and Russel Bigden (who had joined the gang with a 1956 DB 34 Goldie and lived in Maldon, Essex. I had helped him on many occasions sorting out his bike especially the ignition timing which he had difficulty with) were line abreast in the wet and going quite quickly. There was not a soul about and we were stopped at a road block at the next junction and given a severe lecture, but we were eventually sent on our way in good humour after the police had thoroughly examined our machines. They were impressed with the condition of them, and one of the policemen wanted a machine desperately for himself!

First thoughts of racing

Riding on the road was getting more and more hectic and dangerous and the thought of racing was coming frequently into my mind – the love of riding and riding fast was in my blood, the Goldie being fast and reliable helped with this but my competitive spirit was also growing apace. On the next visit to Brands I started timing novices in the middle and back of the field to see what they were lapping and what I would have to do just to be involved.

One minute 15 to 20 seconds seemed to be what was needed for a lap to keep in mid-field in the non-experts race, this represented an approximate average speed of 60mph as the Brands circuit was about 1.24-miles at that time. The bikes I timed were also Gold Stars and I thought, 'I could do that'. However, any thoughts that it would be easy, or that motorcycle racing was not dangerous, were so graphically illustrated to me at a meeting we had been to at Crystal Palace in south-east London. Totally contrary to today's circuits this one had no run off areas, in fact half the circuit was enclosed on the edge of the track with five-feet high concrete walls! The other half was enclosed by a dirt bank reinforced with railway sleepers! If you fell off you got hurt.

In this instance it was a 500cc heat, and one guy at the end of the pit straight going into Paddock bend (later to be called Ramp Bend as they moved the Paddock) lost control and hit the wall with his bike bouncing back onto the track. Six riders came to grief in this accident, two died and the others were seriously injured. As it says on the tickets 'Motor Racing is Dangerous'. Pictures of this horrific accident were on the front pages of the *Daily Mirror* and the *Daily Herald* along with centre spreads, showing the public at large the evils of motorcycling!

The much publicised crash at Crystal Palace, south London, on Easter Monday, 30 March 1959.

This did not deter me, however, and the thoughts of racing continued to grow, and soon my friend Ron Fisher was first to have a go on a racing circuit. Brands Hatch (being our favourite and closest) was chosen, of course. The real reason was that every Wednesday and Saturday when there was no racing the circuit was available for testing. It was open to everyone who paid the fee of £4 10s per day, both cars and motorcycles, and organised with marshals on 20 minute sessions, for example: for bikes 20 mins – 10 min break to clear up. Then 20 mins for cars from 9.30am to 4.30pm with an hour break for lunch – very reasonable. There were all sorts of cars from single seaters to Austin Sevens containing all levels of drivers from first-time novices to GP veterans.

This also applied to the bikes as it was not unusual to see Derek Minter trying out the latest mods to his Manx Nortons or A.N. Other seeing what he could do on his BSA Bantam. All had to have their wits about them as some of the speed differentials were alarming and the first timers' corner lines were totally unpredictable. This, of course, led to many mishaps and some serious accidents, but even then there was no litigation sought or asked for.

Ron readied his Goldie by removing the headlight and centre stand. The second item was obligatory, but all you had to do with glass was put a cross of sticky tape over it to comply with the regulations. We followed Ron down to Brands, his bike had been put into a wooden pig truck and towed down. It was a dry but cold day with not too many people and Ron was excited but nervous.

The next bike session was announced and Ron went off through the tunnel on his well warmed-up Goldie with the red tank. He was waved out onto the circuit down by the start and we all cheered as he went gingerly round Paddock Bend for the very first time. He completed his first and second lap and seemed to be going well when disaster struck. Going up the hill into Druids – the hairpin – someone quickly dived up the inside of Ron, he went wide and braked late. Down he came on the only slippery bit on the outside of the bend. Thankfully, neither he nor the bike were hurt but, I am sorry to say, this was Ron's first and last venture onto a circuit. The experience also seemed to sway the others as well as they never even attempted it!

This proved to most people the theory that as soon as you go on a race circuit you will fall off. Do people still feel the same today?

Decision time

The winter of 1959–60 was the time I made a decision. I do not know why, but I felt committed to going racing and if I was to practise at Brands it would be on a bike fit for racing (as I could have it on my limited budget) and only use it as a learning step for racing, not as a 'try it and see' experience. So the bike had to be prepared.

Space was at a premium – my workshop consisted of a 6ft x 8ft shed in my parents' garden, where the Goldie was normally kept. It was a simple wooden structure with a bench down one side and a big vice mounted on that. Tools were the normal compliment of hand tools – we did not even have an electric drill!

This did not matter as true enthusiasm and commitment were in abundance. Suffice it to say, there was certainly no heating in this cramped space – we just got on with it as we knew no different. First the Goldie was stripped of all its road bits. Seat, lights, mudguards and brackets, dynamo, battery, toolbox and those horribly heavy standard foot rests and side stand, all went. A wooden block was constructed to mount the bike on so it was slightly off the ground and supported well.

As my beloved bike was off the road, I had to have transport and so purchased a 125cc BSA Bantam for £14 from my neighbour. Lots of my pals and my girlfriend Pearl (the sister of one of my rocker friends, Keith Crannes) derided this 'thing' but I did not care. I was mobile and I was going racing. I will add though, that because I pushed the poor old Bantam to, and past, its limits, I fell off it more times than I can remember – and I would rather forget it anyway as it was the source of so many leg pulls from my chums!

Rebuilding the engine

After removing the easy parts I decided to totally rebuild the engine. As I dismantled it, it revealed some problems – mainly just wear and tear but also some surprises. The oval flywheels of the CB engine were all polished, as was the con rod and rocker arms. The exhaust valve was a unique shape with a domed head and cut away rear (I still have this valve – it is an old friend, I look at it often and have never seen another like it).

I finally had this almost fifty-year mystery solved by my friend Mick Walker, who has recently published a biography entitled *Derek Minter – King of Brands* (Breedon). In this, Mick reveals that Derek's Gold Star was a BB (narrow fin) and that BSA development engineer Roland Pike provided Derek (via dealers Hallets of

The ex-Minter Gold Star in all its glory. Originally a BB34, it had been fitted with a later Big Fin motor specially tuned by the famed BSA engineer, Roland Pike. As bought from Monty & Ward's in 1958.

Canterbury) with an experimental CB (big fin) engine during the mid-1950s, which was still fitted when Derek disposed of the machine at the end of 1956. So that explained that. The valves, being worn (as were the guides), had to be replaced as well as the springs, retainers and collets, but the biggest problem was the big-end. It was a little loose and I could detect the slightest up and down movement, it just would not do to go racing. Facilities were not available to replace the big-end and, as I wanted it done properly, there was only one place to take it. That was the mecca for all things to do with Gold Star – Eddie Dow's emporium, Banbury, Oxfordshire. Eddie was famous for his exploits on Gold Stars, which included winning the 1955 Isle of Man Senior Clubman's TT, his shop specialised in Gold Stars, and he also offered all kinds of bolt-on goodies for these bikes. An obvious choice, then, but how to get there? On the Bantam was clearly out of the question so it was a case of 'whose machine can I borrow?'

Travelling to Banbury

During discussions on what I was doing, and where the Gold Star had gone, Derek Cornell came up with the offer for me to go to Banbury on a used Greeves twin cylinder 250 roadster he had in stock. His idea was that if I liked it I would tell all the locals and he would get some free advertising. I jumped at the chance. The Gold Star crankcase and flywheels were put in a box and strapped on to the passenger's portion of the dual seat. On a cold Saturday in November I made the arduous journey to Banbury, mainly on minor roads, from Chelmsford. I used the A414 to Harlow, Hoddesdon, St Albans, Hemel Hempsted, Tring, then the A41 to Aylesbury and then Bicester through to Banbury and the Gold Star Mecca – a distance of about 90 miles.

The Greeves behaved impeccably and sang along happily at 60-65mph (70mph downhill) on the clock and, I must say, the handling really impressed me. It did not put a foot wrong on the three hour, non-stop journey. I left the goods and purchased the other parts, valves, springs, gaskets, etc, had a cup of tea and a roll at a nearby café where I first met Dick Standing (who lived in Ascot, Berkshire), who was to become a lifelong friend and fellow racer, then left for the long journey home in the cold. It was frosty but bright and dry all day.

I arrived back at Derek's shop at 4.30pm and reported a very successful and enjoyable ride. I told him that I would thoroughly recommend the Greeves Twin to anyone even though the forks and the frame looked strange.

Eddie Dow had said the work would be done in seven to 10 days and he would send the completed bottom end back to me by parcel post.

The Marconi 'Scrap Shop'

At Marconi's I had made several friends in different departments and was getting to know my way around one of the most fascinating places, which was the scrap shop where you could buy anything. This consisted of nuts and bolts, any material, cabinets and even scrap transmitters with electrical component valves, resistors, capacitors, etc.

What I was looking for was enough duralumin sheet ¼in thick to make myself a set of engine plates to substitute the steel ones. Dural, as it is commonly known, is as light as aluminium but a lot stronger. Additionally, I needed a piece of aluminium bronze rod to make a new pair of valve guides – the standard components being manufactured from phosphor bronze. Aluminium-bronze is more stable at higher temperatures and works very well, especially on the exhaust side. The right stuff was duly found and for a few pence and a chitty it was mine!

Making the replacement engine plates was relatively easy, using the steel ones as a pattern, but the valve guides had to be turned and reamed with great accuracy and the correct clearances. Once made, my dear old mum's gas oven came into use to heat up the cylinder head, drive out the old guides, reheat the head and drive in the new guides, re-reaming until the valves were a perfect fit. Not a five minute job or one for someone who is nervous, but it worked perfectly.

All was re-assembled as far as possible with the new dural engine plates (which I had engine turned for effect) ready to receive the rebuilt crankcase. I had left new main bearings, which came with the compliments of my father and Hoffmans, with Eddie Dow. When it arrived frankly I thought the big end was rather stiff – but the experts had done it. I finished the bike off with a racing seat and an old piston in place of the dynamo, and it was ready to test on the road.

Problems

At first I was very happy, carefully running in all the new bearings, and had a few good rides until one day when I was going along the newly opened Ingatestone bypass (part of the A12 between Brentwood and Chelmsford). An ominous knock sounded and got worse as I continued the five miles home. Yes, you guessed it, the big end had gone! I was distraught, the time, the work, the cost – all for nothing. Back on the telephone to Mr Dow I explained the situation. He was very good and said if I brought the crankcase back he would put in a new one while I waited. This time my friend Russel lent me his DB Goldie for the journey, and the following weekend I retraced my way to Banbury.

Fortunately, it was dry and not so cold. I certainly got there a lot quicker as I had a good idea of the road and the Goldie would cruise at 80-90mph happily. Dows were as good as gold and replaced the big end, reassembling the crankcase in a waiting time of two-and-a-half hours, so it was the long ride home again and a final rebuild, hopefully. This time I also bought a new set of clutch plates, chains and green linings for the 8in front brake.

Back on the road again it felt good, and I was soon in the groove and with one of the guys in the Blue Star gang. His nickname was 'Bonk', real name Martin Turner, who was very small and light and had a beautifully prepared 500cc Bathtub Triumph T100A sporting a twin leading shoe front brake which he had designed and built himself. He was a very quick rider and we chased each other along the very twisty A414 between Ongar and Chelmsford return – super riding.

A Brands Hatch debut

The time was nearing now for when the track test had to be committed, of course Brands Hatch was chosen and a Saturday at the end of January 1960 picked. Suddenly it was all happening!

Racing is not a 'turn up and do it' situation, it all has to be organised months in advance. The club which puts on the meeting (or the company which runs the circuit) has to advertise in the motorcycling press that regulations are available for their meeting, this is usually three months before the meeting takes place. So in January 'Regs' become available for March/April meetings, the first ones of the year. You had to write off for these 'Regs' and wait for them to come – complete them and return together with your entry fee which was about £3-£5, and then wait again and see if you had been accepted!

Apart from the time, the most difficult part (for me, as I was still only 19) was to get my mother – my father refused to do it – to sign my completed regulations as my parent or guardian. This had to be done until I was 21 years old, the coming of age at that time. To my mother it was like signing my death warrant and she cried every time she did it.

You were certainly not guaranteed a place in the race meeting as most times they were heavily over-subscribed, and it was not always first come first served, as the organisers wanted 'Stars', names and regulars – those with experience – before novices. I was a real novice.

Brands Hatch 1959, with left to right, Mike Hailwood, Ginger Payne, Alan Trow and Derek Minter (all with 500cc Manx Nortons).

King of Brands, Derek Minter, Reg's idol as a teenager.

Finally, I got my first acceptance at Snetterton on Easter Sunday, a day to look forward to. Before the Brands' practice further work was done on the bike. The first thing was fitting proper racing tyres. I had obtained them by writing to Avon's racing department in Melksham, Wiltshire, and telling them about my venture into road racing. They agreed by letter to send me a new pair of Avon racing tyres by rail. When the station contacted me I took a friend on my trusty Bantam to collect them. When fitted they really looked the part and with racing brake linings, new chains and a good rebuilt engine, I was nearly ready to go.

One last job was to fit a fibreglass Dolphin-style fairing which I had bought from a guy at college for £1, he had already tried to fit it to his B31 without any success. Fitting this to get good clearance round the handle bars and to fit snugly elsewhere, was much more of a job than I had anticipated but I wanted it on to complete the picture. What it did not have until I went racing was the perspex screen, which I had to make myself from flat sheet heating it carefully to bend it – also another very tricky job but when you had no money to buy these things you had to do it yourself.

Now to get it to Brands. Ron's friend with the pig trailer was happy to loan it again and another friend, 'Tree' – (I never knew his proper name), who rode an International Norton and lived in Fyfield near Ongar – had access to an Austin 12 taxi with a tow bar attachment. The bike was duly loaded and we all clambered aboard the taxi to enjoy the ride in luxurious comfort, via the preferred route through the Blackwall Tunnel (still no Dartford Tunnel at that time). I had borrowed a set of leathers for the occasion (plastics actually with leather pads on shoulders, knees and elbows!) but had bought a new ACU helmet, and everything was black as it was the only colour then and little else was accepted or available.

By this time I also had grown a very good beard and trained a moustache to curl at the ends, and it made me look older – they were in fashion – I did not have to shave and it stopped the rain stinging my face. At least I looked the part!

On arrival, I signed on, paid my fee and then the bike was 'scrutineered', something I had not known about. An official looking man in a boiler suit checked it over, pulled the exhaust pipe, shook the head stock, checked chain tension and general fixtures and fittings. All was OK and he put a piece of sticky tape on the fairing to show it had been done – all very professional.

We had no briefing of any description, no flag drill, no safety remarks, nothing.

The Goldie was duly started and warmed-up thoroughly as it was a very cold day, and suddenly the next bike session was announced on the tannoy.

The moment of truth

Now the moment of truth – surprisingly I was not nervous but very excited and wanted to get on with it. Dropping down through the hallowed tunnel under the track from the paddock to the centre of the circuit was a moment I shall never forget, and the noise from the open megga (we made it at the Apprentice Training Centre) as it reverberated on the walls was fantastic. Along the path to the pit area I looked around. Brands looked different from this perspective and I enjoyed the moment. A man was stationed on the slip road access to the track. He stopped me then waved me on when all was clear – this was it – goggles down and open her up! At first the bike did not react or respond too well as I had not got the revs high enough, and I had to get over the flat spot to bring her on the megga. Duly done, I made sure not to drop the revs or go slow enough again to let this happen.

As I had been to Brands before I thought I knew the circuit well, and for sure I knew where the bends were and which way they went. What I had no experience of was using all of the road, and I was not ready for the plunge down Paddock Bend or the steep climb up Druids Hill. The hairpin came up quicker than expected, but the bike went nicely round on the megga in the low first gear, down the hill to bottom bend where the camber seemed like the Wall of Death – along the bottom straight, which I realised now was a bend, and into the complex of Kidney and Clearways – at least three or four corners at that speed and no experience. Clearways corner rose and fell alarmingly with several gouges out of the surface where many had fallen. Accelerating along the top straight and past the pits I completed the first lap – great – but where to brake for Paddock Hill Bend? There is a long curve into it, and it drops away, plus the camber. Now I felt it for the first time, a corner that is so fast but must be treated with great respect – the line really had to be learnt.

'Concentrate, ride smoothly, use all the track, get the lines right, learn, make haste slowly', all this was going on in my mind but I was lapping OK. Of course others came by me, even a sidecar outfit, but I would not be diverted from my task.

Suddenly the red flag came out and I pulled off the track, my first 20 minute session was finished and I had completed 12 laps of the track without falling off. It was great, and I just could not wait to get out there again.

A close friend was Martin Hayward, seen here on his Gold Star during the 1959 Senior Manx Grand Prix.

January 1960, the ex-Minter Gold Star on the road, in racing trim.

A feeling of elation

That day I was to complete five 20 minute sessions, and yes, I got faster, smoother, and began to know where I was going and where the breaking points were – the Kidney Clearway complex had been reduced to two bends flowing nicely into one another. I had a feeling of elation, knowing I was doing what I really wanted to do. On a high all the way home, my friends were bored with all the descriptions but I did not care, this was great.

The first practice session at Brands, being overtaken at Clearways by a faster rider.

Reg's first-ever pratise at Brands Hatch, in January 1960, with future wife Pearl.

The next few weeks went by slowly but with a lot of help and encouragement from my friends. John Houghton (with the Velocette whom I crashed into) had been working with Martin Hayward at De Havilands. Martin lived at Walton-on-Thames and we had met at Brands practising. He had already been riding his Gold Star in races and it looked so well prepared – a real racing bike with alloy rims etc. Martin showed me a few tips on preparation and we became kindred spirits. Dick Standing, who I had met at Banbury, was also one of Martin's friends so relationships were already forming.

Brian Wolfendon – who rode a beautiful little 175cc Gilera which went well and sounded like a really sporty machine – and who was with me at college, was also an influence and helped with preparation. The apprenticeship was going well and I was working in the gear cutting department and helping assemble gear boxes for radar aerials, all good experience which complemented the racing preparation and understanding.

Trying to refine my bike, I made a flexible mounting for the rev counter and, doing away with the superfluous speedo, fitted the fairing properly with new and stronger brackets.

She really began to look the part, especially when I painted on my first set of racing numbers (these were allocated to me by the organisers of the Snetterton meeting); the number '32' is indelibly printed in my mind.

Painting the yellow ellipse (again dimensions for this were given) brought the fairing to life, the yellow colour depicted 500cc class (blue for 350s, green for 250s and black for 125s) with black numerals carefully displayed. I was so proud.

And that Snetterton race debut date was fast approaching. One that was to be a life-changing event.

Chapter 3

Racing the Gold Star

Race day, Easter Sunday 17 April 1960, quickly arrived and the faithful pig trailer was once again utilised, but this time it was towed behind a Standard Pennant in sage green, owned by Keith Vine who was the parts manager, salesman and storeman at D.A. Cornell Motorcycles. He had very kindly offered his services for the epic event.

Snetterton

Snetterton is some 65 miles from Chelmsford, via Braintree, Halstead, Sudbury, Bury St Edmunds and Thetford – all A roads but single track and full of bends. Great on a fast bike but very slow by Standard Pennant (1200cc) and pig truck! We allowed three and a half hours for the journey, including a stop for tea – the driver deemed it necessary! This necessitated an early start because scrutineering began at 8am for a practice start at 9am; so we duly left after loading up at 4.30am, with little sleep that night due to excitement. This was the part that in my previous life as a spectator I never saw. Spectators turned up at midday, watched the racing and went home at 5pm – a nice day out. Those who raced and entertained the spectators were usually up before dawn, after working most of the night before getting the bike ready, then having it scrutineered and warmed up. Practising, refettling and preparing the bike for racing was a lot of hard work and, I might add, you were also paying as much (if not more) than the spectators for the honour of doing it.

The meetings were always over-subscribed, so the organisers did have it easy as far as finding riders was concerned – and there were a lot of them at that. This first meeting at Snetterton was

Reg outside his Chelmsford home with the 500cc BSA Gold Star; prior to his first race at Snetterton in April 1960.

an example, only a few of the riders had more than one bike unless they were well sponsored. The classes were 125, 250, 350, 500 and sidecar. Solos were 40 starters and sidecars – 20 per race – but 350cc had three heats and 500cc had two heats. There were about 7 x 40 plus 2 x 20 competitors, i.e. 320 (say 300), which meant 300 bikes which had to be scrutineered!

Each class had its own practice but if you can imagine eighty 500cc bikes in the very congested warming up area, all with open meggas and blipping throttles, the noise was unbelievable (and ear plugs had not been invented!). Trying to get through the opening onto the circuit (which was just wide enough for three bikes) and being stopped after the first 40 had gone through – it was just pandemonium. Everyone was wound up, but this was all part of the scene, again one that the normal spectator does not see or comprehend.

The journey was uneventful; we had the requested stop for tea (brewed up on a primus stove and taken in a layby near Bury St Edmunds), then carried on to Snetterton.

Entering the circuit

Entering the circuit near the Hairpin (not even part of the circuit now) – after our passes had been checked and double checked – we progressed alongside the Home Straight to the Esses (now called the Bomb Hole) and I glanced through the car window. I must say that the surface of the circuit did not impress me too much as it was broken up in places with grass growing through the joints!

We went over the rickety bridge into the centre of the circuit and across to the paddock – a place where I had very seldom been before. Here there were all kinds of trucks, vans and cars with trailers, also tents where the guys who had long distances to travel had slept over night. There was real activity at 7.45am on that Easter Sunday morning, although it was strange as it was quiet – the lull before the storm – as engines were not allowed to be started until 8.45am.

We found a place to park with a piece of concrete access track nearby, luckily, as many people were on the grass, and although the weather was surprisingly good it was wet underfoot and quickly deteriorated into mud.

Offloading and putting the bike on the stand, I donned my leathers in the toilets and there was very little in the way of changing or washing facilities available. These were real leathers, purchased from Dave Mallows who had only used them on the road but had grown out of them. (Dave raced later in life when his roofing business was a success, mainly in sidecar classics with a special Vincent. He had great results and retired at the end of 2004). My racing boots were new and very polished, full length leather ones with a zip up the back – I really looked the part.

This done, it was off to the scrutineering bay, it was at least under cover but had all four sides open to the elements. The time was about 8.30am and the queue was very long, with everyone jostling for position, but we just had to wait our turn. There must have been 100 people with bikes in front of me. At 8.45am it was like a storm approaching as first one, then two, quickly followed by 10-20, 50-100 bikes all started up in the paddock, and it was like that for the rest of the day. What a noise, the only respite was lunch which was taken in the hour between practising finishing and racing starting, when there was relative peace and the local churches had their services. Readers should remember that, unlike today, racing motorcycles at that time were totally unsilenced.

Finally, I got my bike and clothing passed by the scrutineer and the vital piece of sticky tape was put on the fairing, also my crash helmet was given approval of the ACU cut out mark in the leather harness.

It was 9.30 by now and, pushing my bike back to the car, I noticed practise was well under way and the bikes could be heard in full song going down the Norwich Straight. The warming-up area was also jammed full with bikes and the noise was unbelievable.

I checked the oil, petrol and tyre pressures, took the bung out of the protruding large hole in the GP Carburettor (put there so no extraneous objects could get in), and she was ready to start! The gear lever was put into second gear – one push down from neutral with the reverse plate box – pulled the engine back onto compression, pulled in the clutch and we pushed for all we were worth ('we' meaning my friends as I was sitting astride it) up to speed. I dropped the clutch, bumped in the seat and hoped the engine would go over compression and not lock up. Over she went and was fired up and ran OK, starting relatively easily in the cold morning air. I gave it a quick spin up and down the access road and went off to the warm up area to wait my turn for practise – this time with my competitors!

Again, I knew the circuit at Snetterton as a spectator. This was an old World War Two Aerodrome circuit, and the track was mainly the disused perimeter except for the home straight which was part of the main runway – totally unlike Brands Hatch which was purpose-built for racing and in a natural valley. Snetterton was flat and open, windy and cold, had no markers to denote the edge of the circuit and was very wide in places but only with a good surface in parts, making braking and peel-off points difficult. Once the engine (and especially all the oil) was warm, the engine was stopped and the soft engine starting plug was replaced by one suitable for racing such as a Lodge RL47, and the bike was then re-bump started.

Practice arrives

My turn to practise had finally come, and as we jostled and pushed through the gap, suddenly I was onto the circuit and free to give it all I had! I went up through the gears (keeping over to the left for the first right-hander) into a sweeping long fast corner into a short straight and to a section of the circuit I had not seen before

Snetterton, Easter Sunday 1960. Reg (32) going out for practise before his racing debut later that day.

where spectators were not admitted. The next bend was a right-hander also but without any real means of seeing where it started and went, it was so flat. This one was quite tight but followed immediately into a fast sweeping left-hander into the long Norwich Straight which ran parallel to the A11 trunk road. This was a long straight, and at the end were marker boards set at 100-yard intervals before the hairpin bend, the first one stating 400 yards (brake early, change down to first) the hairpin bend still coming up quickly and very sharp – many people came to grief here. I went up through the gears down the home straight, bumpy, rough and grassy, then into the Esses, a sweeping left dropping down into a hole with a good camber followed by an opening out right – it was a great feeling.

Along the short straight to the very fast sweeping right-hand bend called Coram Curve, then up the straight via a flat-out left-hander and past the pits – 2.7 miles completed without mishap. The following four laps went well and I was learning OK but I knew now that my 'fast' Gold Star was not fast when Manx Nortons and G50s just flew past me down the straights and into those fast sweeping corners, going round me as though I was standing still. And the braking! I was sitting up braking when others were still flat on the tank! I had so much to learn – 'just riding' and 'competition' were vastly different.

Practise ends.

These races were national events open to anybody in the UK, so we novices in our heats were riding against the best in the country (and probably in the world). It was really not surprising we got blown off in practice, especially when it was a first. The red flag came out and I rode slowly back into the pits to the car where my crew were waiting – they were happy and patted me on the back – apparently I had done well, I had actually gone past a few riders and also looked good.

Now I faced the long wait to the start of my first race. We fried up a little lunch, I felt alright although my appetite was not that good, my crew ate ravenously though.

The bike was cleaned, checked over thoroughly and topped up with Castrol R and fuel. I found my friend, Martin Hayward, and he told me about the gearing for Snetterton. He was using a 21-tooth engine sprocket, mine was only 19 – far too low – so it was off round the pits to other Goldie competitors to try and borrow such a sprocket! As they were all using their 21-tooth gears, the nearest Martin had was a 22 so I opted for this as my standard box had a lower first gear and other internal ratios. It was preferred to over-revving down the long straights. After changing this (I had to lengthen the primary chain) and readjusting the rear chain, we all went to watch a few races – they were fast coming past

A happy looking Reg opposite the pits at Snetterton.

the pits, flat out and jostling for position – my excitement, pulse and adrenaline was pumping and raring to go, this was the life!

The first race

'Competitors for Event Five Heat One 500cc to the warm-up area' came loud and clear over the tannoy. My heart jumped and my pulse rate went up a gear. Pushing the Goldie (race number 32) into life I rode to the warming-up area and queued up at the entrance with my fellow real competitors for my first real race. This initial queue was to draw for grid positions. Up until now, I had no idea how this was done and to draw seemed to be fair for the heats, and the grid for the finals went on time.

There were eight rows of five so to be in the first three was a help, but I did not care, I just wanted to get on with it. Approaching the official I saw him holding a big bunch of leather strings, one end free with the other inside a bag. This had an aluminium disc with a number stamped on it. One leather string was hanging out to the left and was easy to grab, so I pulled it quickly, you just cannot believe how I felt

Warming up the Gold Star before the debut race.

when I looked at it and found the number 'ONE'! First on the grid for my first-ever road race, was this an omen or what? My friends were happy and Bunny went off to grab his camera, he could not miss this photo opportunity of number one on the grid.

I got the bike warmed up. The previous race had finished and the track was cleared so we were ushered onto the track and to our allotted grid numbers. I went to number-one, gave the bike a good rev up, put it into gear and let it stop gently by letting out the clutch with the front brake on. Silence! I looked to my left, and number two on the grid was Derek Minter! Number three on the grid was Mike Hailwood. I did not look any further – surprisingly they had got good numbers too!

Again, I just could not believe it. Goggles lowered, I bent down, selected neutral with the gear lever, sat on the bike, put it into second, got off and pulled the bike back until the engine was on compression. I pulled in the clutch, made sure it was

Lining up on the front row at Snetterton for his first-ever race, with Derek Minter (Lancefield Norton, 4) alongside. Reg finished 22nd, while Minter won.

free and pushed the bike to the line. I was ready to go, making sure also that the petrol tap was on.

Bunny was in front of me waving to take that vital picture – I was ready but others were still looking round – the starter was not even on his rostrum yet. 'Hurry up, I want to go!' I thought. Sure enough in his own good time the starter got onto his rostrum, looked around to see if anyone was creeping and got the OK to start from the clerk of the course. He raised the national flag, hesitated, and then down it came. I let go the front brake for a moment, more quiet, then pandemonium broke loose, the noise, the movement, activity, bikes everywhere – but me! What had happened?

The start at Snetterton is slightly uphill, a 500 Gold Star weighed about 300 lbs, the rider (me) 133 lbs. Although I pushed I did not move: I got 'bootspin', my legs were running but nothing was moving. A vital part was missing! All the preparation, all the thought, cost, anxiety and elation, all let down by the absence of rubber soles on my boots! So I stopped – pulled the bike back into compression, walked slowly pushing, got up speed, bumped onto the seat, dropped the clutch – boom, boom, boom – the engine fired and was running, I put my leg over the seat, hard acceleration, tucked down behind the screen just in time to see the last person disappearing round the first bend – what a terrible start to my racing career.

'Settle down now' my brain was saying – 'don't panic, enjoy the experience'. Total concentration on what I was doing became engaged. The exhilaration in going down the Norwich Straight and waiting for the marker boards to appear, to brake hard at about 250 was my aim, sit up, all OK down through the box to first round the hairpin, tuck down behind the screen second, third, fourth, the gearing seemed OK. I revved up to 6,000rpm and passed my first competitor going into the

Getting a taste of racing for real during the event, Easter Sunday 1960.

Esses. I was racing, I could see others in front of me – keep going – concentrate round Coram Curve, accelerate hard through the left kink, up into top just before the pits which then flew by, this time I passed someone going round Riches – what a feeling! Head down again, get into a routine, learn the peel off points, hit the apex, try to be smooth, nothing erratic. I was really enjoying this.

Those heats were only seven laps at about two minutes per lap, less than 15 minutes of racing (the leaders were lapping the 2.7 mile circuit in 1 min 50 secs. 89mph average) I passed a few more but all too soon the chequered flag was out, and I sat up and eased off, and my first road race was over.

Cruising round the lap for the first time noticing the spectators – there were thousands lining the circuit, small stands full at the hairpin and the covered one at the Esses. They were leaning on the picket fencing and waving to the riders. I had been there just a few short months ago, but now I knew this was to be my side of things in the future.

Back in the paddock

When I pulled back into the paddock, my friends were very excited – the questions flowed but, of course, the first one was 'what happened at the start?' All were duly answered. Generally the first race had been good and I had finished in 22nd place from the 40 starters – about mid-field from a bad start, but short of the cut-off point of 15th to qualify for the final. My fastest lap of 2m 8secs (an average speed of about 76mph) was not bad for a first attempt on a six-year-old bike. All the packing up was an anti-climax but the drive home took place in good spirits and a lot of chatting was done. I knew then that I could not stop, this was the life which had a lot of teamwork and preparation but was a truly individual participant sport.

A real anti-climax

For the next few days after Snetterton, returning to work was a real anti-climax; although now I was working in the gear cutting and gearbox assembly at Marconi which was very interesting. Also, the education side was taking up a great deal of time studying for my Higher National in maths, theory of machines and strength of materials – one day on day-release and three evenings of 6-9pm. All this added to my understanding of the mechanical intricacies of the motorcycle.

A real downside was the lack of new entries being accepted for meetings, many being returned as 'over-subscribed'. Letters arriving at home were rapidly opened and when the word appeared it really knocked my patience; it was a fact that for every meeting of 300 riders there seemed to be 600 applicants, and the top riders were chosen first.

I belonged to Bemsee which was the racers' name for BMCRC, the British Motor Cycle Racing Club, as you had to belong to a club that was affiliated to the

ACU (Auto Cycle Union) the governing body of all motorcycle sport. This could help as this club also held races just for club members, especially at Silverstone, which were great for novices like me to enter. Finally I got an acceptance letter for a national meeting organised by the Greenwich M & MCC, Rochester & D MCC and Gravesend Eagles MCC, together with the Brands Racing Committee at Brands Hatch – but not until Whit Monday, 6 June. So far away. Maybe I only got an entry because so many riders would be at the TT in the Isle of Man. Whatever the reason, however, I at last had an entry.

ESSA

My friend Brian Wolfendon helped to keep my interest going. He was a real enthusiast, and was in my class studying HNC, so we met regularly. He rode a Triumph 650cc TR6 which had replaced the Gilera. He watched me race at Snetterton and was full of praise, and he came round to help refettle the bike as I had decided to go for another practice session at Brands during May to prepare for the Whit Monday meeting. I was also active at my local club ESSA (Eastern Sporting Sidecar Association) which had many members. This club used to run some meetings at Boreham circuit, an old World War Two airfield near Chelmsford, but, unfortunately, by the time I had begun racing the circuit was no longer in use.

ESSA organised local grass track meetings, all of which were well attended and were very competitive. Local man Derek Yorke was the star and the one to beat on his JAP sidecar outfit, and Londoner Alf Hagon was the leader on the solos. Eric Oliver (World Sidecar Champion on Norton machinery in 1949, 1950, 1951 and 1952) came to the club one evening to give us a talk on his Grand Prix career and (in spite of the weather) came on an International Norton – he was great and the evening was a huge success.

Going to Brands for practice involved begging for transport. This time Ron Fisher's new Ford 5 cwt van was kindly offered. Removing the Goldie's front wheel was the only way we could get it in and still we had to have the back doors open, but never mind – it was in. The session went by without incident and, with the 18-tooth engine sprocket refitted, the gearing seemed fine. The engine was just making 7,000rpm before braking when going into Paddock Bend. My lines became smoother and lap times were dropping into the 1-min 10-sec area, good improvement, but I noticed that the megaphone exhaust had begun to scrape around some of the corners, especially on Clearways. These practice sessions were so valuable as they gave at least six or seven 20 minute periods, far more than I would ever get on a race day. Learning was such a pleasure and was vital if I was to improve.

Derek Minter

It also gave me a chance to meet other like-minded people who practised on a wide range of machines and some of the top men like Derek Minter who also practised there regularly. I introduced myself to him as I was riding his old bike, and I wanted to ask him some questions about it and his riding techniques, but he was rather un-cooperative and said he knew nothing about the engine. He said I should learn my own technique and not get in his way! He was, however, a professional racer and always in much demand. At a recent Brands' meeting he set about winning the 250, 350, 500 and unlimited races took home £130 in prize money alone!

At the time I was still earning under £5 per week and anyone earning £20 per week or £1,000 per year could live very well indeed, so I concentrated on what I was doing but really had no help or advice from anyone, and I certainly had none from my parents.

Brands Hatch race day

When race day finally came round, Ron Fisher was good enough to put the Ford van into use and off we went on a fine June day. Scrutineering started at 8.30am, so we left at 6.00am to ensure being there on time, again a 5.00am wake-up call. After scrutineering we were allowed three (yes, just three) laps of practice, so thank goodness I had had the opportunity of going there before! Brands was very short, only 1.24 miles, compared to Snetterton's 2.7 miles, and was mostly corners. The bottom 'straight' was one continuous bend and the faster you went the more bend it became, with the short top straight giving little respite. Braking had become very important and needed a lot of finesse, much of it being done on the lean, especially going into Paddock bend.

Here we did not draw for grid positions, we were put on a row according to the organisers who made their own choice. Referring to the programme I found I was on the third row of the grid for heat one of a four-lap race, with the first 12 going into the final. Their heats and finals were reserved for novices so, unlike Snetterton, we were not up against the aces and therefore had a chance. Many of the top riders, as I mentioned, were away on TT duty in the Isle of Man but of the 300 or so competitors, names such as Jim Redman, Paddy Driver, Bruce Daniels, Ginger Payne, Lewis Young, Fred Neville, Joe Dunphy, Dave Degens and Ian Goddard were there.

With so many competitors, riding in the paddock area was banned so no 'testing' could take place, which only enabled the bike to be started on the way to the warm-up area, just outside the tunnel. Again the noise of my fellow 30 competitors was making my neck tingle with anticipation. Here were my real competitors: 11 Gold Stars, 13 Manx Nortons, and the odd Matchless, Vincent and Norton Triumph hybrids including two local Southend riders, Brian Dennis and Colin Huff. In line of file we went through the tunnel and on to the grid where silence reigned once more.

This time I had new rubber stick-on soles on my boots and I had been practising starts, so I felt reasonably confident of not making a hash of it again. The grid area of Brands is also slightly downhill, helping the bump start situation, but this time I had two rows of machines in front of me and one behind. It looked and felt so different to Snetterton, especially with the huge packed grandstand to my left, it gave so much more atmosphere and created more tension.

A much better start

Anticipation rose as the starter mounted his rostrum, the flag hovered then dropped (it is so strange that you can hear the Pettering of feet hitting the ground before the first engine fires) then all noise; deafening sound breaks loose drowning out your own engine. I had elected to make sure of the start by running until I had good speed before dropping the clutch, but the engine fired up OK and I swung my leg over the saddle well in time to change up. This was different, I was in the middle of the pack, all hellbent in getting to Paddock Bend first – noise, bikes, jostling for position, acceleration, braking, it was bedlam and something I had never experienced before – it was real racing.

Safely round Paddock Bend, Druids Hill, 'keep left, brake hard, round Druids down the hill, round the bottom bend, accelerate hard, into Kidney and Clearways with the megga scraping the deck and on the twist grip to the stop past the start and finish'. I was 12th at the end of the first lap and overtook another rider going into Paddock Bend, and then I scratched round another on Clearways on the second lap. I managed to pass one more before the chequered flag fell on the fourth lap, finishing a creditable ninth in my first race at Brands and thus qualifying for the 15-lap final.

Reg's second meeting, and his first at Brands Hatch, came almost two months later on 6 June 1960, where he finished a creditable 9th on the Gold Star.

Reg's friends Dick Standing (left), and Martin Hayward in the Brands paddock, summer 1960. The bike is a 1949 Triumph Tiger 100, modified with swinging arm.

A celebratory cup of tea!

Friends and helpers were well impressed, and so was I, and so we had a celebratory cup of tea! Try as I might though, and after racking the brains of friends, I simply cannot recall the final at all. I cannot have finished in the top 12 as I would have achieved International Licence points which I have well documented, but the Goldie being inherently reliable must have finished. This is a real blank in my history – not really surprising as it is almost half a century ago, but most races I have super recollections of.

I just wanted to race and could see and feel already that it was beginning to take over my life, the thrill, excitement, speed, competition – all the ingredients were there. I now definitely had something that replaced my disappointment at not being trained as an RAF pilot, which once had been my dream. My dream now was racing motorcycles and I was doing it of my own accord and need. I did not want anything more, I just wanted to do it at whatever level I could.

Just after that race I had to sit my A1 HNC Examination at the Chelmsford College and one paper took place while the Senior TT was running. I could not bear to miss it as it was on the radio, and I needed to know the result. I was becoming obsessed. Taking my small portable radio in with me I made the excuse during the exam that I had to visit the 'boys' room', and to my surprise was given that sanction. I made myself comfortable and listened to the closing stages, returning to finish the exam. Needless to say that when the results were announced I had failed this part (but only by one percent), but this meant I had to re-sit all three papers and cost me a further year of studying!

In retrospect, it was a real lesson learned that I should concentrate on one thing at a time.

Back in action

Another six weeks had to pass before my next race, which was again at Snetterton on 24 July 1960. At least I knew the ropes this time, but I still had the same problem – transport.

Another lad I had met at Braintree College, Jeff White, came to the rescue with his father's old black 10 cwt Ford van. We all got into this easily – after Ron's 5 cwt version it was comparative luxury!

The race was in the same format as before with two 40-rider heats and the first 15 in each heat going to the final. I did not draw such a good start number and found myself on the third row, but at least the start was much better and I got away with the pack and was in for 10 laps of racing – great!

I soon found out, though, that my Gold Star was certainly no match for speed along Snetterton's three straights compared with the Manx Norton and Matchless G50 machines; 21 Nortons and five Matchless bikes were in that race and there were 12 Gold Stars. In the end I finished in 18th place at an average speed of 71mph. 'Who won?' you may ask – well Mike Hailwood did at an average of 87.4mph, and he lapped me on the last lap! Second was Bruce Daniels and Derek Minter was third, Ned Minihan and Ron Langston followed, Peter Darvil, Frank Rutherford and Tony Godfrey were next, all capable of winning and with some years' experience.

I was actually the fourth Gold Star home and with all those 'Experts' in the race was thoroughly satisfied with my performance and wanted more, having beaten my local rivals, Brian Dennis and Colin Huff.

Crystal Palace

August Bank Holiday Monday 1 August was Crystal Palace day, and I was looking forward to my first race on this notorious South London circuit. On arrival in something borrowed (I have no record of this one), we had our first encounter with the 'gnomes of Crystal Palace' – little brown men! They were the council-employed 'official' officials who would now all qualify for any 'jobsworth' title. They had brown Harris Tweed suits complete with waistcoats, and they were wearing brown trilby hats with bands and square brass plates bearing their number. To finish their ensemble they had brown puttees and brown shoes, also with square buckles.

As we competitors arrived, we were stopped and asked to produce our entry tickets and parking permits which were examined most rigorously. People in the vehicles had to get out and be counted as 'people without a ticket may not enter'. We always had this game with the officials as usually we were only given two tickets and took at least four people, normally with the other two under a tarpaulin in the back! When we arrived at the Palace we knew our van would be opened and inspected so as soon as we were stopped by the little brown men, the two, three or four in the back got out and went round the other side of the van so when it was inspected no one was in there. A cat and mouse game ensued, we were always in stitches over this farce, and sometimes the extras had to run away into the paddock and hide with the little brown men chasing them. We always outwitted them somehow!

In the paddock (which was then at the 'bottom' of the circuit) it was generally well organised, and scrutineering and practice went without mishap, except I found the circuit difficult to learn and I found the walls and sleepers which lined the edge very intimidating.

The left kink before the tight right-hander at the end of the terrace straight was the most demanding, especially getting the braking point correct. I did not succeed in my four practice laps, which was most worrying for the race.

During the 12 laps I started OK but found the enclosed nature of the circuit fearsome and could not get my braking points or lines right. I elected to make my first outing on that circuit 'safety first'. The Glade section I found difficult and also the line going into South Tower ramp, with its 5ft high concrete wall all along the outside edge of the track (this was where the lads got killed the year before). Nevertheless, I still enjoyed the experience, the adrenaline flowed and the racing was great. I did not finish in the top 12 of the 26 starters, but I still felt satisfied and had an addition to my racing knowledge on a circuit so different to Snetterton, or Brands for that matter.

A weekend's racing

A weekend of racing was next on the agenda, really great if you do not weaken and have reliable transport, which I, of course, did not. This was a Bemsee Club race at Silverstone on the club circuit followed by a national race at Brands on Saturday 20 August and Sunday 21 August 1960. What a way to live, always something exciting to look forward to and two days of doing things I really wanted to do, this was the life! In truth it was a lot of discomfort and hard work interspersed with a short period of absolute exhilaration.

The bike was finally readied late on the Thursday night and I kept the gearing I had at Crystal Palace as the Silverstone Club circuit was about the same length and flat, being an old airfield circuit – much like Snetterton only shorter, at 1.6 miles. It was basically triangular in form following the GP circuit from the start to finish (in the same place as now) along the straight round the fast right-hander at Copse, a left kink for Maggots Curve into Beckets where the tight right-hander doubled back on itself down the back straight intersecting Woodcote corner half way round and back to the start and finish – really not very interesting but still another race and more experience.

Silverstone – being near to Banbury – meant another long cross-country trek. Along the old 414 through Hertford then to St Albans, up the A5 to near Towcester

A wonderful paddock shot of Reg (11) and Ken Johnson (Norton, 21), at Silverstone Bemsee Trophy Day, 20 August 1960. Reg finished fifth in a race won by Ron Chandler riding a brand new Matchless G50.

and the back lanes to the circuit, a journey of about 85 miles on difficult roads (all single carriageway and very badly lit – if any lights at all, through the centres of all towns and villages as there were no bypasses in those days). Not only that, but we had to do the journey in a borrowed 10 cwt van which did 50mph at best downhill with the wind behind it! It actually took four and a half hours, and as I did not leave work on Friday until 5.15pm, after packing all in the van we did not leave before 6.30pm, so we did not arrive until 11pm that night.

After an uncomfortable night in the van we brewed up at 6.00am ready for scrutineering. This was made slightly simpler as we did not have our fairings on, as they were not allowed under the regulations which helped to make all the bikes equal. Here we had 420 competitors and 41 in my race of which 17 were BSA and 11 were Nortons. Triumphs and Matchless, a Velocette and a Vincent made up the numbers. So, we were in with a chance!

Three of my fellow competitors were my friends – local rivals who were in their second or third year of racing – Colin Huff, Terry Mayne and Brian Dennis (all on BSAs) but it looked like the one to beat was Ron Chandler on a very new looking G50 Matchless the type of bike about which I could only dream.

This time I made a good start and got away with the front bunch from the second row, and I found the circuit easy to learn and ride after a good practice session. Two laps had gone and no one passed me, so I settled into a good rhythm and concentrated on passing one at a time, mostly on braking when going into Becketts and Woodcote, the gearing just right, peaking along the back straight, third good for Copse and second just right for the other two, Maggots Curve taken as fast as I could in fourth still accelerating – that was a real thrill.

Finishing fifth

Finally the chequered flag and, finishing fifth, I was really elated. Who won? Ron Chandler on the G50 of course, with the BSAs of Terry Mayne, Geoff Sendall and Colin Huff also in front of me (Brian did not finish), averaging 73.39mph. The 12 laps took 15m 46 secs and after packing up and managing to leave the circuit by 5pm we took the long drive home in great spirits.

Arriving back at about 10pm we unloaded and got straight to work, cleaning and checking the bike over fully, changing the oil in the engine, gearbox and front forks, adjusting brakes and chains and putting on the fairing ready for Brands Hatch. We went to bed at 1am and woke at 5am when the pig trailer and Austin 12 taxi were due to arrive (the 10 cwt van was not available for both days) – and we left at 6.15am to go via the Blackwall Tunnel to Brands, so we arrived well in time for scrutineering at 8.30am.

This National meeting was again organised by the Brands Racing Committee with the secretary Mr C.D. Elliott, the large Mr Ridley in charge of the paddock and Ken Philips the travelling track marshal, a great man who became a good friend.

Hailwood, Minter & Co.

Hailwood and Minter were the stars of the day, backed by a host of regulars including Thorpe, Hempleman, Phillis, Daniels, Shorey, Payne, Young and O'Rourke, just to name a few who were all capable of winning. This time we novices had our own race – just one of 15 laps, again about 15 mins of racing. Twenty-eight riders, with me positioned on the third row of the grid. This was my fourth time at Brands, after two practice sessions and one race, and the start of my sixth race proper. I really felt at home and at ease, loving the atmosphere and surroundings, all the noise and THAT smell. Practice had gone well and the Goldie was proving really reliable, which was a real positive as it was hard enough to get into races without having the bike let you down.

Back on the grid I was always nervous but happy, just wanting the flag to drop – then no nerves, just sheer 100 per cent concentration on where I was going. Already the gear changing was physically and mentally automatic, and although the starting was also becoming routine, my first race experience still made me careful. I found going into Paddock Bend on the first lap a daunting experience, and those who got away well really had a great advantage (being 100 yards ahead by the top of Druids hairpin). This time I made a real note of this.

Overtaking was becoming part of the routine and the over/under positioning on the circuit most important. Following, watching for an opportunity, appraising the opposition's lines and braking was taking precedence in my thoughts, instead of just learning the circuit and lines for corners and braking points.

By the time the race was over I was up to seventh place (which again for me was just great) and had lapped at 1m 06 sec, not bad for an old Gold Star and an improvement on the 1m 15secs I was doing earlier in the year! The third BSA home, I also beat my friends – Colin Huff who was eighth and Brian Dennis who was 10th. Notable in this race was one Tom Phillips, who finished third on his Triumph in his second season and was to become a close friend.

Watching this race was Brian Wolfendon. He was always at Bottom Bend at Brands, and he would come into the paddock after the race and give me a pat on the back and some helpful advice. We met socially as well as at the Technical College and we were really good friends. After each race, on the way back to the paddock, we exchanged waves and thumbs up – it was good to have a 'fan'.

What a weekend, two races, two finishes in the top 10, my best finish to date, fantastic! I had done 300 miles of travel over 13 hours, only about 11 hours' sleep, the rest working on the bike, for 30 minutes of racing! Was it worth it? You bet it was, this was my life! Never mind the cost – I still do not know to this day how I possibly afforded it!

Southend racer Brian Dennis (seen here on a 500 Gold Star at Crystal Palace). As Reg says 'we met at Marconis in Great Baddow, he was in the workshop and made parts I had drawn in the drawing office'.

Back to Snetterton

I then had a weekend off to prepare the bike for my next venture, a return to Snetterton on 4 September – another national meeting and my heat containing, again, Mike Hailwood and Co. Mike took part in the 125, 250, 350, and 500cc races that day as he usually did. With heats and finals he had as many races that day as I had that year! I noted that my old school teacher Albert Wiffen was in my heat, so I visited him in the paddock and a new type of relationship began. My friend Joe Iszard was riding his 350 AJS and finished 19th in his heat, and Colin Huff, Brian Dennis, Terry Mayne – all were there. It was like a club, all meeting at weekends with like minds and interests, helping each other, having fry-ups together, in good camaraderie, what a life, it was great! On the track we were bitter rivals, though, only wanting to be in front of the others.

A competitive environment

These races were very competitive, and the start was crucial over a seven-lap heat if you were to finish in the top 15 who went into the final. I drew the second row so was in with a chance, but with 25 Manx Nortons of the 41 starters, it still was a real challenge. This is how the race unfolded in my mind: 'Always watch the starter, be ready for the first twitch for the drop of the flag – down it comes, silence, patter patter of feet, explosion of noise as 41 500s with open meggas roar into life, (a good start, not rushed) but I am about 10th going into Riches, great – round Sears and flat out down the Norwich Straight. First one then two then a third Norton comes roaring past! I try to catch the third one's slipstream but they are much too fast – careful braking into the hairpin, going OK round and holding 13th, still in with a chance. Ron Chandler on his new G50 comes past down by the start and finish, there's just no way the Goldie can hang on. Again Riches, Sears, down the Norwich Straight near the braking point, well over to the left for the Hairpin. Glancing to my right I see Vernon Cottle on his 500 Manx on the 'wrong' side of the circuit'. Suddenly, at that point, my mind said 'what is he doing right over there?'

The crash

Too late!! – I missed my braking point, did not change down into first and tried to get round the hairpin, but much too fast. Both wheels lost their grip simultaneously and I was following the Goldie on its side on my right-hand backside across the road and into the bank! Did it hurt? Well, fortunately not really, my only injury was burnt skin through my leathers down my thigh, elbow and shoulder. The bike suffered a bent clip on, scratched fairing and broken footrest. Really nothing serious except my pride was damaged. What a mistake – still it had to happen one day and, as nothing was really hurt, I put it down to inexperience and learnt from it.

Vernon just went on his merry way and got into the final. I went home with my friends talking of a new experience – crashing when racing. Had it dented my confidence? Did I want to continue? Yes, to me it was part of racing (not that I wanted to do it regularly!) because, provided you did not make stupid mistakes like that, riding a motorcycle to its limits while racing is bound to bring some mishaps.

The year was drawing to a close and I had a month to repair the Goldie before my last meeting again at the Silverstone Club Circuit for the 8 October Club Day – another closed meeting. One small mod that was done was to cut and re-weld a flat portion on the megga where it scraped the ground (also damaged in the crash). This made it look more 'modern' as the new Manx meggas also had this shape. A new clip-on was put on as I did not trust the 'heat and straighten' technique. A real problem for this meeting was transport as I just could not beg, borrow or find any. At the last minute 'Spider', another local road Goldie owner, came to the rescue. 'You can borrow my sidecar combination if you like, Reg', he said. Well I had no choice. I also had never piloted an outfit before!

We removed the sidecar and strapped three scaffold boards to the chassis, and, with miles of rope lashed the Goldie on, it looked a real sight against the M20 BSA

– ancient and modern came to mind. The side-valve 500 had seen better days and power was limited. Lighting was very sparse, and the six-volt system and the corroded headlamp reflector did not help. We could not leave before 6.30pm on the Friday night due to work and the fact that it was cold and raining. They really were not very good conditions in which to start my sidecar riding experience with 85 miles ahead on unlit roads. Still, I thought, let's go for it!

Very quickly I found out that you cannot lean a sidecar to negotiate corners, you have to turn the handle bars, a totally new feeling, and what with the dark, wet and cold conditions, bad brakes and no lights, I had a feeling of foreboding. After 30 miles I was exhausted, soaking wet and very cold. Even with the Goldie aboard, the sidecar wheel kept lifting.

My girlfriend, Pearl, who really did not know what she was letting herself in for, was terrified on the pillion seat. At least I could not go fast. I ran out of road on three occasions during the trip – once up onto the verge into a hedge, fortunately with little damage – the whole journey was a disaster.

We finally arrived at Silverstone at 1.30am – six and a half hours later. Sleeping in a wet tent in wet clothes did nothing to help and at 6.00am it was still raining and it rained all day!

My first wet race

This was to be my first race in the wet and practise was vital. I was used to riding on the road in all conditions so I was not apprehensive, but I was soon to find that just riding in the wet and racing in the wet were two entirely different things. I began by riding around at a speed I thought was sensible under the conditions, and was soon passed at high speed by all of my fellow competitors. This time I had been put in 'Race Two' not 'Race One' as previously and was up against more experienced competitors, the likes of Joe Dunphy, Peter Darvil, Richard Difazio, Ron Chandler, Ian Goddard, George Collis, Griff Jenkins, Fred Neville, A.R.C. Hunter and Ken Watson to name just a few – plus my friend Martin Hayward on his Goldie.

To say I was disillusioned was an understatement. Whereas in the dry I could keep up, in the wet I was totally outclassed. My bike seemed to slip and slide everywhere. So, wet, cold and depressed, I went to the grid with trepidation. It was still raining. I went round at a snail's pace – I was just not able to understand what was happening. I tried to keep up but just got into trouble and lost confidence – I went rigid and was lapped by half distance by people coming past so fast I could not believe it! The 12 laps were finally over and my humility was overwhelming.

Fred Neville on his Matchless won at 70mph, and I finished 23rd, my lowest-ever position, at under 60mph. My friend Martin Hayward managed 10th position at 63mph. I suppose the only thing I could take from this was that I was not last, there were six finishers behind me, the last one by 18 seconds.

The last meeting of 1960 was again at Silverstone, on 8 October. It was also Reg's first wet race – the tricky conditions are evident from the photograph. A lack of fairing did not help.

Going home on the outfit in the wet, cold and dark, completed what was the worst day in my racing career to date. Being the last race of the year made it worse and a long cold winter ahead without any racing made the story complete. Was I dejected? Yes. Was I dispirited? Yes. Did I want to race again? You bet I did! I simply could not wait for next year to come round.

International Racing Licence points

A brief summary of the season revealed that in eight meetings I had nine races and eight finishes, of which three were in the top 10. I had one crash and one race in the wet, which was the low point, otherwise I was well satisfied and gained six points towards an International Racing Licence.

Back at work, I had completed my stint on inspection and was going to Drawing Office School, which really suited me and meant shorter hours (8.30am to 5.00pm). It was nearer home so the Bantam (which was still my everyday transport) was very handy. I rode it ridiculously fast (within its very limited capabilities) and managed to have a head-on crash with one of the other students on his brand new Triumph Tigress Scooter.

All was repaired under insurance but he never forgave me for this and bore a real grudge for years. As no one was hurt it really did not bother me, although I was sorry at the time.

At college I was re-sitting the A1 exam as I stupidly failed it the first time round, and I missed my friend Brian Wolfendon who had passed and was taking A2. We did meet at breaktimes during day release and the three evenings a week when we were still studying, so time was precious. I was still keeping very active by swimming and doing gymnastic circuit training at the local schools.

The Goldie needed some love and attention and a weight reduction to try to keep it remotely competitive. Any thought of changing it for a 500 Norton or G50 Matchless was totally out of the question on cost, although by now I had at least paid for the bike. All of my meagre £5 per week was going on the racing itself and, thank goodness, the BSA had been reliable. Even a modest Manx or G50 would have cost £400. New they were £500, so my £250 a year income was totally inadequate, and without others' kind help I could not even have gone to the meetings! Also, a new exhaust valve for a Manx, the sodium filled type, was at least £5, so again I could not afford to run one. If I broke a Manx engine I would be finished for the year, so for the 1961 season it would have to be the trusty BSA again.

Stripping the engine

The engine was stripped and found to be in remarkably good condition, but the valves and springs were replaced as a precaution, as were the piston rings.

Internals were all cleaned and re-polished, then carefully re-assembled all in my 8x6 garden shed, which included an 18in bench and no stand. Major mods to be carried out were to the wheels which were sent away to Monty & Ward for rebuilding, replacing the steel rims with alloy Dunlops and reducing the front size from a 21in to 19in diameter, which really helped to save weight.

To compensate for the reduced ground clearance, a new alloy top fork yoke was used, pushing the fork tubes lower by one inch, this retained the bike's dimensions. New green Ferodo linings were added to the front brake and the drum skimmed and shoes fitted to ensure good contact within the 8in single leading shoe brake. In the D.O. (Drawing Office) School I had designed a twin leading shoe conversion

Over the closed season of 1960–61 the Gold Star was given a facelift, including a new fibreglass fuel tank and fairing. Reg is seen here with the revamped bike at Snetterton on Easter Sunday, 21 April 1961.

but could not have it manufactured in time, so it never saw the light of day. A lightweight fibreglass tank was purchased as well as a new central oil tank, which although steel, was about a pound or so lighter and held more oil and was less vulnerable. A new fibreglass seat from a Manx Norton completed the major transformation. Other mods included significant ventilation to the primary chain case for the clutch and the addition of a drip positive oil feed for the primary chain, to ensure continuous adequate lubrication.

The rear back brake plate was also cut away for lightness and ventilation. Mostly all of the extraneous brackets and protruding items were cut from the frame and then the whole assembly was given a new coat of black paint.

On re-assembly, with a white fairing and tank lined black and yellow to match my repainted helmet, also with REGS (Reg Everett Gold Star) painted on the tank, the whole machine looked much more modern.

New Avon tyres (the first set had lasted the entire 1960 season as I changed them round so they wore evenly both sides!) and the black-painted megga, now chrome-plated in Marconi's plating shop, completed the transformation. I was really pleased with the outcome and could not wait for the 1961 season to begin, and I was really determined to try and do more races and get my International Licence.

Scanning the motorcycle press

Every week in January and February I would scan the pages of the various motorcycle publications to find out what regulations were announced, so I could write for them on the first day and thus stood the best chance of being accepted. I decided to apply for all meetings which I could feasibly attend within England.

My friend who had a Royal Enfield Constellation, Dave Livesy, had also bought a Morris 10 cwt van which had been used as an ambulance in World War Two. When he bought it there were still four stretcher beds in it and even a flashing light and a bell!

With the beds and frame removed it made a great transporter with plenty of room, and so another problem was solved as it was at my disposal for the season, with Dave and I and others who came along sharing the driving. We gave it a coat of paint to remove the huge red crosses on the sides, and at last we were mobile (I still have the workshop manual for this van, but unfortunately cannot find a photo). The engine was a side valve 1550cc four-cylinder with three gears. Top speed on the level was 45mph with fuel consumption around 22mpg. We did not mind, however, as it was permanent transport.

I received my new licence (number 61/1153) and in *Motor Cycling* on 19 January 1961 was an article by none other than Derek Minter on 'How to Win Races'. At the beginning he said 'I've never learned much from the experts' teaching – you have it in you or you don't!' Sounds like a report of my first talk to him! One thing that pleased me in the article was a picture taken in 1956 at Silverstone in the wet, with me on my Gold Star easily recognisable by the massive front brake air scoop and 21-inch wheel.

First meeting of 1961

My first meeting of 1961 was again at Snetterton, on Easter Sunday, 21 April, and again in my heat were Hailwood, Minter, Godfrey and Robb along with my local rivals Colin Huff, Brian Dennis and Martin Hayward.

I had a terrific scrap for the entire race with Brian on his BSA, and at the end we crossed the line together an equal 15th, with both of us qualifying for the final – the first time for both of us and the first time I had battled for the full race distance with another competitor. The only thing that was disappointing was the race speed, which was exactly the same as it was during the July meeting the previous year – so much for the weight reduction! Maybe we were just holding each other up, though it did not seem like it, but nevertheless the racing was great and our pals enjoyed it. We were the first Gold Stars home. We would not have been because Martin had been in 12th position before he crashed at the hairpin, bringing back memories of my similar fate at the end of last year. On this occasion, Minter beat Hailwood, Tony Godfrey was third and Colin did not finish.

A final for the first time

Well, to the final – great. The start was something else in among all the top guys again from both heats, and going into the first bend the Nortons streamed past down the Norwich Straight. Changing down and braking for the hairpin from fourth to first gear brought to me my first DNF (Did Not Finish). This was because at that precise moment the gearbox broke and I had no drive, and stopped after a scary moment when it locked the rear wheel, but luckily I came to a vertical standstill just after the hairpin. Having this opportunity, I watched the experts; their lines, braking points, etc. and Minter again beat Hailwood with Dan Shorey third and Tony Godfrey fourth. Brian Dennis finished this 10-lap final in a very creditable 22nd place: it was real competition against all the experts on their quick bikes.

Just after this meeting a very sad thing happened on 24 April, when I was told that my friend Brian Wolfendon had collided with an American car, being thrown from his bike and killed just a few hundred yards from his home at Blackmore End, near Braintree, Essex. Brian was just 26 when he died and had been riding since he was 17 years old. I knew him to be a good rider, fast but not flamboyant or dangerous, and he had been a club member and a marshall at local grass track events. He was a Barbour jacket man, not a rocker (although I had nothing against rockers as I was one too!), and a genuine enthusiast. I had lost a real pal, who was both a helper and a fan, and I would really miss him. In July 2007 Mick Walker told me about a sister machine to Brian's Gilera in a local auction, which I subsequently was able to purchase.

Going to his funeral, at the local church, brought it home to me that riding motorcycles is dangerous. Although there were hundreds of other riders there, his mother was so distraught that she wanted me to stop riding. Somehow I knew that Brian would want me to continue and would be watching me, and I thought that when racing at least we were all going in the same direction!

An entirely new racing venture

My second race of 1961 would be an entirely new venture as I still could not get many entries and so was not going to be racing until 20 May at Silverstone. During the closed season of 1960–61 I had often called at Derek Cornell's motorcycle shop which was near my home and listened to his scrambling exploits with local rider Pete Smith on the Greeves. My mind had wandered back to before racing when Derek had kindly loaned me a bike to go to Eddie Dows at Banbury. I recalled how well the Greeves handled and withstood my flat-out riding style there and back.

I used to joke with him about the mud and wet and lack of facilities at the scrambles in local fields, and how he should go road racing instead. Well, I kept sowing the seeds and in the end suggested he should enter a production race to help promote his shop and the Greeves marque.

Finally, he succumbed to the idea, and that was how we came to enter the first-ever Bemsee 'Silverstone 1000' – a 1,000km race for production bikes.

The prospect of doing a 600-mile race on Silverstone's Grand Prix circuit made my mouth water. What a chance to gain some real experience and totally learn the

Reg gained a second ride for the 1961 season aboard the DA Cornell Motorcycles' Greeves 25 DC twin-cylinder production machine. This period photograph shows Derek Cornell's showrooms at 245/47 Broomfield Road, Chelmsford, as it was then.

circuit – but first we had to find another rider. I chose Martin Hayward because he was fast, experienced and reliable (and no doubt quicker than me) as I wanted us to be in the results. A new Greeves 250cc 25 DC twin was taken from the showroom and readied for the race, which only required putting on rear set footrests, changing the gear lever and fixing a pair of Ace drop handlebars in place. I ran the machine in carefully on the local roads for about 250 miles, but apart from doing that and fitting some decent brake linings, little was done. We even used the standard road tyres.

Keith Wash (who was Derek's workshop mechanic and later boss of Hedingham Sidecars) was responsible for all of this, and so it seemed odd to have so little to do. The 'superb luxury' continued as the bike was transported to Silverstone in the DA Cornell van driven by Keith with me as the passenger. We even stayed at a pub in Towcester at Mr Cornell's expense. This really was the life: we had a good dinner, a good sleep in a good bed – it was another world – and I liked it!

Martin arrived in the morning at the circuit. We had a small mishap when leaving the pub as Keith scraped the side of the newly painted van! (Derek never forgave him for this.)

Martin familiarised himself with the bike as it was the first time he had ridden a two-stroke. After practice he pronounced it good and we were ready.

Silverstone 1,000km

My practice was also OK, but Silverstone's wide Grand Prix circuit (with mainly sweeping bends and being very fast) meant that most of the time the little Greeves was flat out and I think we only changed down once each lap (for Becketts). So it was flat on the tank, keep the throttle open and the lines good and smooth. Eighty miles-per-hour was about the best we could get on the speedo and we could average 70mph for the lap. We just had to last for about the seven and a half hours the race was expected to take, with the front men averaging 85mph on their BMWs and Triumph Bonnevilles. Fuel was going to be a problem as the tank was very small (only about two gallons) and by riding flat-out continuously we were only getting about 35mpg (two-strokes not being very economical compared to four-strokes). So it looked like we would have to change riders and refuel every hour. That was our strategy, so we would not be too tired.

In the race there were four classes, A – 1000cc, B – 500cc, C – 350cc, D – 250cc. Our class was the most popular with 19 of the 50 entries, (two of which were Greeves). The programme commented 'not very often raced – today is one of the rare occasions in which they will be seen in this element of competition', could it have been the first? The other 250cc machines were a Norton Jubilee, three Ariel Arrows, a BSA C15, six Enfield Crusader Sports, two Hondas, two NSU and two Aermacchis. It was a real assortment with some good riders, especially on the larger capacities.

Reg leading the riders away from the start of the Bemsee 1,000 kilometre production machine race at Silverstone on 20 May 1961, riding the Derek Cornell Greeves twin (34).

Our competitors included riders who were already household names or future stars – Derek Woodman, Peter Inchley, Cecil Sandford, Sammy Miller, Chris Vincent (of sidecar fame but a fair solo rider also), Bruce Main-Smith, Norman Surtees (John's brother), Denis Gallagher, Colin Peck and David Dixon. Fred Launchbury and Roy Bacon were reserves on another Ariel Arrow.

A new experience awaited at 10am with a Le Mans-type start with yours truly doing the first stint. Fifty riders lined up on the outside of the circuit and when the flag dropped it was a mad dash to the other side where our bikes were – with the kick starter strategically held by the mechanic ready for me to jump on and start, followed by putting into gear and charging off. Being number 34 we were already towards the back but had 16 others behind us, most of which were the 250s.

The race is on

After pulling down my goggles the race was on and most of the slower-starting big bikes soon came past. I settled down into a rhythm but I also attempted to slipstream the faster bikes to get a tow down the straights and had a good dice with G.C. Young on his NSU Supermax. The first hour went by quickly as I was really enjoying it and, despite the lack of speed, was still racing (this was by far the longest I had ever raced).

I came back into the pit and Keith put in another two gallons. Martin jumped on, kick-started the Greeves back into life and we were circulating again. In my stint I did 24 laps averaging about 70mph, a great start, and we were eighth in the 250cc class. This all went like clockwork with Martin and I changing regularly every 24-laps. Martin reported all was fine during his time on the bike, he was also enjoying his first experience of long-distance production racing. After five hours or so, I was just finishing my third session and came in to refuel and change over (we were now lying sixth and had completed 121 laps, or 353.7 miles, in about five hours, so only had two and a half hours left to run) when disaster struck. Kick as

An action shot from the 1961 Bemsee 1,000 Kilometre race, with Reg (34) chasing the NSU Supemax of G.C. Young and J. West.

he might, the engine would not start. We knew we had plenty of fuel as we had just refuelled, there was a good spark, we had changed the plugs and checked the carburettor – all seemed OK but it just would not start. Fortunately, compared to a four-stroke, it was simplicity itself to remove the cylinder heads and cylinders. So this is what we did, only to find the tops of the pistons had slightly collapsed and trapped the piston rings, resulting in much reduced compression. While the engine had been running it was OK but as soon as we had stopped there was no chance of a re-start. Not having spare pistons we retired, but all of us agreed that we must try it again if we could get the use of a bike. We were disappointed as we had been

Being overtaken at speed by the 600 Norton Dominator 99 of Frank Rutherford and Fred Neville.

going so well for so long; although when we reported to Derek Cornell on arriving back home it did not seem to make a good impression on him: 'A scraped van and a new Greeves with a damaged engine does not seem successful at all!'

Who won? Well, it was Bruce Daniels and Peter Darvill on the MLG-entered BMW R69S, the pair completing 215 laps in seven hours 25 mins and averaging 84.7mph. The first 250 was a CB72

Honda (10th overall) at an average of 72.5mph and completing 185 laps ridden by C.G. Peck and J. Somers, with Robin Good/Peter Inchley (Ariel Arrow) second at one lap behind.

Our average speed would have seen about 171 laps completed and thus seventh in the 250 class.

Brands Whit Monday

Three days later (Whit Monday, 22 May) I was back to 'proper' racing on the Goldie at Brands Hatch. It was another race for lesser-known riders but which included Ron Chandler on his beautiful G50 and Ray Pickrell – the latter having his first-ever outing (on a 500 Manx Norton). Poor Ray finally succumbed to cancer after a long fight in February 2006 after becoming a top-flight rider, winning many important races in the late 1960s and early 1970s.

This time I made a fairly good start from my front-row grid position (there were eight people in this row). At least I was in the first 10 going round Paddock Bend. My friend, Colin Huff, now on a Norton framed BSA, also had a very good start. I got into a dice with John Funnell on a 500 Norton and he chased me for a couple of laps before coming steaming by at the end of the top straight and going into Paddock Bend much faster than I was capable of. This success was short-lived however, and he crashed heavily with both he and the bike hitting the high earth bank that went all the way round most of the circuit (and only 6–10ft from the edge of the track) so there was virtually no run-off area! His bike was badly damaged: front wheel forks, frame, tank, bars, fairing etc. and so was he – he had concussion and was carted off to hospital.

Reg on the Gold Star (69) at Brands Hatch on Whit Monday, 22 May 1961.

Norton rider John Funnell crashes out spectacularly during the 500cc race at Brands Hatch, as Reg sweeps past on his Gold Star, 22 May 1961. This photograph was published in the national press the following day.

I, of course, had a grandstand seat of this incident as was clearly shown in the following day's *Daily Mirror*, where poor John's crash photo was spread over the centre pages, but which also showed me calmly going by! I do not think I was affected by this, but suffice it to say I finished in 11th place. This was nothing to get excited about, although I was the second Gold Star – G. Sandall came in eighth on another. Colin Huff finished a great second on his Goldie engined Norton to Ron Chandler on his G50. Ray Pickrell, in his first race, finished in a very creditable seventh place.

My next meeting was also at Brands, where I had entered two bikes for what was called 'Trophy Day'. This was a special meeting put on by the Brands Racing Committee for racers who had not won a race and did not have an International Licence, so you could say it was for novices.

Back on the Greeves

Riders were given only one ride at the special meeting to let more people have a race, so I was only accepted on the Greeves (instead of the Gold Star) we had raced in the 1,000km production race at Silverstone. Derek Cornell had agreed to let me use this bike and again Keith Wash had done some additional work on it. He had designed a set of

Reg going on to finish 11th after the Funnell crash.

Back on the Greeves at Brands Hatch, 25 June 1961. By now Keith Wash (Derek Cornell's workshop mechanic and later boss of Hedingham Sidecars) had carried out additional work on the bike, including fitting expansion chambers, removing lighting equipment, making up a pair of clip-ons and fitting Avon racing tyres.

The Cornell Greeves 25DC twin at Brands on 25 June 1961. Reg finished fifth in his heat, eighth in the final. It was an excellent ride against far more expensive machinery.

expansion chambers to replace the original road-going silencers, removed the lighting equipment, made up a pair of clip-on bars and put on racing Avons.

Sunday, 25 June arrived and again I had the luxury of being taken to Brands by Keith in the now unblemished Cornell Motorcycles van. There were two heats for the 250s – a field of 28 riders – with the first 14 going forward to the final. I was in the first heat which was the first race and which started at midday. This was my first real 250cc race and I was amazed at the wide variety of machine types taking part, so unlike the 500s which were mainly Nortons with a few Matchless and BSA.

The following list is taken from the programme: Ariel, 'Special', Norman, MV, Ducati, Moto Guzzi, Rudge, Triumph, Matchless, Gilera, DKR, NSU, DDS (Dave Downer Special) Royal Enfield, Greeves, NSU/Norton, Norton, Norvel. So, in my heat alone there were 18 different makes of 28 starters. Also in the second heat were Excelsior, Velocette, Anzani and AJS, – another four – which makes 22 in total!

The only other guys who I had 'heard of' before in my heat were Alan Peck and Ron Freeman, the latter was one of the Southend riders, down to race a 250 Norton but actually riding a Triumph Tiger Cub. Brian Osborne also raced his NSU. In the other heat was a certain

W.D. (Bill) Ivy on a 190 Gilera entered by Chisholms of Maidstone, Jim Russell on a NSU entered by Dulwich dealers Pullins, the only rider on two machines, Vic Poore on a Velocette and the American Richard Wyler – who appeared in a Cops and Robbers serial on the television: *The Man from Interpol*. He had managed to talk his way into getting a Greeves from the factory! I met him once and his Greeves was languishing under a tarpaulin up a passage between two houses and he was wearing shoes full of holes. We laughed and I said: 'If this is what you can live like being a TV star then I'm glad I'm poor!'

So different

The race started OK and I got away well and was soon into the rhythm of the race, albeit only for four laps. Racing the 250 was so different as it did not have even half the power of the Goldie (the Villiers 2T engine only producing about 15 bhp). It was imperative that once a good head of speed was attained it was not lost. So, corner line was very important. With the slower speed you had time to line up accurately and try to negotiate all as fast as the bike could go – hence on Paddock Bend it was nearly flat out as I kept flat on the tank as much as I could to eliminate wind drag. The poor Greeves was very slow – not doing much over 75mph, but with all my scratching I managed a fifth place in my heat, equalling my best-ever placing on the Goldie the previous year. Brian Osborne on his very quick 250 NSU won and my friend Ron (on the Cub) was a very good third. E.J. Woodward on another 250 NSU won the other heat and Bill Ivy was fifth in his heat.

Ron Freeman aged 19 in the paddock at Brands, the motorcycle is a 1957 199cc Triumph Tiger Cub converted for racing by Ron and first raced in 1959 by the person making a nuisance behind him; Trevor Incham who used to race a Goldstar.

The final was altogether different and I picked a fourth-row spot from the ballot. I got away with the back of the field and the low top speed of the Greeves was unable to make up the deficit even with my ever-ambitious approach to cornering (as can be seen on the pictures), enjoying the flat out technique where possible. Even so, I managed an eighth-placed finish, with the heat winners first and second and young Bill Ivy fourth.

The other Southend lads on their 500s also had a great day. Colin Huff was runner-up and Brian Dennis was third in their final. So a great day was had by all. The Greeves had really impressed me with its handling as the lap times were within two seconds of the BSA lap time at about 1m 8 secs. On the return Derek Cornell did not seem too impressed with the results as he was used to winning with Greeves at local scramble meetings, and he never went to any road race to see what I was up against, but even so we are still good friends all these years later.

Reg at Brands Hatch, 9 July 1961, leading a group of riders on the 500 Gold Star (most of the others are mounted on Norton or Matchless machines). This was Reg's first race on the full 2.65 mile Grand Prix circuit and he finished sixth 500cc and eighth overall, the race being won by Ken Gawler.

Brands Hatch long circuit

Brands Hatch had opened the new longer 2.65-mile GP circuit in July 1960 but I had never raced there, or practised for that matter, as only the short circuit (now called the Indy Circuit) was available for this. Needless to say I was looking forward to the experience. It came during my next meeting on 9 July 1961. This was a national meeting and we were in a Non Experts scratch race over 250cc to 1000cc. All the stars were at this meeting: Hailwood, Minter, Read, Robb, Hartle, Payne, Neville, Shorey, Thorpe, Langston, Young, Hardy, Duff, Mayhew – just to name a few! It had all the atmosphere of a great racing day and a huge crowd was there. I immediately got to grips with the long circuit with its gradients and fast sweeping bends, they were fantastic, but the practice really was not enough and I completed just five laps with the starting lap and finishing lap included. It really was not enough.

Our race was second in the programme starting at 1pm after the curtain raiser of the 350cc Experts. This was a ding-dong affair which was finally won by Phil Read, with Fred Neville second, Derek Minter third and Mike Hailwood fourth, followed by Ginger Payne and Tom Thorpe at an average just short of 80mph.

There were 35 starters in five rows. This time – in their wisdom – the Brands Racing Committee had put me on pole position in row one, so I wanted that good start. There were 11 350s and only two of the 500s were Gold Stars, so I knew I had my work cut out over the 10-lap race. I did get a good start and had become much better having been really practising them at any opportunity, honing my technique, making a plan of moves in detail and not varying them until it became a drilled routine. Every aspect of carburation and ignition also played its part as did correct chain tensioning and freedom of rotation of clutch wheel bearings and brakes.

Bump-starting

Bump-starting was the only method allowed and it could win or lose you a race easily. I was fourth going into Paddock Bend and kept my position until going down the fast back straight approaching Hawthorn Hill bend. It was here (over the next few laps) that the Nortons and a couple of G50s passed me, but I had a great ride and learnt the circuit to finish in what I considered an excellent eighth place, overall the sixth 500, being the best Goldie with only two 350 Nortons in front, the first being fourth-placed Haynes and a good sixth place and second 350 for Rex Butcher. My friend Dick Standing finishing as the fifth 350 and 16th overall. Ken Gawler won the race as he had the Trophy Day 500 and the speed was fantastic as it was virtually the same as the Experts' 350 – 79.64mph against 79.68mph. I was really pleased with this even though the Experts 500 was won by Derek Minter at an average of 85.82mph. Minter's lap record on a 500 was 89.15mph. My best lap was timed by my friends at 2 min 5 secs so 79.15mph, not bad for a – by now – eight-year-old Gold Star!

Two rides

My last ride on Derek Cornell's Greeves twin was at Snetterton three weeks later, so at that meeting I had two rides. Again the Goldie was out-numbered and out-paced by the Nortons and G50s, so in my heat I finished 18th and did not get into the final. My friend Martin Hayward was in the other heat and finished 19th on his G50; he took 14 min 17.6 secs for the seven-laps to my 14 m 14.2 secs so I felt good. Again I was the first Gold Star home and again that man Minter won (as he did the 500 final). Phil Read was runner-up. My fastest lap was 2 min 2 secs, average speed 79.87mph – it seems that this speed was the limit for the old Gold Star.

I still had the Greeves to race and here the lack of top-end speed really showed up on Snetterton's long straights, but racing is racing and I tried very hard, again using the flat-out technique at every possibility. It was only at the hairpin I changed down to second, and at the Esses one gear to third, all the others were in top. I had a pretty lonely race, finishing 16th out of 40 starters at an average of 69.26mph. The winner, Dan Shorey (on an NSU), won at 80.30mph and put in the fastest lap of 1 min 57.6 secs at 82.96mph winning comfortably, followed by Norman Surtees (Aermacchi) and Arthur Wheeler (Moto Guzzi). Again this race had many different makes, 17 in all, the old NSUs being the best in the field – which was food for thought!

Back to the Palace

The following weekend, myself, the Goldie and friends went back to run the gauntlet of the little brown men at Crystal Palace. It was a lovely sunny day and I had a good race, finishing eighth – and guess what? I won £1! This was my first-

Crystal Palace, 7 August 1961, with the dreaded railway sleepers in the background. Reg finished eighth and won £1!

ever prize in racing – how much I had invested goodness only knows! The picture I have of this race shows the Goldie to good effect and also clearly shows the railway sleepers reinforced by the dirt bank around the edge of the circuit – no run-off area here. Many riders refused to ride there including Derek Minter (after April 1958) as they regarded it far too dangerous. John Surtees rode there on many occasions as did Joe Dunphy, while Mike Hailwood held the 125 lap and race records. I cannot say we had a huge celebration on the way home but, boy, did that £1 feel good!

My total circumstances were now about to make a complete change. The following Sunday was my 21st birthday, and the following Saturday 19 August was my wedding day to my long-time girlfriend Pearl! As far as work was concerned I was still an apprentice, and until April that year I was still learning in the Marconi Drawing Office School, which was very useful. I did so well, in fact, that they decided I was good enough to be a fully fledged draughtsman and so I was appointed to the Marine Navigation section of the Marconi Research Department in Great Baddow. Also, the college work had culminated in me being awarded a Higher National Certificate in Mechanical Engineering for Theory of Machines, Strength of Materials and Metallurgy, all good compliments to motorcycles, engines and racing.

So, by September 1961 I was married and earning proper money as my apprenticeship finished that month. My income had increased suddenly from £6 per week to a huge £624 per year (£12 per week).

Setting up home

Pearl and I moved out of our respective homes in Chelmsford to live at Basildon, as my wife's brother had a council house there but was in the Royal Air Force and could not use it! So we had a house and a lock-up garage and space to park the old ambulance which was being used as transport to meetings. My everyday transport was now a much newer Bantam, the original 125 being replaced by a shiny red 175 model which would commute daily on the 36-mile round trip (Basildon, Marconi Chelmsford, Marconi Baddow, Marconi Chelmsford, Basildon) all on country back roads. It was OK in the dry but uncomfortable in the wet and cold; although it was helping my wet weather riding technique! This seemed hardly an ideal situation but one that had to be contended with for the forseeable short-term future.

We made some new local friends and also introduced Ron Freeman to his future wife Sue (also at Marconi).

1961 season finale

Try as I might I cannot find any accurate records of what happened in my last three races that followed in 1961, but a relatively accurate assessment is as follows: All three races were in September, the first one at Snetterton was on 3 September, where I was entered by Derek Cornell and was number 51 on the Goldie and reserve number 44 on the Greeves. I am sure we did not take the Greeves as, as I have already said, Derek was disillusioned with it. What happened on the Goldie I do not know but I believe I crashed during my heat again at the hairpin. This is

Finishing sixth in the wet at Brands Hatch on 17 September 1961. Reg was riding without a screen as he hadcrashed the bike a couple of weeks earlier at Snetterton.

With the Gold Star during his last race on the bike, this was at Silverstone on 30 September 1961. At that time Reg was very uncertain what, if anything, he would be racing the following year.

possibly confirmed as at the meeting at Brands on 17 September I was riding in the wet with a broken screen (see picture with racing number 73) and according to my licence points record I finished sixth – but unfortunately I have no way of confirming this without either a programme or results.

My very last race on the Goldie was on 30 September 1961 at Silverstone, a Bemsee club day meeting. The weather was fine, as can be seen on the picture with race number 135. No fairings here but the bike looked really good for its last race, and although I have the programme I have no results – so, again, I cannot produce my final finishing position.

The end of my second year of racing left me content with my progress. There was no doubt that I would continue racing as it was now an integral and very important part of my life, in fact it came first – not a good philosophy for marriage! This left me with important decisions to make, the first being what I was to ride the following year. I knew that it would not be the Gold Star as it was just not competitive enough and I wanted to compete at the next level. I now had enough points for my international racing licence, having six points in 1960 and another 14 in 1961, the total of 20 giving me enough to race against anyone, anywhere. I had managed 10 meetings and 13 races throughout the year (four more than last year), resulting in nine finishes, five in the top 10, and one crash. I wanted more and more but how to get it?

The Goldie had done well for me, and I advertised it for sale but only had inquisitive interest. Finally my near neighbour at Basildon, Alan Waterman, bought most of it from me. I say 'most of it' because he wanted to turn it into a 'scrambler'. I cannot say that I was too enthusiastic about it, but he ended up with the wheels, engine and frame from the Goldie. The remaining tank, seat, fairing and old road gear off SKP 647 was sold to all-comers. The only components retained was the 1$\frac{9}{32}$in GP Carb and float chamber which Alan did not want as he deemed it not suitable for 'scrambling', plus the aforementioned worn out one-off exhaust valve. Keeping the carburettor was a blessing, however, as will become apparent. It still exists and is in good hands indefinitely, I hope.

I will finish the Gold Star saga by reproducing the following letter sent to me years later in 1985, following a request in the motorcycle press which was intended to see if the machine still existed.

Sadly, it appears to have gone but if anyone who reads this knows about a 500 Gold Star Engine CB34 GS 114 it has a fantastic history. Ex-Derek Minter race bike, ex-Reg Everett road and race bike and a winning scrambler. Not that many Goldies had such an illustrious history.

Roger Sivyer
Norwich
18 Feb 1985

Re Gold Star

Dear Mr Everett,

Bad news for you I am afraid! SKP 647, your old Gold Star has, I am almost certain, been broken up.

I saw your information wanted piece in the 'Where are they now' section of Classic Bike. A bit of luck really as I only buy the magazine infrequently and it was just by chance that I bought it this month. A spin-off from the previous issue featuring the Gold Star Scrambler.

After you sold your Goldie to the chap from Basildon he started to convert it into scramblers trim. He did carry out about 90% of the work but as far as I'm aware never actually used the bike. From what I can remember he had about 6 kids and couldn't actually afford to race it! So, I assume, to satisfy his frustration at not being able to ride it, he spent the majority of the time polishing it. Every piece of alloy was buffed up to a brilliant shine, including crankcases and gearbox castings, etc.

Eventually I suppose finance caught up with him and he advertised the bike in The Exchange and Mart. At that time I was scrambling a Tribsa that I had built, and I was looking for something a bit more competitive. This must have been in about late '63 or early '64. As far as I can remember I paid about £28.00 for the bike as it stood. Pinching some bits off the old Tribsa I soon had the bike running well.

It wasn't long before I had my first ever race win on that Goldie. Still the best moment ever! Several other wins soon came. That bike was terrific. Reliable and trouble free and also very competitive. I kept it as far as I can remember for about 18 months-2yrs, racing practically every weekend in the Eastern, South Midland and South Eastern centres. Incidentally the money I bought the bike with was originally earmarked for an engagement ring for my girlfriend, but the Gold Star won that race too!

I eventually married the same girl, so I suppose I had my cake and ate it. But after a while the usual financial problems associated with newly weds and mortgages and rates forced me to sell the bike.

I sold it for the same price I paid for it £28.00. The bottom had fallen out of the big bike scrambling scene. Everyone was riding Greeves and Husqvarners. When I think back and realise what I did it makes me want to weep!

At the time I was a member of the Chingford Grasshopper M.C.C. and I sold it to another club member. Unfortunately I cannot remember his name, only that I think his first name was George. In fact the name George Brine keeps ringing bells in my head but I cannot be certain of the person's name. Shortly after selling I moved to my present address near Norwich and I lost touch with the club, which is now no longer in existance. But I am pretty sure that the bike was stripped down for spares and sold off, so I don't think that we shall see it in one piece again.

I eventually bought another bike, a Matchless Metisse, I always preferred the big bikes and continued scrambling until about 1969. I am still active in the sport and at present ride a Suzuki Sidecar trials bike in all the centre events in the Eastern Centre. I still look back on the Goldie, though. It was probably one of the best bikes I ever had and as it was the machine that took me to my first ever win I remember it with particular affection.

I hope it makes the blow a bit easier to bear to know that the old bike at least went down winning and fighting to the end!

I have enclosed a couple of photos of the bike as it was when I rode it but I don't suppose that there are any distinguishing marks left that were carried over from the days when you raced it.

Regards
Roger Sivyer

Chapter 4

The Greeves Prototype Racer

For my next season of racing, the question uppermost in my mind was 'what will I race?' If I kept in the 500cc class it would have to be a fairly new Norton or a Matchless G50.

My friend, Martin Hayward, had bought a G50 to replace his Goldie but had a crash on it which had seemed to slow him up a bit. Anyway, that was out of the question as I really did not have the £500 necessary, and even then, would it be competitive? No, my mind kept coming back to the 250s and my exploits on the Greeves. I was really impressed with the way the bike handled, you could really 'scratch' round the corners on it.

'Scratchers' was what we were called as our bikes generally could not keep up with the front runners, so we had to try especially hard to scratch on the limit with our feet on the ground, but even then bikes such as the Greeves were woefully short on power – that was the problem.

The 250cc class

The 250 class had many makes and some fantastic specials, in particular the REG twin built by Bob Geeson, a real winner in the hands of Derek Minter, Sid Mizen, Ray Fay, Fred Hardy, etc. Geoff Monty had a special 250 Gold Star and there were 250 Manx Nortons, old 250 Velocettes, Pike Rudges and the best NSU Sportmaxes – but all were heavy old bikes, and did not appeal. What I wanted was a lightweight 250 with some power. This would also suit me as I was only 5ft 7in and weighed in at 9st 7lb. Keeping the overall weight down was important, as the power to weight ratio had to be good. This helped very much with the braking as it obviously takes bigger and heavier brakes to stop more weight and these are unsprung items. It appeared to me that what I needed was a good powerful engine put into a Greeves frame.

The Greeves factory

Although I was now in Basildon, my previous relationship with Cornells in Chelmsford had also given me a contact directly with the Greeves factory. This was Bob Mills of the competition department who always related great stories of the firm's exploits in European Championship Moto Cross.

Travelling previously on the Continent with Brian Stonebridge and later with Dave Bickers, the Greeves 250 24 MCS Motocross machines were well known and had been European champions (the forerunner of today's world series) in 1960 and 1961, and I had asked Bob what engines they used. Generally it was a Villiers 34A crankcase with Alpha crankshaft and flywheels, and their own designed single-cylinder, square-finned barrel with porting and piston to suit. These lightweight bikes were regularly beating 350 and 500 machines in open local events, so the engine really had some 'go' in it.

Living in Basildon, the Greeves factory at Thundersley was only about four miles distant. I found out they were looking for a draughtsman and wrote to them for an interview. During November 1961 I visited the factory and saw J.L. Ralling (the works manager) and was shown around the drawing office and assembly line, but he deemed my Marconi experience not suitable for motorcycle construction and I did not get the job. Having enthusiasm, being a good draughtsman and having an HNC in mechanical engineering obviously did not seem to impress Mr Ralling.

The more I thought about the situation the more I became convinced that by using a Greeves road frame and fitting a 24 MCS engine into it I could form the basis for a good little lightweight 250 with enough power to be competitive. With Derek Cornell as a contact, I arranged a meeting with Bob Mills just to put forward my idea to him. He was positive and enthusiastic, but said it was a non-starter as Bert Greeves was very against it when Bob had mentioned road racing to him before. However, he said I should try to meet Derry Preston-Cobb to discuss it, who was much more amenable. So I duly wrote to Mr Cobb on 26 December 1961 – Boxing Day – you could see how keen I was! His reply dropped on my mat on 3 January 1962 and he suggested a meeting at his home the coming Friday at 7.30pm – I was elated.

The meeting

The meeting went well but it was rather difficult as Mr Cobb was a paraplegic who had a speech impediment, but he was a great guy with huge enthusiasm and his laugh was infectious. His three-wheel open invalid carriage (in which he sat in his wheelchair) had been specially built in the factory for him, and guess what? The old Villiers 9E engine that drove it had been replaced with a 24MCS unit and, boy, did it go! He wanted to take it round Shrublands Park scrambles track when he was there with Dave Bickers, but Dave had to tell him that it would never get through the 'Bomb Hole'. He was most insistent that he wanted to experience the thrill and Dave obliged by putting the three wheeler into the back of his pick-up truck and taking the whole assembly through the Bomb Hole!

What people! what times! – they were great. However…I digress.

The meeting ended with Derry Preston-Cobb agreeing to talk to Bob Mills 'off the record' to make the necessary parts, including the latest engine available to me, and suggested that I should keep it quiet and wait two to three weeks before doing any more.

Well, if any of you readers cannot remember the winter of 1961–1962 I can tell you it was very severe, with a lot of snow and ice. Days of below zero temperatures and the journey on the Bantam to and fro was very bad. I used to put a hot water bottle inside my waterproof jacket to try to keep me warm, I wore silk gloves, wool gloves, leather gloves and plastic overmittens for the ride which took nearly an hour each way. When we got home at night, at about 6.30pm, I used to light the one small coal fire that I had laid before going to work at 7.15am. Some way to live and work!

One night, when going home, the bike just slid down the camber of the road on the sheet ice. I managed to keep it upright until we hit the kerb and took a nasty tumble. This was in Galleywood and luckily Ron Fisher (from the Gold Star days) lived nearby. I crawled round as I had twisted my ankle badly and could not walk. When he opened the door he could not see anyone, then he looked down to see me moaning on the ground. His little cottage was warm and cosy and he was most hospitable, and I stayed over – I think this was the only time I was warm in about six weeks during that winter!

The adventure begins

My meeting with Bob Mills had been arranged for a Saturday morning (Mr Greeves was not there), so off I went to the factory at the end of January 1962. I had no idea where to find Bob so I called in at the factory entrance reception. Here a charming lady called Pam (who I later found out was Bob Mills's wife) told me that he was in the Research and Development shop of the competition department and pointed outside across the road and explained how to get there.

'Wow!' I thought, 'I have arrived!' To go to the R & D of a European Champions motorcycle manufacturer! I felt very important and went to find the building. My euphoria, however, was short-lived, as all I found were some decrepit-looking wooden sheds. I saw a guy outside dressed in a Barbour suit, who I later found out was the Greeves competition manager Bill Brooker, and asked him where I could find Bob Mills. 'In there', he said and pointed to the small wooden door in the end of the hut. On entering, the illusion was totally shattered – it was dark and dingy, lit only by one or two single unshaded bulbs dangling from the roof, the floor was black with oil-soaked compacted dirt and the only heat was from the very small single 'tortoise' coke-fired stove in the middle of the hut (nicknamed 'Central Heating'!). The ingenuity of the 'Development Engineers' was present, however, as strapped to the 6in pipe (which passed for a chimney and which disappeared vertically through the corrugated iron roof), was a one-gallon can. This was modified by the addition of a simple petrol tap soldered into a hole in the bottom and a straight piece of $1/8$in diameter copper pipe about 1ft long. This was strategically placed over a door in the top of the stove. The can was full of 'dope' and the petrol tap cracked open to allow about one drip per minute into the coke's glowing embers, producing a 'poof' of flames each time, augmenting the meagre heat – so much for health and safety! The wooden shed was affectionately referred to as 'The Chicken Shack', as you could still see the side flaps from which the eggs were collected!

I found Bob in the gloom and was made welcome with a warming cup of tea – I just wondered how they survived and worked in such atrocious conditions – but in those days we knew little better. Bob had been busy and had started getting together parts we needed: a frame, forks and a special modified engine cradle of steel plates which was, in fact, a sub-frame connecting the typical Greeves aluminium beam to the rear down-tube and swinging arm mount. The standard road version was no good as it was made for the Villiers 2T unit, and mine had to be fitted with the 25 MDS. This had to be designed carefully to give enough rigidity but also provide adequate ground clearance; it was a really one-off unit.

The engine

Bob also showed me the engine, which looked the part with its large, square-finned, air-cooled barrel. It was assembled, except for the carburettor. We designed a transfer piece for this to connect the cylinder to the $1\frac{9}{32}$in GP carburettor I had kept from the Gold Star (I would just like to add here that the Goldie's carb is safe and sound and is, possibly with the float chamber the only part remaining in situ on the Greeves – but more of that later).

We had a pair of front and rear hubs that were given to Greeves to try out from the Midland Hub Co. They were full-width alloy units of $6\frac{1}{2}$in diameter; the front having a more centrally placed brake and cooling duct, looking adequate for the job and quite light. We found cables for the front brake and clutch and lots of Nyloc nuts and bolts, (inc. engine studs) and I took this basic kit home.

The assembly shop

The front room in the Basildon house became the assembly shop – at least it was not sub-zero temperature – and I sent the hubs to my friend, Derek Yorke. He built the 19in wheels and fitted a new pair of Avon racing tyres. Basic assembly was quick and I soon had the forks with their tapered roller-head bearings fitted, the cradle and the engine/gearbox unit went together well and when the wheels came it began to really look the part. I was excited and very elated. The project was a reality and I was 'on track' – well, very nearly!

I went back to Greeves for the carburettor/barrel transfer piece and looked down the list of 'still wanted for the job' parts. Things like clip-on handlebars (which had to be drawn and made to fit round the large fork tubes), quick action throttle and cable, tank, seat, footrests, gear lever, rear brake lever fittings and cable, and rear alloy guard. There was some slight concern shown by Bob as it appeared Bert Greeves had got wind that something was happening. Bob was in fear of losing his job which he liked immensely, but he still found me a used alloy trials tank (only 1½ gallons and very small). It really did not look the part but I did not mind as it was light. A quick-action plastic throttle assembly with cable followed and a trials rear brake lever with handle bar clamps to modify as cable holder, a standard road gear lever and again various nyloc nuts and bolts.

'This', said Bob, 'is it. No more!' With this he presented me with an invoice for £130 dated 12 February 1962 which I paid cash for and was signed by Mr Bennet. Now I was on my own. The other parts needed were drawn up by myself and made at either Hoffmans or Marconi by various volunteers in the Baddow R & D workshop.

The seat from the Gold Star was utilised, which was made from fibreglass for the Manx Norton. The top-frame tubes over the rear wheel allowed this to fit properly and I had coupled the two ends together with a loop of tube to give more rigidity to the frame rear. A small piece of alloy guard was cut to go behind the engine up under the seat and a large quarter-inch alloy bracket was constructed to mount the float chamber to ensure flexibility and accurate levelling. The fuel level in a remote device has to be accurately adjusted to ensure good running and, if not more important for short circuit racing, easy starting.

Clip-ons fitted with throttle, cable ('modded' to fit GP carburettor), tank, seat, rear set footrests and rear brake were all installed, and fortunately I put the standard gear-leverunit on backwards and it fitted well. This made the gears 'up' for 'up' and 'down' for 'down' – as it was on the Gold Star – because also we had reversed the lever and not changed the internal plate to reverse the mechanism. So far no mention of the exhaust system – well, by this time the middle of March was approaching and my first accepted entry was at the Brands Hatch 'Trophy Day' for non-winners on 1 April – a day not to be fooled with!

The riding position

Sitting on the bike in the front room was fine and the shortened and straightened ball-ended brake and clutch levers were adjusted to my liking as were the gear change and brake pedals. It did feel strange without a large tank between my knees but, apart from having one made or putting a heavy 2½ gallon steel tank on, I had no option. I thought about the jetting for the carb as there was no reference and I left in the 410 main jet as in the Gold Star, figuring a 250 two-stroke would consume as much fuel as a 500 four-stroke. Knowing the race was at Brands' short circuit, where top speed was not paramount but good acceleration essential, I decided on a rear wheel sprocket which I calculated at max revs 7,500. Note that I had no rev counter – there was no place to fit a drive, and afterall a two-stroke would not over rev, they just ran out of steam. There were no valves to hit the piston and the weight saving was useful. Maximum speed on the Brands gearing was in the region of 85mph. I fitted a Motocross stubby megaphone exhaust which I knew would work.

Bursting into life

Well, would it run? I enlisted the help of Alan (my neighbour) and we decided to bump it between the garages and the backs of the houses in Feering Green, the street we lived in. So one Saturday morning I wheeled her out and put in some four star two-stroke mix at 25:1 for the first time, tickled the float chamber (I had already checked spark timing etc. set by Greeves), put it into second gear, pulled back on compression, freed the clutch and Alan and I pushed. We got up to a good speed, dropped the clutch and after a few silent revs she burst into life. I pulled in the clutch and selected neutral and warmed her up. What a noise! Blipping the throttle it seemed clear and ran up the rev range well, it was just terrific and I was very happy (I cannot say the same for the neighbours!). Nice and warmed up, I gave her a thorough check over for loose fittings but the nylocs had done a good job (thanks to Greeves' MotoCross experience).

The chain tension was OK, the brakes statically worked well, so no more ado – the road test was imminent. I donned my riding gear, bumped her into life again and went off gingerly, trying not to make too much noise out through the estate, round the edge of Basildon and onto the Southend Arterial Road where I could let her go. This little bike really surprised me, the acceleration was fantastic and in top she really flew. I just could not believe how well it went and just wanted to keep on riding, down through the box round the roundabouts. The steering and brakes all seemed OK so after 20 minutes or so I brought her home, thinking I had run the gauntlet enough (it had no tax, insurance, it was unsilenced, had no horn etc.) but I knew then that I had created something really special.

Bill Roberts Fairings

I just could not wait for my first meeting, but I had to first go to Bill Roberts Fairings down the Arterial Road to see what he had that would fit. I told him it had to be light and he said 'come and look at this'. He had just made a replica of a Peel Fairing as a trial which had handlebar surrounds and he made it a one-off one layer trial. This appealed to my sense of adventure, it was also cheap and I took it away and fitted it. It looked like a real racer now! With the numbers (153) painted on, I was really ready to go.

Finally 1 April 1962 arrived, though the only practising I had done was starting which, I have to say, was really good. By pushing hard against the front brake I was able to drop the clutch within three steps and 'bouncing' on the seat side saddle brought the engine immediately into life, starting in second gear the acceleration and pick up was fantastic, Moto Cross style. It left only just enough time to get my leg over to change into third, but I thought this should do well for the four-lap heats on the short circuit at Brands.

We loaded the old ambulance which had lain dormant all winter and needed most of the day before it would start again. In both of the heats there were 28 starters, again a total mix of various makes and specials, 20 to be exact with one other Greeves (a twin). The favourites in my heat were an Arthur Wheeler MotoGuzzi, E.R. Cooper on a superb NSU Sportmax, P.R. Butler also on a NSU, Ron Freeman (Southend friend) with a new 250 Honda CB72 (the only Japanese bike in the race) and six other NSUs. I had my work cut out – only time would tell!

Our heat was race number six in the programme at 1.15pm. Scrutineering and the four-lap practice session went well, the bike handled well (if not better than I had hoped) as nothing scraped due to the more than adequate ground clearance and high footrests. The acceleration was fantastic, the braking was sure and solid. It just seemed a little under-geared. It ran out of steam along the top straight but this was mainly due to the stubby MX megaphone exhaust which definitely limited the top end revs (something had to be done about this and a proper expansion chamber manufactured).

We picked our grid positions by ballot and I was on row two. I was really fired up but not nervous, just wanting the race to start.

The debut race

'Go through the drill – push hard against the brake!' – the starter hesitated and dropped the Union Jack flag – 'release brake, one–two–three steps, drop clutch' and 'pow' we were away up through the box and well tucked behind the screen!

First into Paddock, up the hill, first into Druids – where were they all? – this was a new experience, racing in front, behind no one – a clear track was fabulous, what a feeling!

I concentrated on making my lines smooth and clean and still nobody was coming past down the top straight; although I certainly could feel where the peak power was and, going past the start and finish, I was flat out. I did not look behind but just kept riding as fast as I could, and suddenly the chequered flag came out and dropped as I went the past the line again – four laps gone and the new Greeves and I won! I just could not believe it – what a feeling, a dream come true, exhilaration, elation, I cannot describe it. I knew I had made the right decision and calculations as my one-off special was a winner, albeit in a restricted race. Still, to win in my first race in my third year of racing was more than I ever dreamed about.

The centre of attraction

Back in the pits everybody patted me on the back and the crowds gathered to see the Greeves which had won. My friends congratulated me and we had a great laugh. I was told that I was being caught by E.R. Cooper on the NSU and Trevor Barnes, but never mind. While we were chatting and reliving the race Ken Phillips the travelling marshal came up and congratulated me. Then came the clerk of the course, Mr Lovett, who explained that a protest had been lodged against me. I actually laughed and asked 'what for?' 'Illegal fuel' was his reply. 'I have been told that you are running this engine on dope', (a methanol-based concoction sometimes used in Moto Cross, grass track and speedway, which gave a significant increase in power). Of course, I knew this was not the case but the officials had to check. To this day I do not know who put in the protest but I took it as a compliment as others did not believe my bike was so quick on pump fuel, but it was.

A sample was soon taken from the tank and proved it was just petroil mix, the officials shook my hand and the incident was over. Back then to reality, I checked the bike over and prepared for the final at 2.45pm. The other heat had been won by Jim Russell (Ariel Arrow), not surprisingly as he was a known and sponsored rider by Pullins Motorcycles and had two rides in the day (the only rider to have two rides). He had already won the 125cc race on his Bultaco.

The final

For the final I got a second row draw and again had a fabulous start – well in front at Paddock Bend, getting more and more used to the handling and the brakes.

The then relatively unknown Reg Everett sprang to instant fame on 1 April 1962, when on his home-built Greeves special he won his heat and then finished runner-up at Brands Hatch in the final.

Reg taking his 249cc Villiers-powered Greeves special to victory in its first-ever outing, at Brands Hatch on 1 April 1962.

Especially the angle of lean to the limit of adhesion which, compared to the Gold Star, seemed limitless.

My lap times equalled the best I did on the Goldie of 1 min 6 secs. I was doing a speed of 67.64mph average, and again, to my surprise, I continued to lead the race for lap after lap. I was feeling great and really enjoying this feeling of racing in front. After four of the six laps I was given the 'hurry-up' sign by my friends standing at the top of Paddock Bend and knew that the faster bikes were catching up. Well, I managed to keep them all at bay except one E.R. Cooper, whose NSU steamed past me just before the flag on the final lap – the Greeves just not having the top-end speed to do anything about it, but first in the heat and second in the final really was not a bad day's work, and I was given a nice little silver cup to look at forever more.

Making history

Little did I know then that what I had created was to become history, and what had been achieved would be re-told often. The press (*Motor Cycle News*) came to me and wanted information on me and the bike. For such a small meeting we got a good write-up and a picture in the paper on the following Wednesday. What a start to my third season! Now I really knew I had made the right decision and that racing to win and winning were within my reach – life seemed just great!

As soon as I could, I went to the Greeves factory to see Bob Mills – they, of course, had already heard of the success and had prophesied the lack of top-end performance with the 'megga' exhaust. To my surprise, Bob handed over a sketch of an expansion chamber but said they could not make it due to overwork in the development department. Bob was over the moon with my success though, and found and gave me new pistons, rings, clutch plates and special tools they had made for removing engine sprockets, and a new clutch, plus what was most valuable – a full selection of rear sprockets for the gearing. This was all confirmed in a nice letter of congratulations from Derry Preston-Cobb.

The expansion chamber was manufactured as a sheet metal project by John Tarrant (who raced a sidecar outfit) in the Marconi apprentice training school and was attached to a suitable exhaust header pipe found and given to me by Bob Mills. I gave the bike a quick run up the road and found it different in both noise and performance, estimating another 1,000rpm at the top end. Well, that was just great!

The second meeting

Doing a plug chop revealed a mixture weakness, so the main jet was upped two sizes to a 430. All of this was completed in good time for my second meeting which was to be at Snetterton on Sunday 22 April. This was a totally different challenge as it was a full national meeting on a fast, flat, open circuit against all-comers – the best in the country and Grand Prix competitors. This would be a real challenge.Practice was utilised ensuring that the gearing was correct on this fast circuit, the 250s averaging over 80mph! The smallest rear sprocket given to me by Bob seemed OK and a plug chop confirmed the mixture.

By now I knew my way well around this circuit and I was loving the fast, open bends. The Greeves handled really well and it was now much quicker down the straights, but it still lacked a little in this department. After practice a long wait ensued. As the 250cc race at Snetterton Nationals was the last one on the programme (it always was, starting at about 5.00pm), I had plenty of time to look at my opponents' machines and watch the other races.

Mike Hailwood started the proceedings by winning his 350cc heat from Derek Minter and Dan Shorey. My friends on their 7Rs, Joe Iszard and Dick Standing, finished 19th and 23rd respectively – about 9mph slower average than Hailwood's 88.78mph. They should have been in the second heat which was won by Roy Mayhew at 85.83, then would have been in the top 12 for the final. The third heat was even slower at 82.58mph. Hailwood romped away with the final, with Mayhew second and Minter third followed by Dan Shorey, Lew Young and Tony Godfrey – in all a great race was had by legendary names. Hailwood won his heat and the final of the 500 race, again followed by Mayhew, Godfrey, Minter, Shorey and Dave Degens. It was great to see Martin Hayward back to his old form on his G50, too, making sixth in his 500 heat and 17th in the final at 85.41mph. Dan Shorey won the 125 on his Works Bultaco closely followed by Tommy Robb and Bill Friend similarly mounted.

My race had Hailwood down to ride a 'not specified' and he subsequently did not ride, but I had Shorey on his Works Bultaco and Tommy Robb, V. Chatterton, B. Clarke, P. Inchley, K. Watson, E. Cooper (who beat me at Brands), N. Surtees,

V. Poore, T. Grotefeld, A. Wheeler, R. Denny, and G. Collis to contend with, to name just a few. This was a real quality field of 'smaller machine' specialists on proven racing machines, a daunting task but I was really looking forward to this one; although a third row grid position did not help in the draw.

A great result

The Greeves did not let me down and I was up with the front runners into Riches – down the short straight into Sears then via the swooping left-hander down the Norwich straight fearing the worse. Two or three of the quick guys came past but I also overtook, much to my surprise, and I became embroiled in a race-long dice with George Collis (LCH) – this was really fantastic wheel-to-wheel racing. George finally beat me by only .02 sec and I averaged 77.74mph and finished in sixth place, a great result for such a circuit. Dan Shorey won at 81.79mph so I still had a way to go but this was my best-ever result in an open national race for all-comers. So again I went home very happy in the knowledge of a job well done.

My next race was the following day at Crystal Palace on Easter Monday. It was an open national with heats and final, the first 12 from each heat of 25 going into the final. I had changed back the gearing to Brands as the circuits were roughly the same length and average speed, and practice went well.

Attracting attention

The bike was beginning to attract a lot of attention, as at Snetterton – the only Greeves there – and looking good in its 'Peel' type fairing. The white of the fairing showed off

On the Greeves special at Crystal Palace, Easter Monday, 23 April 1962; 4th in heat, 9th in final.

the distinctive Greeves Blue (note: most bikes were black). It appeared, with the exception of Dan Shorey, that many of my competitors that day were the same as the day before and only three of 50 machines were two-strokes.

I had a great ride in my heat, finishing fourth to Fred Hardy on an NSU, Norman Surtees on a special Reynolds-framed, Ducati Desmo twin and J.F. Harper on another Ducati (220 dohc single), but I was slower than the first four in the other heat won by Alan Pavey, Ken Watson, Brian Osbourne and Carl Ward. Although I had a good and informative ride, the final was not the success I wanted and I finished a lowly ninth. Brian Osbourne won easily.

My bike seemingly did not to have the real zip that I had quickly become accustomed to – perhaps I was already expecting too much from my special. In the post, though, to my surprise, I received a cheque for £1 for my fourth place in the heat! My sixth place at Snetterton in a national scratch race gave no such rewards and paid only to fourth place, with the 250cc winner receiving £12.10s. The prize money for racing in those years was a disgrace as we were paying about £3 to £4 for fees. So many people wanted to race that all meetings were still over-subscribed, and the organizers/circuit owners had the upper hand and took advantage of the situation.

Bantam Racing Club

Back at Snetterton for the next weekend, I was riding in a closed meeting organised by the Bantam Racing Club. At this meeting they had a special race for 'British' 250cc machines so I was back to my not-so-exotic competition, Velocettes, Ariel Arrows, Rudges, various specials, BSA C15s, Royal Enfields and a very new looking Cotton with a Villiers twin engine ridden by Jim Curry (Jim and I were to become good friends and rivals).

It was an eight-lap race as against the previous six for the national event, and I had a good start and took the lead. All seemed OK but at the end of the second lap going down the Norwich Straight this Velocette (a KTT) came steaming past and the rider, a semi-toothed slightly older gentleman, was looking my way and grinning like a Cheshire cat! We had a great race together, he passing me on the straights, me catching and passing him in the corners. What a great time and what a teacher he was. I was still learning and he showed me how to slipstream by tucking in as close as I could behind him when he passed me to help my speed down the straight. Every time he passed he gave this toothy grin and we laughed together – what competition, what sport, in the true sense of the words. It was, I am afraid, inevitable that he would win as he always passed me along the start and finish straight by the finishing line. Try as I may, I just could do nothing about it. So it was Mr Ray Cowles of Pontypool, South Wales, first, Reg Everett second (Ray was to become a good friend and later still the sponsor of several top-line riders including his fellow countrymen, Selwyn Griffiths and Malcolm Uphill). Third was J.R. Blackwell on a BSA who scratched round like a demon on fire and F.J. Curry was sixth on his Cotton. A great day was had by all. For some reason the Greeves was not as quick in this race as before, only averaging 75.22mph over the 77.74 of the previous Snetterton outing. I thought that it must have been getting tired already, so I should have a look inside.

Actually, I now had plenty of time as my next race was not until 11 June at a new circuit for me – Thruxton in Wiltshire. I had visited as a spectator at a previous 500 mile production races and this was also an old airfield circuit, similar to Snetterton. It had flat, wide, open, fast corners and was a very fast track. A six-week wait was too much to bear after such a hectic season start of six races in four weeks.

On stripping the Greeves I found signs of detonation which appeared as small marks in the top of the piston, which usually indicated too soft a plug. I had been running on Lodge RL47 so decided to up it to RL50 and changed also to the new piston and rings given to me by Bob. The gearing should be OK as I would leave it on the Snetterton set up. Otherwise just a general check over was needed, taking the wheels out to check the brake linings were well bedded in and making 100 per cent contact, checking the bearings and adjusting the chains. There was little else to do but work and wait.

Testing at MIRA

One other trip was planned as I had to go with Bob Mills for a test day at MIRA, the motor industries' test track at Nuneaton. This was to test the Greeves road bike which the factory wanted to race in the 1962 Thruxton 500-miler and would actually be entered by Comerfords of Thames Ditton who were one of Greeves' best (if not the best) dealers. Although I never saw anyone from Comerfords even at the race.

Martin Hayward and I were due to ride the Greeves after our outing at the Bemsee 1,000km race effort last year. This bike was a Model 25 DCX, a 250 twin again, but in a new Greeves colour scheme of light blue and yellow with a handlebar fairing and chunky looking tank made from fibreglass, a real departure for Greeves. The bike went and handled well and was a pleasure to ride even on the high-speed banked track at MIRA, but for me it all added to my racing and riding experience. I was still riding daily on the round trip to work (Basildon/Chelmsford/Basildon) on the 175 Bantam, as the old ambulance was far too thirsty and not very reliable to use on a daily basis. On the way home from MIRA in the Greeves Development Transport (a BMC Atlas, which must have been about the slowest van on the road) we got a puncture at Gants Hill roundabout on the North Circular in the rain and got soaked repairing it. The visit to MIRA turned out to be a very long day, leaving the Thundersley factory at 6am and not returning until 8pm. It took a long time to go anywhere in those days.

Thruxton, short-circuit style

Before the 500-miler came the first Thruxton meeting – National Road Races on 11 June 1962. So, when the time came, we loaded up the old ambulance – this was to be its longest journey to date, about 145 miles (on the A12 through the centre of London, Hammersmith, Egham, out to the A30 to Basingstoke then the A303 to Andover and on to Thruxton). At an average of, say, 25mph, as it would only do 45mph flat out downhill, we allowed six to eight hours including a stop to make a cup of tea and eat a prepared sandwich or pork pie – real luxury! Fortunately we got through London without mishap apart from stopping for fuel – the 10 cwt Morris fully loaded and only having a five-and-a-half gallon tank and a small 1550cc engine and very low gearing did at best 20 mpg. All was ok until we got to Egham. I had noticed the 'performance' dropping off and a noise getting louder. Finally the exhaust pipe broke and dropped off with the silencer. We all got out, picked up the offending part and with the help of hacksaw, hammer and odd nuts, bolts and wire duly rigged the modified exhaust across the front bumper and were on our way again. We plodded on but the poor old van got slower and slower and finally on a hill near Andover we had to stop and investigate. Dave Livesy, the previous owner who was with us, thought he knew the problem. We lifted the bonnet and he cranked over the engine with the starting handle (a most important part of equipment) only to find no compression. 'The exhaust valves have burned out' he said. Surprisingly, we had one with us – or, rather, Dave did – he must have known something! This was just as well as the one we found was completely burned out. After we had removed the cylinder head, the other three only needed regrinding in. As it was a side valve, the head was easily removed and the remedial work started. New valve for one, three others reground in, head back on, hose and plugs reconnected, refilled with water, we started her up and we were on our way again, after only a two-hour delay! Finally we arrived late and tired out at Thruxton, brewed up and had a fry-up in the van for dinner and grabbed a few well deserved hours of sleep.

The atmosphere

Travelling and being at races was like being part of a very large and exciting club. On arrival, all the faces were familiar and friendly and the place had a great atmosphere: excitement, smell, noise, comradeship, help and real rivalry. There was playfulness and pranks but it was coupled with the seriousness of good engineering practice and skilful, safe, but very hard racing competition – this was really becoming not just a sport or fun pastime but a way of life and one to be followed at all costs: physically, mentally, monetarily and socially. Other concerns had to take second place.

Practice went very well and I liked the circuit with its challenging flat-out corners and 2.2-mile length. I learnt it very quickly (as you had to) with only five laps' practice! Speeds were relatively high, the 250 record by John Kidson on his Moto

Guzzi stood at 76.15mph but Mike 'the Bike' Hailwood had done 87.32 on his 500 MV, lapping 1 min 30.8 secs, some 14 secs quicker than Kidson. There were 36 riders in each of the two four-lap heats. Again I was the only Greeves – there were 13 NSUs, five new Aermacchis, nine Ducatis, seven Ariels, Guzzis, MVs, Adlers, Cottons, Villiers Specials, Velocettes, Triumphs, Royal Enfields and Rudges, plus all kinds of one-offs being ridden by the regular specialist protagonists. After referring to the programme I must admit I had the easier heat, as the only ones I recognised were dear old Ray Cowles on his Velocette and J.R. Blackwell on his Beeza from Snetterton. The generally more recognised names of J. Kidson, B. Lawton, T. Jeffrey, G. Collis, R. Williats and A. Wheeler were in heat one. A front row start in the heat saw me grab a lead which was not to be contested and I won with relative ease.

The final was different – I was on the third row and was baulked at the start and not able to find a way through. I was enjoying the competition but finally finished in 12th position. I was not quick enough to make any impression on the leaders. Just how important is a good start?

Going home we took it really steadily. It became more and more obvious that better and faster transport was becoming a necessity and something would have to be done before other far-flung race circuits were contemplated.

The Norwich Trophy

Back to Snetterton again for the next weekend, 17 June, for the BEMSEE Norwich Trophy meeting, which was a closed meeting with trophies and exclusively for BMCRC members. Nevertheless, there were good riders involved in a six-lap scratch race. Mick Manley, a great and fast Welshman, won this race on his superb gold-finished 220cc Ducati. He had a great scrap and won by only 0.2 seconds from R.D.L. Denny on his NSU Norton, and I finished a lonely third, eight seconds behind and 10 secs in front of Keith Powell on his Parvel, averaging 76.60mph. I was still not as fast as my first outing of 77.74mph, but I just could not work out why. This time I won a silver ashtray for my efforts. Poor old Martin fell off at the start and Dick Standing finished 20th in his race. Lew Young won the 500cc event and a certain D.L. (Dave) Croxford and Ray Pickrell were ninth and 13th respectively. Lew also won the 350cc class in which Tom Phillips was fourth.

Thruxton the 500-miler

I went back to Thruxton the following weekend for the 500-mile production race. This time I rode to Martin's on the Bantam and stayed at his house in Walton-on-Thames overnight. His father drove us to Thruxton the following morning and he and Dick Standing were our timekeepers and lap scorers. This was a request from the organisers who were the Southampton and District MCC. They were trusted to sit in a tent marking off our laps and did it in one-hour stints.

The competition had a new manufacturere in the 250s. There were six Honda CB72 four-stroke twins entered, one of them ridden by Minter and Bill Smith, and seven Ariel Arrow Sports two-stroke twins, one ridden by Cecil Sandford and Mike O'Rourke, out of the 24 250cc participants.

We elected to ride in one-hour stints, me doing the first from the Le Mans-type start. This was pretty hectic and consisted of a 25-yard dash to the bikes. There seemed to be people everywhere, and as we were to the rear of the line up – behind the 11 500s and 25 650s – we were well behind the faster bikes at the start. The race was expected to last approximately six and a half hours, and with the weather being good a 70mph average was well within the capabilities of the top 650s. The worst part of the race was the speed difference between those 650s and our modest mount, which meant the top runners came past at an alarming rate showing no consideration.

Disaster

We went well for over four hours and were circulating in about ninth place of the 250s. Martin took over and continued lapping consistently until disaster struck. Coming through the straw bale chicane near the pits, (designed to slow the machines down for the lap scorers but unliked by the riders) Rufus Broomfield on one of the Hondas ran wide and forced Martin into the straw bales. He went over the top in a nasty accident. Some pandemonium ensued as the debris was cleared. Martin was taken to the first aid post by the St John Ambulance men (what a great service they all gave for free – I still support them now) and I ran across, picked up the bike and pushed it back to our pit. Bob Mills examined it and we straightened out what we were able to and removed the damaged screen.

Not knowing exactly what shape Martin was in, it was decided that I should quickly remount and get on with the race. After circulating again for about 30 mins we got the black flag, and on stopping were informed we were disqualified. What for? Apparently it was because Martin had not completed his lap and I was not allowed to complete it for him even for about the 100 yards or so back to the pit, even though he was in no state to. No amount of argument would change this so our ride was over. As I was allowed to ride for two hours we would have probably completed the race, but it was not to be.

Martin was taken to hospital with bad cuts on his nose and face, which he caught on the Perspex screen when going over the handlebars, and a huge bump on his hip that was lanced – ouch! The 250cc class was won by the Minter/Smith Honda, certainly the first sign of things to come. Overall, the Norton 650 SS sponsored by Lawton and Wilson with Phil Read and Brian Setchell aboard took the honours. A very good ride was had by Tom Philips and Ellis Boyce on the superbly prepared Geoff Dodkin 499cc Velocette Venom, they took the 500 class and were a fantastic second overall. Bob Mills was upset with our outcome and went away despondent, but I have to say I just shrugged my shoulders and realised that disappointment was just as much a part of racing as elation.

Home-Built Special v Works Honda

Our next outing on 8 July at Brands Hatch was back to short circuit scratching at its most intense. The eight-lap scratch race had Derek Minter as its favourite on the Grand Prix-winning 250cc Honda four, some competition to my front-room-built special. Imagine going to Brands now and finding Rossi on his Moto GP Yamaha and you on something you had built in your front room from parts!

I was up against the best of the best, but felt excited rather than daunted by the challenge. Ernie Wooder, Brian Clark, Len Rodda, Fred Hardy, Brian Osbourne, Alan Pavey, Phil Read, Ian Goddard, Ken Watson, Terry Grotefeld, Barry Lawton and my friend Ron Freeman were all in the race, so it was clear that this would be a hard one. The 36 starters lined up and the Brands organisers had graciously put me on the second row, so I just had to make a good start.

The eight-lap race was on the long circuit and that meant a distance of 21.2 miles, which was going to make it more difficult for me but I was determined to make a good showing. Of course, Minter won easily and set new lap and race records at virtually the same speed as the 350 times on the same day (also by Minter and Read), averaging 86.72mph. I rode my heart out, scratching as hard as

Brands Hatch, 8 July 1962. The Greeves special awaits action.

Reg heeling his Greeves special well over at Brands Hatch on 8 July 1962. He eventually finished seventh.

I could and flogging the little Greeves to its absolute limit. I made a good start and more or less held my position finishing a fantastic (for me) seventh place and in front of many of the established 250cc stars. Behind me were Osbourne (Aermacchi), Fred Hardy (REG), A. Pavey (NSU), Grotefeld and Lawton (both on Aermacchis). The only Greeves in the race had certainly not disgraced itself and I felt now I could live with the top riders. We went home well pleased with ourselves and I also won £2, Minter receiving £15 for his win.

Minter that day won the 125, 250, 350 and 500cc and unlimited races, netting him a total of £114 plus his appearance money.! O,h what I would have given to get another bike, one pound per meeting would never be enough to really become established and win enough to survive, especially with the meagre prize money on offer (though £114 was equivalent to about six weeks' wages at the time).

Attracting the press

To say that the Greeves was a help is an understatement because it had taken me from lowly positions in non-experts' racing to the top-10 position in open all-comers' racing in just a few short months, and this soon brought attention from the press and photographers.

This was new to me and apart from accepting it by being helpful and polite, I really did not pay much attention to it or have the understanding to use it. In fact I never did, which I believe was to my cost. At the time my friends and I were just happy to be competing for the love, fun, excitement, the travel and camaraderie, doing what we really wanted to after the austere upbringing and hardships endured during and just after the war. That was enough for us.

According to my records, I returned to Snetterton on 21 July for another closed Bantam Racing Club meeting, finishing sixth in the first race and third in the

Reg leading his friend Ron Freeman (Honda) at Brands Hatch, 7 July 1962, on the approach to Druids Hill hairpin.

second. This was due to the dreaded detonation and partial seizure during the first outing and not having a new piston for the second race. Using a file and emery cloth to take off the high spots had to suffice.

Brian Woolley

Having the engine taken apart in the pits attracted the attention of a moustachioed gentleman with a Midlands accent who exclaimed, when looking deeply into the barrel, 'how the hell does this bike go so quickly with this porting?' I just informed him that it came that way direct from the factory. He then said he would get in touch with the factory and tell them how to make it quicker. I gave him Bob Mills' name and then asked for his. 'Brian Woolley' was the reply and we struck up a friendship which was to last many years until his recent death.

The Honda outing

We all returned to Snetterton again for a National Open meeting on 29 July. It was a horribly damp, wet and cold day and my Southend friend Ron Freeman had convinced me to have a ride on his race-kitted CB72 Honda by way of a change and to make comparisons, to see what I could do on his bike as generally I had beaten him on the Greeves. Well, the conditions did not help and I found the Honda very heavy in comparison. The acceleration was slower, but it was certainly quicker down the straights which was good in the wet. For a modified road bike I was impressed and enjoyed the ride and experience; although I was still not a wet-weather rider and was very cautious on someone else's bike.

I eventually finished seventh at a very slow 62.94mph (my general average on the Greeves was 76mph) and the race was again won by Dan Shorey on the Works 196cc

Bultaco at 68.25, with Terry Grotefeld second and Horace 'Crasher' Crowder third, both on Aermacchis. I was just behind Ernie Wooder on another Honda.

Ron was happy and admitted he was glad he did not ride on such a rotten day. Dick Standing did not finish in his 350 heat and Joe Iszard was 14th in his, so they did not qualify for the final. Now recovered from his Thruxton crash, Martin Hayward did well and finished 11th in his heat and qualified for the 500 final,

Reg racing Ron Freeman's Honda CB72 to seventh place in the 250cc race at Snetterton in July 1962.

where he finished 13th in the torrential rain. This 500 final was won by Derek Minter at only 72.093mph (he won his heat at 91.32) so you can see the conditions were really bad. (Remembering that then we only had one set of tyres for hot/cold/wet/dry conditions – practice and race, so it was usually down simply to rider skills.) Phil Read took the honours in the 350cc final.

Going to Crystal Palace on Bank Holiday Monday 6 August was to be one of my worst results of the year. It was very wet and I just could not get my act together. I still could not ride fast in the wet. I was not relaxed, much too rigid and did not

July 1962 and Reg is seen here on the ESSA (Eastern Sporting Sidecar Assocation) float at the local Chelmsford Carnival. At that time he was the club's chairman.

flow like I could in the dry – would I ever learn? I finished a lowly 10th at 54mph and was lapped by the winner Mick Manley's Ducati, which still only managed 62.9mph – very slow. The lap record was held then by John Surtees on a NSU Sportsmax at 74.24mph which he had stood together with the 350 and 500cc records since 17 August 1957. Ron Freeman on his Honda finished seventh. The whole day was a washout and even Joe Dunphy, a great rider and course specialist (although he won the 500 race easily), could still only manage 65.28mph against Surtees's record of 79.43. I went home wet and miserable and determined to beat my wet-weather bogey – but how?

At Brands Hatch on 19 August, happily in the dry, on the long circuit I had a great race and regained some lost confidence by finishing sixth in this open national meeting. Brian Osbourne, Terry Grotefeld, Norman Surtees, Ian Goddard and that Welshman, Mick Manley, beat me, but over eight laps on the long circuit it was a good result.

The 350 race that day was won by Phil Read – Minter was absent having been injured in a crash at the Ulster GP on 11 August on the 125 EMC, as Lew Young

Reg enjoyed a tremendous day a Snetterton on 25 August 1962, winning both his races on the Greeves special.

In one of the winning races on 25 August Reg even has time to stick out his tongue for the photographer.

Snetterton again, this time on 7 October 1962, chasing Ron Freeman's Honda CB72.

took the 500 race and Dave Downer won the unlimited race from Tony Godfrey, Chris Conn, Rex Butcher and Lew Young. Dave was not a new face but he achieved a remarkable victory on his 650 special Norton twin.

More help from Bob Mills

Shortly afterwards, I met up with Bob Mills again and he had a replacement barrel and piston for me to try (I believe that this was one that had been worked on by Brian Woolley) at the next outing, which was again at Snetterton, and another Closed Bantam Racing Club Meeting for British 250s with two races to try the new barrel and piston. This turned out to be really successful and I won both events with relative ease, leading from start to finish and averaging nearly 77mph in both, with a best lap of 2 min 4.8 secs, which was 78.17mph, my fastest to date, the very best on the Goldie being just over 75mph.

Suffice to say, I had three more meetings on my Greeves. Another national at Snetterton finishing a good sixth and averaging the race with a speed of 78.45mph,

a national at Brands on 14 October 1962 for which I can find no result and a Bemsee Guinness Trophy race at Snetterton on 7 October 1962. Here I finished fourth and won a shield. This was won by Terry Grotefeld, second was Trevor Barnes and third was my friend Ron Freeman on his Honda, beating me fair and square after a race-long duel by only .06 of a second, squeezing past on the home straight to pip me on the line! This time I averaged 79.17mph – the fastest of the year, a terrific result and a great finale to the season (my fastest lap of 1 min 58 secs making 82.68mph).

And so, finally, the 1962 racing season drew to a close. Certainly, it had provided a massive jump in my racing career, and its success had – for the first time – brought me into contact with both the press and the public. But it had also made me more determined than ever to succeed in my chosen sport.

By now the Everett Greeves was a well-known machine after a season in which the combination had a a number of excellent finishes; pictured here at Snetterton on 7 October 1962.

Chapter 5

The Silverstone

My results had been causing rumours which abounded about me and my Greeves. The word 'prototype' was written in the motorcycling journals on many occasions. Other factories, such as Cotton and DMW, had noticed the results of my motocross-based project and all could not have failed to have been impressed. Mr O.B. Greeves himself had requested to ride my machine – 'at last some recognition from the boss', I thought!

Bert Greeves

A Wednesday test day at Brands arrived and Bert Greeves circulated well on my bike, completing about 10 laps of the short circuit at a steady pace (about 1 min 20 secs to my best of 1 min 4 secs). He said he liked the bike and that I had done a good job – that was that. *The Motor Cycle* in their 18 October issue headlined 'Greeves on Greeves', relating that Bert Greeves had ridden Reg Everett's machine (which they referred to as 'a privately owned prototype').

The Starmaker

Soon after this, at the end of October, came the first news of a new racing engine from Villiers called the Starmaker to be used in a Cotton production racer, which was scheduled to make its debut at the November Motorcycle Show at Earls Court. Just before the show the press had another story, *Motor Cycling* featuring a 'Greeves production racer'. This was not my bike but rather a factory effort based clearly on my concept. Bert Greeves at the launch said he wanted to see British motorcycles establish supremacy in the 250 class, with a machine all could afford and have a chance to win in club and national events.

I was actually invited to the show to see this bike, it was to be the first time I saw it but I still had to pay to get in the show, and I was not even offered a cup of tea or a drink!

Beart and Dunphy

Bob Mills was there and was very subdued when he explained to me the proposed tie-up with Francis Beart as the Greeves' expert tuner and advisor for 1963, with Joe Dunphy as the rider of the

O.B. (Oscar Bertrum, but more simply 'Bert') Greeves, the autocratic boss of the Thundersley, Essex, motorcycle marque which bore his name.

Bert Greeves pictured at Brands Hatch in October 1962, riding Reg Everett's home-built Greeves special.

Four-times World Champion Geoff Duke pictured on the Greeves stand at the London Earls Court Show, 9 October 1962. The machine is the Greeves Show prototype.

factory-backed project. The bike at the show, plus the news of the tie-up with Beart and Dunphy, provided the press with a lot to write about. At the show on 10–17 November even Geoff Duke was photographed on the bike. Now I cannot compare myself with either Beart or Joe, and Geoff Duke was already a legend, but I wondered how much publicity they would have got without my bike, my idea and my efforts, not to mention my costs and riding efforts garnered by my 1962 results. I had carried the flag for Greeves but now I seemed to be ignored. There were rumours of me receiving one of the new Silverstones (the official name Greeves had been given to its production racer) for 1963 but nothing for sure.

Beart took delivery of the first machine and Joe was impressed by the speed of the bike at a Brands Hatch test session, but this was one of his first outings on a two-stroke, being used to the armchair ride of 350 and 500 Nortons.

Beart lightened the unit and paid a lot of attention to the exhaust system (I did not think at the time that Beart had a lot of two-stroke experience), which he redesigned and made from thin-gauge steel and saved 4lbs in weight. The Silverstone, when it appeared, bore little resemblance to the show bike and had a revised Villiers 36A Unit developing a reputed 30bhp. Whereas the show machine designated 24 RAS was

Much publicity was generated with the announcement that the 1962 Senior Manx Grand Prix winner Joe Dunphy would be riding a Francis Beart-tuned Greeves Silverstone RAS on the British short circuit in 1963.

fitted with a modified 246.33cc (66mm x 77mm) 34A unit which produced around 25bhp (similar to my bike – the real prototype?).

The 1963 season was now rapidly approaching and the news or information regarding me was non-existent, but the press was full of Beart and Dunphy and the machine which went to Frank Higley for Tom Phillips. I had no objection or fear about these guys getting one, but thought that as I had been the instigator, maker and rider of the 'prototype', at least I should be offered one. Even at a price?

An uncertain winter

During that long and uncertain winter my new-found wealth of £680 per year had allowed me to get rid of the poor old ambulance (sold for £10), which had finally come to the end of its road, and to buy a Mini van from a garage in Pitsea to use as transport to work instead of the flogged-to-death 175 Bantam (sold for £20). The Mini cost £275 on hire purchase but it made my life so much easier and more comfortable. I was also amazed at its handling and corner speeds which were greater than I could imagine. I had so much fun in this, going to and from work, that the journey was really enjoyable and was, at 45-50mpg, quite economical. Having a van, although small, meant I could carry all manner of goods and household effects around and so, to supplement my wages, I started doing small delivery jobs for all concerned – in fact, for absolutely anybody!

The 1962 season was drawing closer and I had started making entries on a '250 Greeves', not having sold my own 'prototype Silverstone'. I was still not sure what I would ride as there had been no decision from Greeves – even as late as the beginning of March when the first batch of Silverstones were starting to be delivered at an ex-works price of £285, which included a set of sprockets and main jets for the carburettor (way over my price range) and were, of course, going to those people who had placed their firm orders and paid a deposit. Speaking to Bob gave no indication, and he said I should approach Derry Preston-Cobb again, which I did by phone at the factory. I think he was embarrassed to hear from me but he said he would see what he could do. A week later Bob Mills contacted me and told me there was no chance of a Silverstone, but that they had decided to let me have the ex-show bike as I had been some help to them. This I would be able to collect from the factory one week before my first outing at Snetterton on 23 March 1963.

With no ambulance and the Mini van certainly not big enough for transport, I returned to the garage in Pitsea to see if they had anything suitable. To my delight they had a newly resprayed (in light grey) a 15 cwt Ford Thames van (of dubious provenance), which was full of small dents from the inside and had a badly squashed and dented base below the rear doors (indicating a lot of heavy loads and ill treatment). To me it looked great – a Thames van for transport just like the top riders of the day used and, with a £200 price ticket in the window, I just could not resist it.

The road test went OK, the 1700cc engine seemed to be performing well and mechanically all was quiet. We soon did a deal and I actually came away with the Thames plus £20, getting £220 back for the Mini which I had owned for just six short months. I had my own good reliable transport now and I figured with a 15 cwt and plenty of space I could at least use it well, making a few extra pounds to subsidise the racing effort by doing jobs in my spare time.

I was also about to return to live with my parents in Chelmsford as the house in Basildon was needed by its rightful owners, so for a little while I would not have much rent to pay, which would be a great help financially.

Collecting the 'new' Greeves

On the arranged day, I visited the Greeves factory to pick up my 'new' racing bike. It really looked nice but was still untried. Unlike the Silverstone it had a chromium plated, high-level exhaust system, no fairing, a different seat, gear linkage and no rev counter but a speedo driven from the front wheel; although it did have a 36A engine.

A bill of sale from Invacar (Greeves) for the 1962 Earls Court Show bike.

I was also given some paperwork to sign which said 'Sold to Mr R. Everett – one Greeves Racing Motor Cycle – Ex works, Frame No. 24RAS101 for the sum of £185.00'. Bob said it was the best they were prepared to offer me and could do nothing else. He did say he would try to get parts for me and I should let him know what I wanted when I saw him at race meetings, as he would be there to assist Mr Beart. He also mentioned the official invoice would be sent by post and I should pay on receipt (it was actually sent on 2 April 1963 and I still have it). I can say now that I was happy to get a bike of any sort but really disappointed in that, for all my efforts, I was not more appreciated. Moreover, I did not know how I would pay for this bike as suddenly my homemade bike had become really superseded by the Silverstone and had very little value. I would have to try anyway.

During practice at my first race of the season at Snetterton on 22 March 1963, in very cold conditions, I was able to assess my new acquisition in this closed-to-club Bantam Racing Club meeting. Top speed and acceleration appeared similar to my 1962 bike, but the riding position and handling certainly were not as stable or positive (recalling that in the 21 races I had, four were wins in eight podiums and 14 finishes in the top six); although I could not recall having a bad slide or crash or any handling problem. Some would say I was not trying hard enough, but I was happy with my efforts.

Problems

The seat was too high, making a higher centre of gravity and, with a longer tank, the riding position was further back making the weight distribution too much toward the rear. In the race, though, I took an early lead and put in the fastest lap of 2 min 04.6 secs at 78.29mph, which was not too bad but below my last race average of 79.19 on the 'prototype' back in October 1962. Also, the race was shortlived as the bike seized and I had to retire. Not the outcome I had hoped for with my new expensive Greeves! Tom Phillips won on his machine at the national meeting at Oulton Park, a tribute for this great rider and the new proper Silverstone.

We went to Mallory Park on 30 March and I told Bob about my handling and seizure problems. He said that the steering geometry was different on my bike as it was really only a model put together for the show, but he gave me a new piston and information on the carburation they were using on their bike.

In my heat I finished a lowly 13th, although I recall this was the first time ever I had been to Mallory Park as they would never accept my entries previously. But I was far from happy with the handling (especially on the ripples coming out of Gerrards) as the front went very light, not a good feeling on this very fast exit. On pulling off the head and barrel after the race, the engine was again shown to have had a partial seizure and I would be out of the final. Joe, on his Silverstone, led for 13 of the 15 laps until that lightweight expansion chamber split and the clutch gave out as well – a good show but a bad result.

The International Hutchinson 100 at Silverstone on 6 April 1963 was the next outing, and it promised to be a huge challenge as the field read like a 'who's who' of talent. Hailwood, Redman, Hartle, Bryans, Robb, Woodman, Shorey, Young, Osbourne and Darvil, just to name 10 of my competitors out of the 51 in the race, were to be my opposition. Practice on the Friday before race day was just something else. It rained, it snowed, it blew, it froze – it was unbelievable.

Freezing practice conditions

We practised in the slush on our 'All Purpose' tyres, stopping as soon as our obligatory three laps were over. We were covered from face to toe in frozen slush, soaked to the skin and were very miserable on returning to the 'comfort' of our 15 cwt vans to try to dry out and get warm. Tom Phillips on his Greeves was absolutely elated though, as he had given Jim Redman and his Works Honda four a run for his money during the practice and had finished with times that were virtually the same. This was the talk of the paddock; the Greeves had really performed and Tom was on top of his game.

Fortunately the following morning was dry and it remained so throughout the day; although when we awoke the inside of our van was frozen (including the milk which had come out of the bottle like some grotesque neck from a dead turkey with a silver hat on!) – what we endured had to be experienced to be believed. Our Calor gas two-burner cooker was put on to warm us up (and for the four-stroke boys to warm their oil a little), to brew up the tea and to cook the inevitable, and immensely enjoyable, eggs and bacon for breakfast.

Exotic machinery

As my race was not until 4.25pm we had plenty of time to go round the paddock and see some of the exotic machinery there, especially the works four-cylinder Hondas and the Scuderia Duke Gilera fours of Minter and Hartle in the 500cc class. In my race there was a Yamaha which Dave Degens was riding sponsored by Monty and Ward. Being the very first of the Yamaha's production racers it looked interesting and was a two-stroke twin, model TD1.

The 350cc Championship race was a real scrap as everyone was either on a Norton or 7R AJS, and it was finally won by Mike Hailwood at 92.47mph. The dice of the race for the runner-up spot finally went to Mike Duff, beating Read by just 0.2 of a second. Fourth went to Paddy Driver and sixth to that man Dave Downer, and Tom Phillips came 10th. Still, at over 90mph it was a good ride. Florian Camathias won the sidecar from Duebel and Seeley and the 125 went to Rex Avery on the EMC, who beat Tommy Robb.

The 500cc race was a real exhibition with the two Gileras circulating at close to 100mph, both of them (Minter and Hartle) sharing the fastest lap at 99.41, the final result being: Minter, Hartle, Read, Hailwood, Dunphy, Duff, Degens, Cooper. Tom Phillips was a creditable 11th.

The 250cc race

And so, finally, came the 250cc race, which was easily won by Redman at 91mph followed by Hailwood on the twin-cylinder John Surtees Desmo Ducati and Ralph Bryans on an ex-works dohc Benelli single, entered by Fron Purslow. Tom's luck ran out on the Greeves and he had to retire after a great showing, but Dave Degens finished eighth on that Yamaha and I was the only Greeves (in 11th place) at an average of over 80mph, just behind Ray Williats on his Adler. This was about as

At Silverstone's International Hutchinson 100 on 6 April 1963 Reg faced a huge challenge with a field which read like a 'who's who' of world ranking stars.

good a result as I could hope for – especially as I found out that the piston rings had broken – and it showed me that, as far as the bike and handling and my ability was concerned, I still could do with some improvement to mix it with the real stars. I now felt I was getting there but the journey had still a way to go.

Before going to Brands Hatch the following weekend for the Good Friday meeting we had time to alter the clip-on handlebars on my bike. This was an attempt to put more weight on the front end to alleviate the tank slapping handling problems, and we gained two-inches forward positioning. My bike still had no screen of any form, unlike the little handlebar fairing on the Silverstone, so the only modification that had to be carried out was to fit the rev counter and throw away the speedo.

Good Friday, Brands Hatch

The weather was fine and dry. As I knew the Brands Hatch circuit well I could give the bike a good workout; although Brands generally was a very smooth circuit (especially the new fast part) and should not cause too many problems. Practice went well and so did the race – even though I was put on the third row of the grid. Hailwood was down to race but could not as he had crashed in the 350cc race at Clearways after being pressurized by Minter, who won. Minter (Cotton) and Tommy Robb (Honda) both retired and I had a great scrap with Trevor Barnes on the ex-Arthur Wheeler 250 Moto Guzzi. Brian Clark (Aermacchi) won relatively easily but I kept Trevor at bay, passing him on the last lap going into the hairpin and beating him to the flag to finish a great second. Barry Lawton was fourth on his Aermacchi, Mick Manley (my Welsh rival) was fifth, Jim Russell on a good Ducati sixth, Ray Williats Adler seventh,

Alan Pavey NSU eighth, Sid Mizen ninth and Dave Degens again on 'that' Yamaha came in 10th.

So I had well beaten all my competitors who had previously beaten me! I went home very happy having won £20 (one-and-a-half weeks' wages) and the bike had performed well; although I had a few exciting moments chasing Trevor. The handlebar mod helped but did not cure the problem, and sitting as far forward as I could was still necessary to try to keep things stable.

The Easter holiday weekend was a very important time for racing. Following my exploits on Greeves' machinery, entries to meetings were accepted with more regularity, so this Easter I had Brands on Good Friday, Snetterton on Sunday and Crystal Palace on Bank Holiday Monday – very hectic for travelling. Going to meetings was OK as we left very early in the mornings to be at the circuits, parked up and were ready for scrutineering by 8.30am, and at least Brands was easier now with the Dartford Tunnel open and so the trip to the Woolwich Ferry or Blackwall Tunnel was avoided.

Brian Clark (Aermacchi) who won at Brands Hatch on Good Friday 12 April 1963, with Reg on the Greeves show bike second and Trevor Barnes (Moto Guzzi) third.

Snetterton and Crystal Palace

After the success at Brands I had a day to prepare the bike for Snetterton which, being a circuit I liked, I was looking forward to. 'Wet and cold' was the order of the day, and although I did well in practice, the bike suffered detonation in the race and I was forced to retire. Back home that night we worked until late to ready ourselves for Crystal Palace.

Running the gauntlet of the little brown men again, we established ourselves in the paddock and got to work. I finished fourth in the heat, although the expansion box split again. Joe Dunphy on the 'Works' Beart Greeves won, with Fred Hardy (NSU) second and my friend Ron Freeman from Southend third in a damp race. The 10-lap final was drier and quicker. Joe, who was a course specialist and lived locally, won easily (as he did in the 350cc race) and only narrowly lost to Griff Jenkins in the 500, even though he broke the circuit lap record during the race at 79.68mph. He also won his 350 and 500 heats. I managed a creditable sixth this time, beating Ron who was one place further back.

During the race I suffered with gear change problems as well as some hairy handling going up Annerly Ramp – a right-left flick. Again I won some prize money, £1 for fourth in the heat and £3 for sixth in the final, making a grand total of £25 for my weekend efforts – at least it paid for the petrol and entry fees.

Reg riding the Greeves show bike at the Snetterton International meeting, Easter Sunday 14 April 1963.

After setting the second-fastest lap in practice at Snetterton on Easter Sunday 1963, Reg was forced to retire with detonation in a wet race.

Joe Dunphy with the Beart Greeves, Mallory Park, 27 April 1963.

Now having two weeks to my next race at Mallory Park on 27 April, I had time to visit Greeves and see Bob Mills, who was thrilled with Dunphy's success at Crystal Palace and, of course, knew of my problems, especially with the 'one off' high-level expansion chamber fitted to my bike. He supplied me free of charge with a standard Silverstone exhaust system which they had put on the Beart bike, as the Beart special suffered from splitting and denting as well. I also got a standard gear-change linkage to modify mine as well. What I did not get was a steering damper, which had been supplied as an extra with the production Silverstones and was needed in certain circumstances to combat handling problems.

Mallory Park

With the new parts fitted, we left for the long drive to Mallory Park on another cold, grey, but not wet, day. Practice went well, with no exhaust or gear problems, and the bike was running reliably; although I did not notice any performance improvement with the new exhaust or handling, in fact it seemed worse. I did not know Mallory very well only having been there once before, and then only completing a total of six laps! So as I got quicker, especially on the very fast Gerrards Bend with the bumpy ripply exit, the handling just got worse. I managed a sixth place in the heat with several exciting moments, and even sitting on the rear of the tank to keep the weight forward only helped a little – it definitely made it very exciting!

I made a good start in the final and was lying third behind Chris Vincent (by no means only a sidecar racer – he was also a very quick solo rider) mounted on an

After finishing sixth in his heat at Mallory Park on 27 April and experienceing handling problems around the bumpy Gerrards Bend, Reg suffered a major crash in the final, which resulted in the Greeves show bike being, in his own words, a 'total write-off'.

Aermacchi. On the third lap I made an attempt to overtake him on the exit to Gerrards Bend so I had to go off line and onto the worst of the ripples to do it. The Greeves got into its, by now, predictable tank slapping handlebar antics, and I shifted my weight on to the tank to drive through it as I had on previous laps. This time though it just got worse and worse until the whole bike was jumping from side to side while going along the track at about 90mph. I knew what was going to happen. I was going to crash and it would be a big one, my mind was living every moment, and I was wondering what to do. My brain said 'get off!' so I let go of the bars and pushed with my feet against the footrests, and got off. What happened next I will tell first from my point of view, and then from onlookers and St John's Ambulance men.

The crash

As I flew through the air I thought 'this is it!' and made a short prayer. I hit the track with an almighty thump after feeling the bike hit me while in the air. I slid along the track then rolled and rolled off the track to the inside on the grass coming to rest near the lake. I lay still for some time believing I was dead. Slowly I started thinking again and saying to myself 'try to move your feet', still with my eyes closed as I made this movement. Then I thought 'move your hands' and again I went through the motions and all appeared to be working OK – so maybe I was not dead after all! The real test, I realised as I lay there still motionless, would be when I opened my eyes to see which world I was in. I do not know how long it took to open my eyes but when I did – I could see!

I jumped up cheering and waving my arms, I was alive, I could not believe it – still the medics had not arrived and I noticed another bike and rider who had crashed on the outside of the circuit while trying to avoid my crashing bike. I had pain now between my legs and the lower part of my leathers was hot and wet – I was really bleeding. 'Oh my!' I thought, 'maybe I have lost a vital part of my anatomy…oh, no!'

Without thinking, I removed the top of my leathers and pulled them down to my knees – then my underpants – I was covered in blood but could see that the vital parts were still attached. Again I jumped up and down and cheered. By this time the crowd (outside the circuit watching) had seen what was going on and they also cheered and waved. Now the St John's men arrived and bundled me into the ambulance to make an examination.

Generally, by a miracle, I was OK except for a bad cut between my legs which needed stitching, and I was taken back to the paddock to have this done in the medical centre. Sore and bruised, with my crash hat split open, I sat in my van until they brought the bike back. I was told that, after I had parted company with the bike, I flew up and over it until it cartwheeled end on end and we collided. The bike continued to cartwheel – not only end on end but sideways – several times until it came to a halt still on the track, but at a distance of about 100 yards from where I ejected. I landed about 50 yards away to the right.

The bike

When I saw the bike I just could not believe it, both wheels were bent and buckled, as were the front forks. The front wheel hub was cracked, the frame very bent and twisted, the tank and seat detached and badly damaged, the gearbox casing and crankcase cracked, handlebars, footrests, rev counter smashed beyond repair – in fact, a complete and total write-off!

What a day – my first major accident. 'Motorcycling racing is dangerous' said the signs and warnings, you bet it is! Damaged I might have been but I was not broken; although I was lucky to get away with it. All my friends and other competitors came to see me and the bike before we finally packed to go home, slowly, that evening. I knew how lucky I was, but in my mind I could hear my words over and over as I said, 'it did not handle'.

After recuperating for a couple of days I got back to reality and found myself upset and angry and, in this mood, I did something that was not going to help matters (but I suppose in the short term made me feel good). I re-loaded the written-off bike back into the van and drove down to the Thundersley factory and parked outside reception. I unloaded the wreck and, with the help of a friend, carried it in and left it there. I said to the receptionist, Pam, (Bob Mills' wife) 'Tell Mr Greeves that I said it didn't handle', and walked out.

So, no bike, no money – where do we go from here? In spite of this crash my one burning ambition was to get back racing as soon as possible. Not for one single second did I even contemplate stopping racing. I felt that I had reached a point in my racing career when I had finished my apprenticeship and learned my trade well, could race with all comers and put up a good showing, but I needed more experience and polish to take it to the next level and challenge the establishment. This is what I wanted to do and it was my aim to win against the best. I had tasted modest successes but wanted more. This was my life now.

Woolley to the rescue

It was this crash, and others to that amiable character Horace 'Crasher' Crowder, that kick-started a liaison which would be good for the rest of the 1963 season. On hearing of my plight, and because a bad crash had injured Crasher, Brian Woolley was left without a rider and he contacted me by letter. Remember we were not on the phone at my parents' home and they still did not have transport, only pedal cycles, things then were very basic. They did have a second-hand 9in television in black and white of course, and you had to turn off the main light (notice I said 'light' as it was still a single 40-watt bulb in the middle of the ceiling) to view it.

Brian requested that I visit him at his Leicestershire home in Shepshed (near Loughborough) to discuss the situation the following weekend. Talks with Brian went well at his bungalow which was near the sock factory his family owned (at least now I would get some good socks and I went home with several new pairs).

His Greeves (a production Silverstone) looked OK, the seat had been broken at some time and was re-covered in suede, and it had a steering damper. Crasher also had trouble with the handling but otherwise it looked very standard. Brian said he had been playing with the porting and assured me it went well.

We went to the local pub – where he was well known – for dinner. There I discovered his profound love of bitter and whisky, which he consumed in generous quantities and which were part of his everyday life. Brian was quite a character and a very accomplished clarinet player. In fact, he was good enough to rival Acker Bilk!

Aberdare Park

My next race was at Aberdare Park – in South Wales – the following weekend, 11 May. So we changed the gearing and loaded the van and I took the bike home. Brian would not be coming to Aberdare, in fact he rarely came to any of the meetings except Mallory Park, his local circuit.

After the Mallory crash, Shepshed, Leicestershire, tuner/racer Brian Woolley came to Reg's aid with the offer of a ride on his Greeves RAS Silverstone for the rest of the season.

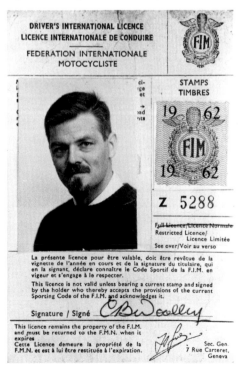

DRIVER'S INTERNATIONAL LICENCE
LICENCE INTERNATIONALE DE CONDUIRE
FEDERATION INTERNATIONALE
MOTOCYCLISTE

STAMPS
TIMBRES

Z 5288

Full Licence/Licence Normale
Restricted Licence/
Licence Limitée
See over/Voir au verso

La présente licence pour être valable, doit être revêtue de la vignette de l'année en cours et de la signature du titulaire, qui en la signant, déclare connaître le Code Sportif de la F.I.M. en vigueur et s'engage à le respecter.
This licence is not valid unless bearing a current stamp and signed by the holder who thereby accepts the provisions of the current Sporting Code of the F.I.M. and acknowledges it.

Signature / Signé

This licence remains the property of the F.I.M. and must be returned to the F.M.N. when it expires
Cette Licence demeure la propriété de la F.M.N. et est à lui être restituée à l'expiration.

Sec. Gen.
7 Rue Carteret,
Geneva

The handling of the Woolley Silverstone was much more to my liking but this was my first meeting at the very short park circuit, which was only 1,320 yards! (exactly ¾ of a mile). It was quite a journey to get there on the Friday night, taking nine hours! By the time we finally found the circuit it was 2am, and the gate was locked, so we parked in the road and fell asleep in the van without unloading it. At 6am there was banging on the doors

ABERDARE PARK
NATIONAL MOTOR CYCLE ROAD RACES

SATURDAY, MAY 11th, 1963

PADDOCK

SEE OVER

D. J. Pryse and Son, Printers, Ffrwd Cres., Mountain Ash. Tel. 2191.

and in a very strong Welsh accent 'get up you lazy b******s, get in the paddock, we need help'. Very tired and disorientated, we went in and parked with the rest of the lads. Mrs Marion Pryce, who was the secretary of the meeting announced on the tannoy – 'Warning! Warning (her Welsh accent was even more pronounced than he who woke us) you boyos! there won't be any scrutineering or practice until you have rounded up all the sheep and cleared the track, so get out there now'! Her husband David was clerk of the course and Roger Pryse was chief paddock marshal, which was organised by the Aberaman and District Cycle and Light Car club. Note also the programmes were printed by Mr D.J. (David) Pryce – printers of *Mountain Ash*.

After some laughter, and some pandemonium, eventually the job was done and everyone was in great high spirits. This little circuit was really challenging and unlike most circuits was run in an anti-clockwise direction, so all the corners but one and a kink were left handers. Down the straight to the sharp 100-degrees left, past the toilets, left kink, sharp left followed by 90-degrees sharp right through the rhododendron bushes, 80-degrees left, left, left, round the boating lake, cafe and toilets, slight right kink, 70-degrees left into the main straight with the start/finish of about 450 yards! Some lap, and about 50 seconds long or an average of 54.5mph.

So acceleration, hard cornering and braking were the order of the day, action all the way – very difficult to learn in the five laps' practice! The difference between the fastest lap from the 125cc bikes of 52 secs to the 500cc of 47 secs showed that sheer power was not of great importance.

The racing

John Cooper, Tony Godfrey, Tom Phillips and local heros Selwyn Griffiths and Mick Manley were the big names. Selwyn won the 350 from Cooper and RAF man Chris Conn. The 500 was Cooper, Godfrey and Griffiths, and the unlimited finished Cooper, Phillips and Griffiths. I did OK in my five-lap heat, finishing fourth behind winner Griffiths, Chris Doble and Barry Lawton, all on Aermacchis. Tom Phillips and Robin Good on an Ariel Arrow won the other two heats with only the first five getting into the final. Robin also won the 10-lap final with a great ride but the dice of the race was with Tom and George Collis who crossed the line in the same time, Tom getting the verdict on his Greeves for second place. Griffiths was fifth and I finished as best I could in 12th place, but my bike was overgeared and try as I might I could not improve – but still, a great day was had by all.

We could not leave the circuit until the end and our final did not start until 5.30pm. It was nearly 7pm when we left to travel to Brands Hatch for the race the next day – also a nine hour drive – so most of us raced to Brands in our Thames vans to arrive by 4am Sunday morning, eating while driving, then readying ourselves for scrutineering at 9am. Great fun if you can stand the pace of having to change the gearing and clutch plates for the long circuit race.

All the usual stars at Brands

This Brands Hatch meeting was full of the usual stars, but was destined to end in tragedy. Bill Ivy was well beaten in both the 50 and 125cc races by Dave Simmonds on his superb little Tohatsu, imported from Japan by his airline steward father. The 350 race went to Phil Read after a great race from Derek Minter, Peter Preston and Dave Downer, who was flying. Derek turned the tables in the 500 when he beat Read, Downer and Degens. Chris Vincent won both sidecar races on his 650 BSA and in my race he finished a good fourth. Derek also won the 250 from Brian Clark, Terry Grotefeld, Chris Vincent, Alan Pavey and John Cooper on the Works DMW. I finally finished ninth but I led for over four laps from my front-row starting position, gained by being second in the last Brands race, beating them all and feeling really good, comfortable and in control. This was the first time I had led the big names, especially Minter on the Works Cotton who was in a class of his own, and especially at Brands he was the acknowledged master. Alas, in my case it was not to be – as the expansion chamber split again and I lost at least 20 per cent of my power and hence finished ninth. It was a great disappointment after such an excellent start, but reliability was becoming a deciding factor.

Tragedy

The main race of the day was the last to be raced, which was the unlimited – for machines up to 1000cc – and Dave Downer was to ride the very fast, Paul Dunstall-prepared 650 Domiracer. I really did not want to miss this so went to watch from the riders' small grandstand at the top of Paddock Bend. This was a great place to watch from and was provided by the organisers for riders or mechanics and their guests.

Minter made a reasonable start, which was unusual for him as he was generally a poor starter, having to ride through the field showing his fabulous riding ability to the full, passing all his competitors. Soon he and Downer became embroiled in a race that got faster and faster with Downer keeping with him and passing him both inside and outside. Minter regained the lead at every chance, what racing! The whole crowd was spellbound at the spectacle but sensed that neither was about to give in. Downer wanted to prove his ability and beat Minter, and Minter did not want some young pretender to show him the way home. Lap speeds increased until Minter, on his 500 Norton, was virtually equalling the time he set up on the Gilera earlier in the year of over 90mph.

As the 15-lap (39.75-mile) race progressed, the crowd tension became electric, you could feel it; all sensed it could not continue without mishap as neither would give in and, inevitably, it happened. We would all watch each lap with eagerness and hope to see them both reappear from the back of the long circuit into Clearways – who would be in the lead to get the vital advantage to the flag? The crowd was hushed – where were they? The third-placed man who was well behind was now leading? When Dave Degans, the third rider, came into view, a huge gasp was heard from the crowd as the seemingly inevitable had happened. Downer and Minter had collided and crashed. Downer was dead and Minter was very badly injured. The quietness that came over Brands that day will always be remembered by those who witnessed this race to the death. All went home very subdued and thoughtful; again I thought of the signs and warnings 'Motor Racing is Dangerous'. I had time during the drive up to Loughborough to return the bike on Sunday evening, and the drive back to Chelmsford, for reflection. I knew Dave Downer, we had chatted on many occasions and become friendly. Derek was a different matter. I had known him since the Gold Star times and although we had talked, it was a more remote relationship.

A 'Racing Incident'

What had happened was a 'racing incident' and had to be accepted as such. Of course, we all knew the dangers but never thought of them or considered the consequences. We just wanted to race, it was somehow in our blood. The next race would come along and I (we) would be there, especially as now on similar machines I knew I could compete with the best and maybe one day beat them. It was a great feeling and one I wanted to repeat, regardless of the risks.

My next meeting was again at Brands Hatch, but it was nearly a month away on Whit Monday 3 June and was an international. Some of the riders from overseas were combining this meeting with their annual pilgrimage to the Isle of Man TT races. I also had an entry for this as it was part of the deal I had with Brian Woolley, he wanted me to ride there and who was I to argue with that? A two-week motorcycling holiday racing in the TT was what dreams were made of for me!

Brands International was just that, although many top names were absent. Minter was out through his injuries, and there was no Read or Hailwood. Redman did not ride, but Hugh Anderson (Suzuki) put on a great display and won the 50cc race. Dave Simmonds again on his Tohatsu beat Browning and Sven Gunnarson on Bultaco and Honda respectively. Griff Jenkins won the 350 and Peter Preston the 500, so it was a great day for the locals. In the 250 my old adversaries on the Aermacchis, Brian Clark, Mick Manley and Barry Lawton, took the honours with me being fourth on the Woolley Greeves in this 20-lap race (John Blanchard on another Greeves was fifth), so I had an excellent, although uneventful, race and took home £15 for my troubles. I was feeling happy with my performance as I acknowledged that the Aermacchis were just too quick for my Greeves, so fourth position was about right.

The Island

Over to the Isle of Man for the TT – we did get some help to pay the way by the Isle of Man tourist board, which just about covered the cost of the boat crossing for the van, bike and occupants. Beforehand, though, imagine our surprise when each rider entering on a Greeves received a company-headed, signed letter from Bert Greeves himself.

Suffice to say Mr Greeves was nervous in the extreme about we boys 'racing' his bikes and so, although you had to pay for mudguards, tanks, brake linings and sprockets, you could get a steering damper fitted for free! My friend Bob Mills was there to help and was based in Geoff Duke's motorcycle garage on the Esplanade.

The trip to the Island was a long one as we left directly from Brands Hatch on the Holiday Monday to drive all night to get the boat on Tuesday. Driving through the Black Country and The Potteries was a new experience as this was the furthest

Greeves factory mechanic Bob Mills in the firm's TT garage, 1963.

north I had ever been. Eric Hodgkinson was my helper on this trip, he was keen and liked the idea of two weeks in the Isle of Man. He was an avid biker and worked in RPM's, one of our local motorcycle shops, and he was 21 and weighed 21 stone! He was very strong and a great character who only ever wore a T-shirt and slacks, whatever the weather.

On arriving at the docks in Liverpool, the van had to be loaded on the boat. I was instructed to drive onto some planks of wood, one either side of the front and rear wheels. These planks were connected to a kind of sling under a huge crane. When I jumped out, the command of 'hoist away' was given and the whole lot was lifted, swinging precariously. Watching this made us very nervous, as when it swung everything inside the van shot to the back. We could imagine the rear doors bursting open and the whole lot, bike and all, dropping into the Mersey!

Thank goodness it arrived on deck OK and was stowed for the trip, but I still wanted to ensure the doors were secure for the off-loading. Waiting on the boat before it sailed was a good experience, meeting many of our competitors and friends who were also making the crossing, including some of the overseas riders. One we immediately made friends with was Sven Gunnarsson from Sweden, who was riding 350 and 500 Nortons. He was a great character and a fantastic wet-weather rider who fed us with buttered biscuits while we were waiting, which was a real treat.

Florian Camathias arrives

Suddenly the air was filled with a deep throated, echoing, roaring sound. We all listened for some while. It turned out to be the noise of a twin-cylinder open megga BMW racing sidecar outfit coming through the Mersey tunnel and skidding to a halt on the dockside. It was none other than the Swiss Florian Camathias at the controls with his passenger, toolbox and various other bits on the chair!

The police pulled up shortly thereafter. Apparently his Citroën Safari Estate had broken down on the M1 between London and Birmingham and, not wanting to miss the boat, he decided he would ride his machine to Liverpool instead – and probably broke every traffic law in existence on the way. There was much cheering, arm waving and shouting, but eventually he was loaded on the boat to another great cheer and we got underway.

When we arrived we made our way to the paddock near the grandstand and found a parking/camping place in among the many others who were camping as well. Eric got out of the van this time with a lot of trouble as he tried to climb over the engine cover to get out of the driver's door. Why? I have no idea! His bulk did not allow him to do this easily and he got firmly wedged between the steering column/wheel and the seat.

Giving assistance, one guy got in the passenger's side and pushed, another pulled a leg and an arm from the driver's side and I turned the steering wheel, which had the effect of squeezing him out. We were all in hysterics. He promised he would not do it again and started putting up his tent. This gave us even more laughs as it was a 'one man survival' type. Now, in no circumstances could Eric be described as 'one man'. Once the tent was erected he finally squeezed in but looked like a balloon inside a paper bag, and as the tent was canvas when it rained he got soaked. He never seemed to mind or complain, and when the sun came out he steamed and dried off!

Learning the course

I had already missed some of the practice by doing Brands and by arriving on Tuesday 4 June, so my first practice was to be on Wednesday and we still had to prepare the bike. We collected our sprockets from Bob and put the gearing right and had a new set of Avon tyres fitted by the company's staff who were on duty there – they provided a really great service. There were several Greeves in the race, one being Tom Phillips. As he had ridden over there before and wanted to do it again himself, he kindly offered to take me around the circuit and give me a few tips in his van. This was a huge help, as to learn the 37.73-mile circuit is quite a feat on its own, the sequences of the bends being very important. It takes well over an hour to go round and, as you cannot do it often, every lap and every chance to do

Reg at the bottom of Bray Hill on the first lap of the 1963 Lightweight (250cc) TT on the Wooley Greeves. It was his first experience of the 37.73-mile Mountain circuit.

it helps. It is so vital to definitely have your brain engaged and not to try to break the lap record first time out. I have to say I really enjoyed it as it was like riding round our country lanes again, only much better as now we were able to use all the road and did not have to worry about something coming the other way (or a parked car, tractor or mud etc.).

You could really ride as you wished; it gave a feeling of freedom going flat out through the trees and villages, the town squares, up hill, down dale, over the mountain – truly a fantastic experience, it was great. Some practice sessions were early morning at about 6am. To get an early start some riders would be in the queue at 4.30am. The main problems with this early start were damp or wet roads, especially under the trees, morning mist and the rising sun which sat like a ball of fire in the middle of the road when going down the Sulby Straight. Just think of the locals being woken by a screaming Honda four on full song going past their houses at 6am – some alarm clock!

One evening, Horace Crowder – who was Brian Woolley's choice of pit crew for me – suggested he would take us round the circuit to help to learn our way around as he was entered on Brian's 50cc Kreidler.

Max Deubel

We were about to leave when chaos broke out in the paddock when World Sidecar Champion Max Deubel's tent caught fire while he was cooking dinner on a primus stove. First the stove flew out followed by the dinner and bedding – fire extinguishers came on the scene and we got it under control and put out, but what a mess! Poor old Max had a rough night under his van but again with our high spirits we laughed it off. Horace, however, was determined to go round in his van and off we went. It was getting dark and the Morris 1000 van's lights were, to say the least, poor. Horace drove like a man intent on self-destruction and Eric and I hid in the back as we thought this was the safest place! We did eventually get back in one piece but I had not seen any of the circuit, the darkness and my fear saw to that. Horace seemed happy and boasted he had lapped in 45 mins – but to me it was like a lifetime and an experience not to be repeated.

My further learning of the circuit was to be by driving my van or in official practice, or watching the experts on certain corners in their sessions.

Race day

Finally, Wednesday 12 June 1963 came and it was my race day. Riders set off in pairs at 10-second intervals so, as my race number was 85, I had a long wait in the Glencrutchery Road. I had decided to ride my own race and after the start got into a rhythm, concentrating hard on where I was going rather than making it a short circuit scratch round every corner.

The last two starters in the 1963 lightweight TT, with Reg on the Woolley Greeves RAS (85) and Irishman E. Goosen on the 196cc Bultaco, 84. Goosen went on to finish 17th, whilst Reg retired on the last lap at Windy Corner when the clutch burnt out.

The weather was dry and sunny and, as it was afternoon, it was dry under all the trees, so there were no problems. At the end of the second lap I pulled in to refuel (Brian did not buy one of Mr Greeves' three-gallon tanks so I had to refuel twice during the race, therefore never doing a flying lap). The whole race went really smoothly and my lap times improved as I learnt the circuit. Most of the time on the Greeves I was flat out at about 100mph and averaging about 80mph. It was a lonely race and I did not really see many of the other competitors. The worst moment was seeing poor Tony Godfrey lying next to his crashed Works Yamaha after hitting a wall. He did recover but was very badly hurt in the head and face, which affected him long term.

On my last lap I was in the top 20 – about 13th – but when going over the Mountain the clutch finally just expired. At the 33rd milestone I cut the engine and coasted home – other than that the bike had behaved impeccably. By the time I got to the finish line the roads had been opened, so officially I did not finish – but I actually was number 23 over the line, which was not bad at my first attempt. Alan Harris from Southern Rhodesia finished in eighth place on his Greeves. He was the first and only Greeves to finish. Jim Redman on his Honda won at 94.85mph, just 27 seconds ahead of Fumio Itoh on a Yamaha which showed great promise for that marque if they could cure the unreliability which showed up in practice and race. Bill Smith's Honda was third, with Takehiko Hasegawa on another Yamaha fourth and Tommy Robb fifth. Mike Hailwood won the Senior on his MV against Hartle and Read on the Gileras, and my friend Sven Gunnarsson did well and finished 14th at 93mph after a great ride.

We did not actually see the 500 race because I had to be back in Essex on the Friday evening for a grass track meeting at the Essex Showground, but my friend Martin Hayward had a fantastic ride on his G50 and finished 25th at 90.14mph.

Redman won the 350 on his Honda from John Hartle on the Gilera, 125cc honours went to Suzuki who were first, second and third, Hugh Anderson the winner, followed by Frank Perris and Ernst Degner – the Japanese invasion was surely underway especially in the smaller classes, 50, 125, 250, 350 – where was it all leading?

Well, what about the sidecar driver who had to ride his bike to the meeting and through the Mersey tunnel followed by the police? Well, he won of course. Florian Camathias just beat Fritz Scheidegger, the first five being BMW-mounted. Our local Sidecar Ace Eastern Centre grass track champion Derek Yorke finished a great 11th place on his Norton and also left early to ride at the showground. The TT experience as a whole was most enjoyable and not to be missed, but I preferred the cut-and-thrust, the side-by-side, on the limit, knowing what position you were in of the short-circuit racing.

Back to Brands

We had a bit of a break for the rest of the month as our next ride was not until 14 July and it was back at Brands Hatch. It was strange to be there without the significant presence of Derek Minter, who was still very poorly and unlikely to race for some time. This allowed Phil Read to win with Joe Dunphy runner-up in 350, 500 and unlimited classes.

I had an enjoyable 250 race on the Greeves, having a great dice with Tom Phillips on his Silverstone, and Lew Young on an Aermacchi. Swapping places and riding side-by-side all race long and chasing Tommy Robb on his Honda and Brian Clark

Brands Hatch, 14 July 1963. Reg (on the Woolley Greeves, 76) battling over the GP circuit with Tom Phillips (Higley Greeves, 5). Tom finished third, Reg fifth. The race was won by Tommy Robb (works Honda), while Jim Redman on another works Honda was seventh.

Reg (86) on Joe Iszard's father's 350 Gold Star at Snetterton, 28 July 1963, leading Norman Archard on a 350 Norton. Norman was also a Southend racer..

on his very fast Aermacchi. Finally finishing fifth, I still beat Alan Pavey, Jim Redman, Terry Grotefeld, Bill Smith, Chris Doble and Trevor Barnes. This being in a 10-lap race on the long circuit gave me a lot of confidence as I was able to run with the best and beat some of them. I was getting there but still felt I had a way to go.

The trip backwards and forwards to Shepshed in Leicester, collecting and delivering the bike, was a real chore and made me think of making other arrangements. At the next meeting at Snetterton (28 July 1963) I did not have a 250cc ride for some reason. I was not entered but I did have an entry in the 350 class – perhaps it was an error, I do not know. Anyway, my friend Joe Iszard's father said I could ride his old Gold Star 350 so I did and, although I had a good day out and a ride, going back to an old BSA (and a 350 at that) did not make for an exciting experience. Try as hard as I could, I did not do better than 24th even though I still beat Norman Archard on his Norton. I really thanked Joe and his father but politely declined any repeat performances. Out of interest there were nine Greeves entered (without mine) – about 25 per cent of the field – what a difference from the year before when I was the only one.

Reflections

July 1963 had now come and gone and I was over halfway through my fourth racing season. The year had been one of highs and lows. I was very pleased with my level of performance – now being confident enough to run up to the front and dice with some of the best. The TT helped more than I knew, giving me a great deal of experience in a short time, covering – as I did – over 500 practice and racing miles. This equalled about 20 short-circuit races so it was well worth the effort.

Just having one bike did not help but it was really all I could afford and, of course, the more meetings I did the higher the costs were. Plus, as I mentioned, the return journey to Shepshed for each meeting did not help especially as Brian seemed to be an absent sponsor who just supplied the bike. He got all parts free from Greeves but I still paid all the entry fees and costs. So far this year, having won the princely sum of £46 helped, but it did not even cover the entry fees of the 13 meetings (so far contested) of £52. Never mind, I was racing and that was all I wanted to do, every weekend, come what may, rain or shine, hot or cold, it was a way of life and in my bones.

The rest of 1963 on the Woolley Greeves went much the same as the first part. I felt I was riding more and more quickly and more consistently, but machine reliability fluctuated as the Greeves was pushed more and more to its limit and beyond.

A précis of the final meetings will suffice here to show what I mean. On 17 August at Silverstone, in a Bemsee Club Meeting I won the 250cc race and was awarded a tankard. At Aberdare on 24 August I finished third in the heat and fourth in the final, the clutch again having given out.

The long journey to Brands on the following day (25 August) saw me having an excellent ride in the wet in third place when the clutch let me down again. On 8 September at Snetterton I was a non-starter, as I was told the bike would be taken there but for some reason it did not turn up. At Brands, on 29 September, I had a great ride and finished fifth; although I lost the expansion box tailpipe. I also rode Brian's 50cc Kneidler on which I had to retire.

Another Bemsee meeting at Snetterton on 6 October 1963, this time finishing runner-up to my old rival Trevor Barnes on his ex-Wheeler Moto Guzzi, even though I holed a piston through detonation at the end. My lap/race speed was now rising to 83.22mph. A good improvement on my best with my old bike of 79.19mph. This time I was awarded a Bemsee Plaque.

50cc Enduro

Brian insisted now that we should enter a 50cc Enduro of 200 miles around Snetterton, a very fast track on which it would be all flat out (except for the hairpin) for the poor little motor. He obviously saw something in this that I had missed, as he brought the bike and was enthusiastic all day. It was some experience as I said, being mainly flat out but equally demanding when lining up the bends for as high a corner speed as possible so you did not lose momentum. This was vitally important, as was keeping your arms and knees tucked in to reduce air drag going down the long straights. I noticed if you stuck your elbows

Reg, far left in as his role as chairman of the Eastern Sporting Sidecar Association, presenting awards in the summer of 1963. Next to Reg is Dave Pearce, then Dick Barton, and on the far right (in the white polo shirt) is the grass-track legend Alf Hagon.

out then the revs dropped and you lost speed, so being well screwed up behind the screen was most important, albeit very uncomfortable.

Co-rider 'Crasher' Crowder and myself led this race for 55 of the scheduled 74 laps, completing 148 miles, when the piston broke to leave me in 18th place at the finish. Brian was pleased we led for so long and it appeared for him a bigger achievement than anything we had done on the Greeves.

The last meeting of the year on the Greeves was at Brands Hatch on 13 October 1963; although I did ride it again later in a sprint event. This was to be a not-so-grand finale to the Everett-Woolley relationship.

Tom Phillips, pictured here with the Frank Higley-sponsored Greeves Silverstone RAS during summer 1963, was not only one of Reg Everett's big rivals, but also a close friend. Later they joined forces to ride for Velocette specialist Geoff Dodkin in long-distance events.

By now my name was known and my results, especially at Brands, were good. Good enough to be put on the front row by the organizers. This felt good as my fellow riders were no less than Derek Minter on the Works Cotton, Phil Read (Aermacchi), Tommy Robb (Honda), Joe Dunphy (Works Greeves), Rex Avery (EMC), Brian Clark (Aermacchi) and Chris Doble on another Greeves, which meant three Greeves in the front row – what had I started? Even the second row was good, especially Tom Phillips on Frank Higley's Greeves and my old Welsh rival Mick Manley who was now on, yes, a Greeves! In fact, there were 10 Greeves in all. What a line up. I was really excited and just wanted that race to start, wanting the opportunity finally of mixing it with the stars over 10 laps of the long circuit.

Tension on the grid

The tension on the grid was great and banter followed. I had not noticed this before but the rivalry between top riders led to remarks on the front line, like Minter's to Read: 'watch out, there's oil on the track at Druids', Read replying to Minter: 'did your mechanic put any oil in the petrol?' with each trying to unnerve the other. This was something new to me as I did not realise how important it was for these riders to win, they were real competitors and it was almost win at any cost. Minter was only

On the Woolley Greeves at Brands Hatch, 22 September 1963.

just back from his serious accident back in June and while he was out Read had been winning and had beaten Derek into second earlier in the day in the 350cc race – the knives were out! The grandstand to the left of us alongside the track was completely full and the crowd was cheering with expectation, trying to motivate their favourites, this again was something I had not noticed before. The atmosphere was electric – what a feeling – I was soaking up these moments.

Everything went silent as the starter mounted his rostrum, and the anticipation was almost an ache. He hesitated, then the Union Jack dropped. All hell broke loose: bodies, bikes, noise, leg over the bike, tuck behind the screen, chin on the tank and up into third. Wow, what a start, the front row seemed to be going into and around Paddock line abreast. Up we went into Druids. I was third behind Robb and Read approaching the bottom bend, but my line out of Druids was tighter and I passed Read going into the turn. He dragged past me along bottom straight and I tucked in behind. Round the left-hander and into the long straight on the new part of the circuit. I slipstreamed him all the way as his bike just had the edge on top speed. Then on the downhill stretch into Hawthorn Hill bend he 'brake tested' me and I had to take avoiding action to miss hitting him. Minter, Clark and Phillips came by all at once. We were all together for the next lap, what close racing, until Westfield when I regained third position and went diving inside Read to try to retake second.

Race and season over

What happened next I am not sure, but the rear lost adhesion. I corrected it and went into a highside, losing contact with the bike, and it veered onto the grass on the inside of the circuit going down into Dingle Dell, while I, by some miracle, fell back on top of it. I tried to regain control but lost all grip on the grass and mud, and fell in a heap. My race was over.

Tommy Robb went on to win in front of Read, Brian Clark, Tom Phillips and Minter, who was fifth. Well, this truly was my inauguration to racing the aces.

Fortunately, neither I nor the bike was damaged. The remark I got from Minter after the race was 'I see you fell asleep going round the back', but it did not affect me as I felt I was among them when I did – maybe I got carried away by the atmosphere, who knows, but I felt ecstatic and could not wait for the next race. Though I knew it would not be until next season, I really did not realise just how long it would be.

Oh, by the way, that sprint at Duxford on 20 October 1963 – it was wet and cold but the bike did well and I finished runner-up in the 250 class with a time of 15.23 secs for the standing start 440 yards, which was not bad, but it was not 'real' racing. I returned the bike to Brian Woolley and he informed me that he would not be supplying it next year as he wanted someone 'more local'. So where would I go, what would I do? I really just had not thought about it, so it was to be a very long winter lay off.

South Bank Bend, Brands Hatch, 13 October 1963. Brian Clark (Aermacchi, 87), leads Derek Minter (Cotton, 11) and Tom Phillips (Higley Greeves, 5).

Chapter 6

An Interim Period

In summary, 1963 felt like my final 'learning' year and the first time I had been fully supported. This helped hugely as the burden of much of the finance had been removed, although transport costs still proved a major expense. The Thames van was reliable, if not very comfortable, but had its foibles. No heating was one and no washers was another although to be fair they were just being invented! It had windscreen wipers working from a vacuum pump that went like the clappers when you took your foot off the accelerator and stopped when accelerating hard or going flat out. It had a good turn of speed, possibly up to 75mph when draughting the motorway coaches going from Birmingham to London on the M1. At that time there was only 30mph and derestricted speed limits.

Chairman

I was now chairman of our local club, ESSA, and with committee meetings and organizing dinners, club nights, etc, it took up a lot of my time. Swimming and gymnastics with Bob Mills at Thundersley school on a Tuesday meant further commitments, but I found that the jobs in the Thames van helped with my finances. My work at Marconi was still my main earnings, especially when doing all the overtime I could: three evenings until 8pm and Saturday mornings too. Generally my time was full, and I had moved back to Chelmsford renting a Marconi House in Great Baddow. Life was good and full.

As 1963 came to a close it became uppermost in my mind that something had to be done to secure a ride for 1964 – but what, and how? Several options had been discussed, one I was excited about was with George Collett and his motorcycle shop near Basildon with whom I had met on several occasions. He wanted me to ride a Honda 125cc CR93 for him in 1964. This was great, as the CR93 introduced at the beginning of 1963, had gone on to dominate the class in British short-circuit events that season.

Another was direct with Greeves again, as I was in contact via Bob Mills with Derry Preston-Cobb to whom I wrote requesting a ride in 1964. I received a reply which included the words: 'I am sure an arrangement can be arrived at whereby you ride a Greeves this year'. So, with these options and some discussions I had with Peter Inchley, who hoped to field riders with Villiers' engined Cottons or Villiers' own machines, I felt reasonably happy with the prospects.

I actually still had my own old 'prototype' Silverstone but, with the other options pending, I sold it to a great guy called Laurence Casey for £150 and I transported him and his new bike back home to South London.

Problems

Of course, by February 1964 the regulations for meetings started coming in, and not wanting to miss the start of the season I started making entries on the 125 Honda sponsored by Colletts and a 250 Greeves. Discussions with Bob Mills, however, revealed that the new Greeves-designated 24RBS was a long way from being ready and that they were still selling last year's model, the 24RAS. Bob thought the new bike would not be even ready for the start of the season. This was not good news. Also, by the beginning of March, no good news from Peter Inchley could be obtained and dear Mr Colletts's Honda had failed to put in an appearance. This was turning into a disaster!

Earlier that year I had entered Brands Hatch on Good Friday, Snetterton on Easter Sunday and Crystal Palace on Monday. This was my fifth season of racing and I had not missed Easter meetings before. Try as I might I was not able to persuade anyone to let me borrow or buy suitable bikes for these meetings, even those which were promised. What use is a racer without a machine?

A real anti-climax

Easter was a real anti-climax – something really had to be done. The following weekend I decided to go and watch the Silverstone Hutchinson 100 and travelled up with my workmate Ray Parker in his car. It was a good meeting and I spent all day in the pits talking to friends and rivals, it was good to be in their company again as this was my scene and I felt part of it and really did not like being without a bike. Most people showed some sympathy but racers are individuals and I am sure they thought 'great, at least I don't have to beat him!' This made me more determined than ever.

I watched the 250cc race with interest as I wanted to see how my opposition had progressed and what had changed. Well, the race was won by Alan Shepherd on the Works MZ, who was closely followed by Tommy Robb on a Honda. Bruce Beale on another Honda was third but Ginger Malloy (Bultaco), Luigi Taveri (Honda) and Derek Minter (Works Cotton) were close together in fourth, fifth and sixth position respectively. It was the next two bikes that interested me, Dave Chester was seventh by five seconds from Bill Ivy who was eighth, both of whom were on new TD1A Yamahas similar to the one Degens had ridden for Geoff Monty the previous year. These were sponsored by Ted Broad and Geoff Monty respectively and beat all the 'normal' regulars, I was most impressed.

Afterwards, I took a good look at the two Yamahas in the paddock and liked what I saw – impressive-looking brakes, full duplex frame, twin cylinder two-stroke engine with very low centre of gravity and lightweight – in fact, a bike made for the job of racing.

On 15 April 1964 I moved house again having purchased a small detached bungalow on Broomfield Road, near to Greenways where I was born, for the princely sum of £3,000 (a huge amount in those days). I paid a deposit of £350 and the remainder over 25 years. So with the repairs and repayments I was surely back to having no cash again; therefore buying a bike was out of the question.

On 19 April I went with my great friends Joe and Joyce Iszard (of the 7R) to Brands Hatch as Joe was riding, and I had entries on Honda and Greeves. What happened in the 250 race I do not know but in the race were 13 Greeves, four Yamahas, Minter on the lone Works Cotton, nine Aermacchi and seven others. It was so different from when I started. Again I looked at the Yamahas – how could I get a ride on one?

The following weekend I had a new rear axle fitted to the Thames van with a higher final drive ratio so we could cruise at a higher speed. That seemed to work fine but, with only a three-speed box, first gear was very high and pulling away demanded more clutch slip – but overall it was a worthwhile improvement.

Riding Brian Woolley's Kreidler 50cc at Brands Hatch on 13 October 1963.

No Greeves, no Honda

Bob Mills informed me that the new Greeves was unlikely to be ready before the TT. I had been entered this year by my old friend Derek Cornell on a Greeves so I booked the ferry again for the crossing but noted that even this could be in doubt.

April passed and the May Bank Holiday weekend was upon us. I went to work on the Saturday morning and watched the Cup Final in the afternoon. On Sunday 3 April I had an ACU Eastern Centre meeting to attend on behalf of the ESSA at the Red Lion in Colchester. This was no good, I should be racing! My mind was made up that something had to be done.

I called my friend, Stuart Hull, who had a BSA Super Rocket and worked in Hoffmans. He had helped out on several occasions and was very reliable. 'Could you come on a fact-finding mission tomorrow?' I asked him. We had some decisions to make and people to find. Yes, he was free, so on Bank Holiday Monday 4 May off we went. Our first call was to Mr Collett – he was actually at his shop and was surprised to see me. I told him I had come to find out what was happening about the Honda. After a long sorry tale about business, etc, he admitted he could not afford one and that I should forget it. I must say that, although disappointed, I rather expected it, and at least he gave me the entry money back that I had spent over the past few months. I also asked him if he knew where Ted Broad lived, to which he replied: 'Billericay, I believe'. I said thanks and that was the last time I ever saw Mr Collett.

Finding Ted Broad

At least we were on a trail, and we had to go through Billericay anyway to return to Chelmsford. How could we find Mr Broad's address though?

As we approached the town I thought I would visit the police station to make some enquiries – by now it was about 1.30pm. I must say the policeman was very cooperative when I told him I was looking for someone and demanded to see the electoral roll (Mr Broad was not in the telephone directory). A copy was duly found and passed over to me, apparently it is a legal obligation and we all have rights to examine it, although I did not know it at that time.

I thumbed through the book and finally found Mr E.R.J. Broad, 22 Perry Street. I politely requested directions to Perry Street and the policeman obliged. Stuart and I set off not really knowing what our approach should be. Anyway, we duly found number 22 and I walked up and knocked at the door.

A very large moustachioed man opened the door, who did not look too pleased at being interrupted, and on seeing us said: 'Who are you? What do you want?' I meekly told him that I was Reg Everett and, to my relief, he told me that he knew of me as a racer. I explained to him I did not have a ride at this time, and he simply

Reg spent much of the 1963–64 closed season with promises of rides for George Collett with a Honda CR93 (a sister bike to the one shown here, ridden by Steve Murray) and also the Greeves factory, via Bob Mills and Derry Preston-Cobb. Ultimately, nothing came of either project.

said 'See you at Brands next Wednesday!' and shut the door! Stuart and I wandered back to the van rather shocked and dazed by the abruptness, but ecstatic about the contents, of this very brief first encounter. Little did we know what was to come.

We talked and speculated about it all the way home. I could not wait for Wednesday to come – it had been nearly eight months since I had raced or even ridden a racing bike and I was nervous, but elated.

Chapter 7
The Yamaha Connection

The drive to Brands for that first Yamaha ride was filled with expectation of the unknown the people, the bike, my lack of practise – just what would happen? Poor Mr Marconi and my job never got even a consideration, I just had to be back riding. The weather was kind – overcast, cool but very dry – the circuit looked great was and strangely quiet, with no crowds as it was lunch break.

What a picture

I soon saw the Yamaha, with its bright red tank in stark contrast to its white fairing and white faired hump-backed racing seat. It looked a picture.

I parked next to Mr Broad's yellow Thames van, got out and formally introduced myself to him as he was bent over readying the machine. 'Jump on' he said and I duly (eagerly!) obeyed. We made a few minor adjustments to the handlebars and brake and clutch levers, then repositioned the rear brake and gear lever to suit my own riding preference. It just felt right, when adopting the racing crouch it fitted like a glove – perfect – as if it were made for me, I just could not wait. I put on my leathers, boots and helmet and sat on the bike just to make sure, once again, that all was in its correct position.

Reg and Ted Broad – a great combination. Flanking the two are Jerry Honeyman, Ted's friend (behind Reg) and Brian Moss, Reg's friend (behind Ted).

The marshals and track staff were back in position and the first bike session after lunch was ready to go. I held the bike as it was taken off the stand, selected second gear, pulled it back on compression, sat on and with the clutch held in and with a thumbs up from Ted let it roll down the hill in the paddock. At the right moment I dropped the clutch and bumped the seat and it burst immediately into life. The twin-cylinder power unit responded as I declutched and revved the engine. It sounded fantastic, a much higher pitch than the Greeves and, of course, twice the frequency. I stood with the gear in neutral and Ted Broad came and took over the throttle, giving it several blips until he was satisfied that it was warm enough and sounded right, then he shouted 'don't take it over 9,500rpm', I nodded, thinking that this was about 2,000rpm more than the Greeves! 'Keep it above 5,500,' shouted Ted, 'now off you go!' I selected first gear, wound up the revs to 5,500 and slipped the clutch to get away. It just felt so great and natural to be back in the saddle again, it was just like home.

Out onto the circuit

Down through the tunnel the noise was fantastic. I accelerated and went up into second, going towards the start-line area. It just felt so responsive.

The track was clear so the marshal waved his green flag to allow me access to the circuit. Accelerating up the gears I was in third by Paddock Bend and then up Druids hill into fourth on the five-speed box (one more than the Greeves). I tried out the eight-inch twin leading shoe front stopper going into Druids hill and boy, did it work well – progressive, responsive and very powerful. Round the bend in second, keeping the revs up, it was smoothly up into third for bottom bend, accelerate, fourth, briefly fifth before the Clearways complex, then down into fourth and the left, right, hard brake, into second for Clearways corner then three, four, five going past the Grandstand on the top straight. I was back in the groove, it felt natural and easy – total enjoyment. Two more laps feeling my way, getting to know more about the acceleration, braking points and handling abilities of my new machine and beginning to know its potential – it felt fast, safe and secure, I was sold. So now to give it its head and to ride as fast as I could, as this was not a test for the machine but for me in Ted Broad's eyes. I had to be able to do it justice. He knew I could ride a two-stroke, in fact at that time I had as much experience as anyone on two-stroke machinery, but would the two go together? The next few laps would tell. 'Watch the rev counter' I would say to myself, going up through the gears as 9,500 came up quickly and easily, peaking in fifth just before braking for Paddock Bend. The gearing was perfect, the bike was singing. I got more and more confident and having a great outing on this machine I could not think or dream of anything better – I felt as if I was flying. I completed 10 laps in this first session, the bike did not miss a beat and I returned to the paddock elated – but was Mr Broad with his stopwatch?

Ted is pleased

I pulled up next to the van and Ted was there, a huge beaming grin on his face. He pushed the stopwatch into my face so I could see where it had stopped – 1 min 3 secs, it read. He slapped me on the back and said 'Fantastic, when can you race it?' I replied that I had a 250cc entry at Snetterton the next Sunday, and he simply said 'it will be ready'.

Ted Broad's motorcycle shop was very close to Gants Hill on the North Circular road and I had arranged to collect the Yamaha from there on Saturday afternoon. It was an easy journey from home, taking only about 30 minutes, so it was very convenient.

The shop

The shop was neatly laid out with a counter and a bell with a sprinkling of new and used Yamahas and Ducatis on display. Seeing no one there, I rang the bell and Ted Broad appeared at the back of the shop, emerging from a flight of stairs below. We politely greeted one another and he beckoned me into the inner sanctum – a subterranean workshop. This was filled with lathes, mills, drills, work benches and bike benches with a few machines in various stages of build, plus a 350 and a 500 Manx Norton. In pride of place on the bike bench was the Yamaha. Ted explained he had changed the gearing for Snetterton and, apart from me putting on the correct number (3), it was ready to go. He made it clear at this meeting that he would not work on dirty bikes. It was solely my responsibility to return the machine to his workshop no later than the evening after the race in as clean a condition as I had received it, otherwise words would be said. Ted was not a man to be messed around with and his request would be obeyed.

We took the bike off the bench and out via a back door in the cellar workshop. This opened onto a rudimentary concrete drive that did a 90 degrees turn on a 45 degrees hill (it felt that steep anyway) to the front of the shop through a large, solid double door gate. This was the only way in or out of the workshop. Pushing it out took some effort, though Ted was at home doing this. Fortunately, compared to some road bikes and the Nortons, the Yamaha was very light. Ted said he would be at Snetterton at 9am and that the bike should already have been scrutineered.

Excitement

I was really thrilled to have such a fabulous looking bike in my van and was really happy on the drive to Snetterton on Sunday, 10 May 1964. Parking, unloading and scrutineering went without a hitch, but many of my friends and competitors had plenty to say about me and my new mount. Some were not very complimentary and the phrase 'Jap crap' was heard on many occasions. I must confess all this went over my head, I did not care, as I was still just thrilled to have a bike to ride. There was still no Greeves available, but the Broad Yamaha most certainly was. I was a racer and all a racer wants is a reasonably competitive machine to ride, and I truly did not care where it came from.

Ted arrived promptly and immediately began 'tinkering' as he always did. We warmed it up and changed to hard plugs and set off for practice. Knowing Snetterton very well, by now it was just to familiarise myself with the bike and ascertain new braking points and correct gearing. I was, though, amazed at the speed along the straights and with the acceleration, and I was impressed with the handling on Snetterton's fast corners.

Debriefing

I was very happy and practice went without mishap. Ted and I 'debriefed' after practice. This was a new experience for me as up until now there had been no one to do this with. Ted was really knowledgeable as he had been sponsoring for a few seasons, beginning with Geoff Tanner on two Nortons who had already achieved 90mph-plus Isle of Man laps on Ted's 500, so he knew racing and racing bikes and riders. This I found to be a real asset and we struck up a good relationship straight away. Ted re-adjusted the brakes and checked the machine over thoroughly. I did the tyres and made sure the pressures were correct, this was always my job. We had a bite of lunch and began the long wait until the 250 race which was, as always, last of the day at Snetterton, starting late afternoon at approximately 5pm.

The Achilles heel

We had a good feeling about the race as in practice I had lapped at 1 min 53 secs (over 86mph – three miles-per-hour better and four seconds a lap quicker than I ever had achieved on the Greeves). All the euphoria was to be shortlived, however, as on the warm-up lap coming out of the Esses I had no drive and had to coast into the pits. Ted soon diagnosed the problem as a broken crankshaft. This was truly the Achilles heel of this engine. The designers, in their wisdom, had mounted the clutch on the end of the crankshaft which, via a gear, drove the gearbox instead of the conventional primary chain layout. The gear system in itself was good but the clutch, a heavy item, was mounted on the outside of the gear and rotating at engine speed, i.e. approx. 10,000rpm, instead of about half of this for a conventional layout. This caused inertia problems and on changing gear down suddenly before violent acceleration, which was normal during racing, tended to 'wind' the clutch from the crankshaft, which is what had happened.

Ted did not seem too fazed by this. It had occurred before, but I was disappointed and still had not raced this year. 'It will be ready for Brands next weekend', Ted told me. 'In fact, we should take it on Saturday for at test, so come and pick the bike up next Friday evening and I'll see you at Brands Hatch on Saturday afternoon'.

A positive attitude

This attitude from Ted was just what I needed to lift my spirits as it was all positive. Nothing worried him, and his commitment to racing, the bike and me was 100 per cent, and so that was what I was determined to give in return. The bike had obvious potential but it was new and was bound to have problems, especially as the materials used from Japan were still slightly suspect. We hoped as engineers that these problems could be overcome.

The test at Brands went well and I managed a lap on the short circuit in under 1 min 1 sec (by Ted's watch), which was better than I had ever achieved before and was a speed which could win races, as was the Snetterton time. Reliability would be the deciding factor.

More reliability problems

The Brands meeting was an international on the full GP circuit on Whit Monday, 18 May. In the programme I was entered by Collets on the Greeves and 125 Honda. Most of the local aces were there and there was also a terrific overseas international contingent. After a good practice and getting a front row of the grid starting position, the bike let us down. This time it just would not start. It fired and ran on one cylinder. I pulled off the circuit and again pushed the bike back to the pits. I just could not believe it that, so far, my Yamaha racing experience read: two races, two-DNF – or, more accurately, two-DNS (Did Not Start)! Ted again took it philosophically and showed no kind of emotion, instead he just set to in the paddock, stripping the bike to see what the cause was but without a confirmed diagnosis.

Reg with the Ted Broad-entered TD1A at Brands during 1964.

We loaded up and left the circuit early and I dropped the bike off at the shop on the way home. Ted was informed that I would be racing at the TT on a Greeves and that my next short-circuit entry was not until 27 July, a national meeting at Snetterton (more than two months away). He assured me that the Yamaha would be ready and available for me to race. It was a definite and I knew already with Ted if he said it would be so, it would – no ifs, buts or maybes. We parted and he wished me luck for the TT.

On Friday 29 May we left to travel to the Island. It was a much easier trip as we had no bikes to carry. The new Greeves, the 24 RBS, had still not appeared but Bob Mills assured me that they would be on the Island as they already had promised machines to Dave Simmonds, Alan Harris, Barry Smith, Sid Mizen and Griff Jenkins.

The Greeves camp

Catching the 4pm boat, we arrived in the island at about 1am and by the time we offloaded and got to the paddock we were just in time to see the end of early morning practice. Later in the day, after a brief sleep, I went to track down Greeves and Bob Mills specifically. Arriving at the garage, no one was to be seen and after asking around I found out that they were having problems with the bikes and had gone to Jurby Airfield, a disused RAF aerodrome, to do some testing. So off we went to find out what was going on. Well, everyone was there who had anything to do with Greeves. All the riders with their new bikes, all the sponsors, Brian Woolley the guru and, of course, Bob Mills. The bikes looked different, somehow higher and with a new engine with much larger finning, different crankcase and primary drive, plus a totally redesigned expansion chamber and larger GP carburettor. Everyone was totally perplexed, the machines would start and run OK up to about 7,000rpm and then a horrendous misfire would set in which made the bike unrideable.

Much head scratching ensued – they had tried and checked everything over and over but nothing worked: plugs, points, coils, timing, petrol, pistons, carburation – all sizes of jets, slides and remote float levels, now they were all at a loss what to try next. Obviously, the machine or engine had not been tested on a 'brake' before being taken to the Island as the fault would have shown up then (as the problem turned out to be elementary to someone who really knew two-stroke engine theory).

Luck plays its part

Luck eventually played its part when Dave Simmonds decided to give his bike one more try down the runway after more 'fiddling'. Even when revving the throttle before he went, the misfire was still there. In fact you could hold the throttle wide open and it would just pop and bang – anyway, off he went and his run out was just as bad. He turned round for his return run and, as if a miracle had happened, the engine suddenly was revving cleanly up to its maximum in each gear and flat out. Dave did two more runs to make sure he was not dreaming and the misfire did not return and he pulled in to the applause of the onlookers. 'What had he done?' everyone asked, he replied 'nothing'. The guru and Bob put the machine on the stand to examine it and crouched around the engine. Finally they noticed that the large long bellmouth of the Amal GP carburettor had come unscrewed and fallen off. They jumped up and unscrewed and threw away those of other machines, and lo and behold all started and ran beautifully as if by magic. Their problem solved, everybody congratulated themselves, packed up and returned to the garage to ready their machines for the 250cc practice the following evening.

'Sorry, this is the best we can do'

I, however, had other problems – it was obvious from Bob's demeanour that not only did he not have time for me, but that he also had no bike. He was very embarrassed and asked me to come back to the garage on Monday morning. It was then he said 'Sorry, but this is the best we can do'. It was a machine from early the previous year owned by Reg Orpin (of London dealers L. Stevens; Velocette and Greeves specialists and race entrants) and taken to the Island as a 'hack' machine – one that can be ridden by anyone for general extra practice if needed. It looked rough to say the least. However, beggars cannot be choosers. I scrounged from Bob whatever he had in the way of parts but as most were for the new machines, they were meagre. So I said 'Thanks and goodbye' as I knew no further assistance could be had and returned to the paddock to work on my hack.

I covered the name 'Orpin and Stevens' (which was written on the screen) with black tape, not only for my interest but as I was officially sponsored by D. Cornell and the fact was that advertising was banned except for the names of the manufacturers of the machine.

Preparation

The wheels were removed and taken first to have new tyres fitted, then next to Ferodo to have new linings for the brakes and the drums skimmed – these were the great trade facilities available on the Island for all riders. New chains were also fitted by Reynold and I put in new clutch plates and gave the bike a good general check over in readiness for Monday evening's practice, which went well but steadily as I completed two laps OK. I did three other practice sessions. One lap only on Thursday morning when the exhaust pipe fell off at the Gooseneck Friday morning when the throttle stuck open going into Bradden Bridge and the last session Saturday morning when I did a plug chop to see if all was OK at the end of the first lap – and only just completed the second lap when the motor cut out at Governor's Bridge. I pushed in and found a lead had come off the coil. So, six laps in all, except for as many as I could manage in the van. I never did a flying lap (either starting or stopping) but I averaged in the high 70s with one lap at just over 80mph, about 28 mins. Here, I must add, my bike (along with others) was officially timed for top speed by the Highlander. Jim Redman's Honda four was fastest at 154mph. My bike was slowest at 97mph so I thought to average 80 was pretty good, and gear changing was almost unnecessary. This was definitely the slowest Greeves I had ever ridden.

Sunday 7 June was spent preparing the bike for the race and I again had fitted new tyres and chains. I also fitted a complete new clutch, remembering last year's race when it let me down only four miles from the finish.

At 3pm the bike was wheeled into the weighing-in tent to be locked up overnight, with no access being allowed to it until just before the race the following day.

Race day

Monday 8 June, race day, dawned and fortunately the weather was good. In the morning we watched the sidecar race which was won by Max Deubel followed by Colin Seeley and George Auerbacher. Our local sidecar road and grass track hero Derek Yorke on his Norton with George Mason in the chair did very well and finished ninth at 76.1mph, and we were very pleased for him.

My bike was released and we fuelled it up and gave it a quick check over. A great guy, John Williams (a friend of Dick Standing), had agreed to be pit crew. He was knowledgeable and very reliable and equally enthusiastic, what more could I want? Lining up with the other starters in pairs, I was number 63 so had 31 pairs before me,

Quarter Bridge during the 1964 Lightweight TT. Reg was riding a spare 'hack' RAS Silverstone which the Greeves factory had loaned him – instead of a new RBS model originally promised.

starting at 10 second intervals, so I pushed off 5 mins 10 secs after the first and fastest bikes at 1.30pm. So, unlike the massed start of short-circuit racing there just did not seem the urgency as you pushed away, just wanting to make a sure and clean getaway in front of the packed grandstand. Then into concentration mode flying down Bray Hill. I was just getting into a nice rhythm going through Glen Vine, about five miles out when a very ominous rattle started. Fearing the worst, I pulled over to the nearside and stopped. I could not believe it, the cylinder was completely loose and the rattle was it jumping up and down. This was not normal, it had never happened before – had I been nobbled? 'Get on with it' my brain said. I whipped the plug spanner out of my

A panoramic view of Ramsey Hairpin, with Reg going well.

At Grovernor's Bridge, almost within sight of the finish.

boot (carried in case I had to change a duff spark plug), knowing this fitted the large aluminium long bolts that held on both the head and barrel, and I tightened them up as quickly and efficiently as I could. Without further delay I re-bump started the bike and got on with the race – even knowing I would be well out of it I was still there and wanted to continue to gain experience and have a lot of pleasure racing in the Island. In fact, I relaxed and really enjoyed what was a very lonely ride. At the end of the second lap I refuelled, and it all went very smoothly. John was great and the bike bumped into life again. Two more laps, and then coming in at the end of the fourth lap John was very excited. He patted me on the back and screamed, 'you're 12th, you are on the leader board!' I thought he was having a laugh so I just restarted and got on with it again, going through most of the corners flat out and only occasionally changing gear. Going up the Mountain on the last lap I did not dare use the clutch, wanting to save it as much as possible, but in the end it felt good and the bike did not miss a beat. Towards the end at the Creg and Sign Post people were waving and I was enjoying the moment, especially through Governor's Bridge and down to the finish and the chequered flag – I had made it – fantastic!

Eighth and first British bike home

I pulled into my pit where John was waiting. He was beaming, waving his arms and jumping up and down patting my back, he was ecstatic. 'What's up? I asked. 'You've just finished eighth in the TT!', he replied. It sounded impossible but it was true, and I looked at the board to confirm it. For sure I was eighth, the first and only Greeves and the first British machine home. Jim Redman won, followed by Alan Shepherd

(MZ) and Alberto Pagani (Paton). But I also noticed a Yamaha TD1A (ridden by Roy Boughey) had finished in fifth place, so did that meant it could be reliable?

There were 96 starters including 12 Greeves, so we were all happy going to the presentation at 9pm that evening at the Villa Marina to collect my award, then to an excellent party afterwards.

The following day it poured with rain all day long but the day was brightened by the *Motor Cycle News* report which had a large photo of me and the headline: '250 Greeves is Eighth'.

Mr Greeves is not happy

I returned the Greeves to Bob at the garage. He was pleased for me but was very dejected as all the other 11 machines (including the five new works machines) failed to finish, and Mr Greeves was not happy. On Wednesday we watched the 125cc race from the start area and it was a real Honda benefit, with Taveri, Redman and Bryans the top three and only two other makes in the top 20, with my friend Jim Curry finishing a good 15th. In the afternoon we went to watch the Junior (350) from Hillberry with a finish of Redman, Read and Duff. Harry Rayner was a good 30th and my pit crewman John Williams finished 36th with Dick Standing 39th. It was a creditable day out for all the lads on their own machines.

Reg's close friend Dick Standing with his AJS 7R in the warm-up area prior to the start of the 1964 Junior TT.

Thursday saw us return home having a typically very rough crossing – many of the passengers felt very poorly. Fortunately, I am a good sailor and I ate heartily during the voyage.

Unfortunately we had to make a detour in Liverpool to the Walton Hospital as poor Tom Phillips had been transferred there from Nobles after a very bad crash at Greeba Bridge. Tom had a badly mangled foot and, what was worse, also had a punctured lung. During our visit his wife Norma was by his side and Tom was very ill, having been diagnosed as suffering from pneumonia. This, of course, gave us real concern for his wellbeing and we left the hospital in a very sombre mood to continue our long journey directly to the Essex Show Ground at Great Leighs where ESSA had organised a grass track race.

As I was the chairman I was there to present the awards, with a special mention to Derek Yorke who had also returned from the Island to win the sidecar event. We were all true enthusiasts and racers – motorcycles were our lives.

In contrast Derek Cornell was very happy

Derek Cornell was very happy with my TT results despite the bike situation, and we saw it as an opportunity for him to get some advertising mileage for his entry

Opposite: A letter Reg subsequently received congratulating him on his TT success; unfortunately this was not to be followed up by any form of concrete help.

ESSEX BUILT!   ESSEX MAN!   ESSEX SPONSORED!

The Only English Machine to Finish

REG. EVERETT

8TH

IN THE ISLE-OF-MAN T.T. ON THE GREEVES 250 c.c. Production Road Racer

SPONSORED BY

D. A. CORNELL (MOTOR CYCLES) LIMITED

245-247 BROOMFIELD ROAD CHELMSFORD ● TELEPHONE 55935

GET YOUR NEW OR USED GREEVES MACHINE FROM THE SPECIALISTS

Advertisement from DA Cornell Motor Cycles publicising Reg Everett's eighth-place finish in the 1964 Lightweight TT.

Reg pictured with Derek Cornell after the TT. Originally, Cornell's, as the main Greeves dealer for the Chelmsford area, had been promised one of the new RBS models for the TT. This never materalised, so although the machine shown here is an RBS, it is not the bike used in the TT – for publicity purposes only, one could say.

fee, so he contacted the local newspaper, *The Essex Chronicle*. They were very enthusiastic and told us that a photographer and reporter would be on the way. Derek also contacted Bob Mills and Bob brought along one of the new Greeves 24RBS machines.

On the following Friday the paper was out with photos and headline 'Town's TT King' and a good write-up. There were also two large advertisements – one from Greeves, stating the success of the Silverstone Racer in its first year, and one from Cornell's, 'Essex Built, Essex Man, Essex sponsored', which proclaimed my eighth position. Well, I suppose this was some sort of fame? I did not feel as though it was, however. It was the last time while racing that I sat on a Greeves – he bike which I had started but for whatever reason the factory did not want me to continue to ride. I had a letter from Derry Preston-Cobb dated 12 June, sincerely congratulating me on finishing so well in the TT. It mentioned that they still had problems to 'iron out' with the new racer but he hoped I would know something definite before very long. This was the last communication I had with the Greeves factory; although Bob Mills and I were to remain friends.

Back to the Broad emporium

Visiting Ted Broad at the shop at the beginning of July, he really showed his pleasure with my TT result and was keen to get me back on his bike, which was much to my liking as I could not wait to be racing again, even with the previous disappointments. Ted had been working on the machine and it was all ready for our next outing on 26 July at Snetterton. Practice went very well without any kind of problems. The weather was kind, we again were optimistic and I posted a very good lap time. Once again, I had to wait for the last race of the day before lining

Motor Cycles *Church Road, Thundersley, Essex*

DIRECTORS : O. B. GREEVES, M.B.I.M
D. PRESTON-COBB, A.M.B.I.M., D. K. GREEVES
(PROPRIETORS : INVACAR LTD.)
TELEPHONE
SOUTH BENFLEET 2761-2-3-4

Our Ref: DPC/JR.

R. Everett, Esq.
10, Hampton Road,
Great Baddow,
Essex.

                                12th June, 1964.

Dear Reg,

I thought I must drop you a line to sincerely congratulate you
on finishing so well in the lightweight T.T;   quite naturally,
we are all thrilled that you piloted the first British machine
home.

As you may be aware we still have some troubles to iron out in
the new Racer, but I do hope that it will be possible to let
you know something definite before very long.

Kind regards.

Yours sincerely,

D. Preston Cobb.

Winners of the 1960 and 1961 European Moto Cross Championships up and because I knew where the low numbers on the draw strings were, I got a front row grid position. It felt great to be in the line up with Joe Dunphy on the Works Greeves, Bill Ivy on Geoff Monty's Yamaha (which was the same as my bike), Derek Minter on the Works Cotton, Mike O'Rourke, Terry Grotefeld and all the other regulars.

A great start

I was really keyed up at the start, not nervous but excited, every muscle taut with anticipation. No anxieties, no fears, just pure adrenaline pleasure. The regular tall, thin starter mounted his rostrum (I knew him well by now, and his technique) and I was ready. The Union Jack fell, and we were racing. This time the bike fired instantly and I made a great start, going into the first corner in second place behind Ray Watmore on his very fast Adler. It was difficult to keep with him down the Norwich Straight so I had to slipstream him. He was flying and we passed and re-passed all race long, what a dice! Lap after lap (it just had not occurred to me that none of the others had come flying by). We both were embroiled in our own battle. This was perfect sport.

The first Yamaha victory

On the last lap I managed to outbrake him going into the hairpin – he pulled alongside down the home straight but I went through the Esses first, round Coram Curve on the absolute limit, flat on the tank, and up into fifth gear through the left

At Snetterton on the 26 July 1964 Reg gained his first victory on the Broad Yamaha, after a great battle with Ray Watmore on his very fast Adler (shown here). This was against top liners, including not only Joe Dunphy on the Beart Greeves, but Bill Ivy (Yamaha) and Derek Minter (Cotton).

kink up the hill to the finish line, I could hear him but he could not get in my slipstream to be able to overtake and I crossed the line with the chequered flag hailing me in first place. Was I elated? Well, it was the best feeling in the world – my first national win against all-comers. At the time I just did not care where the others had come. Ray and I shook hands on the return lap back to the pits. To see Ted's face when I pulled into the paddock was reward enough – what a smile, what a welcome, I had arrived.

The crowds all came round the van, all my friends were there, everyone was smiling and laughing and patting me on the back. It is something I will never forget. So now Ted and I knew it was a race winner and so was I. The only disappointment was that Minter had retired so I had not beaten him, but Bill Ivy on an identical machine was fourth and the first Greeves came ninth. I had also put in the fastest lap at 1 min 54.6 secs, 85.13mph and averaged 82.45mph for the whole race, beating Ray Watmore by 0.4 secs. To say we went home in high spirits is an understatement and for our efforts I won the princely sum of £12 10s. This was probably the first national victory by a non-works Yamaha in the UK.

On Monday I returned the bike to Ted's shop and, of course, we discussed the weekend's triumph – it was good to talk of success rather than failure. Ted knew now that many components could not be trusted and that even the coils had a short life and had to be regularly replaced. However, despite the bike's shortcomings, both of us were looking forward to Brands Hatch in three weeks' time with great anticipation.

Nice weather for Brands

Nice weather greeted us at Brands on Sunday 16 August, just three days after my 24th birthday in my fifth season of racing. I felt in great shape. This time the race was at 1.20pm, race number four on the programme with Minter already having won the 350cc on his Norton, coming in ahead of Paddy Driver, Chris Conn and Mike Duff. He, of course, was in the 250cc on the Works Cotton, with Tony Godfrey, Dave Simmonds (Works Greeves), Omar Drixl, Dan Shorey, Alan Harris (Works Greeves) and Bill Ivy (Yamaha), plus all the other top runners. But this time there were no less than eight Yamahas! I had been demoted to the second row as I had not had a great result at Brands since the previous year. In fact, it was only my second Brands race of the year and in one of those recent races I had been a non-starter. This race was a 10-lap event on the long circuit so about 20 minutes of very hectic racing was about to take place.

Again, I got a great start and was fifth or sixth going into Paddock Bend, overtaking another going up the hill and braking into Druids. By the time I went round Hawthorn Hill bend I was in the lead and there I stayed for five laps, until Minter on the Works Cotton came flying by at the end of the straight going into

After victory at Snetterton, Reg and the Broad Yamaha were entered at Brands Hatch on 16 August 1964. Again the competition was stiff with a host of star names, with the race being won by Derek Minter, with Reg second – still a great result.

Hawthorn. I tucked in behind him to take advantage of his slipstream and just about hung on for two more laps. Try as I might, he gradually pulled away and at the end of the 10-lap race distance won by five seconds. However, for me this was a fantastic result, second at Brands Hatch to the master Minter and beating Drixl, Simmonds, Pladdys, Rodda, Godfrey and Barnes. My old Welsh rival, Mick Manley, was down in 11th place in front of Basil Keys on another Yamaha. To sum up, Minter went on to win the 500 race getting his hat-trick and £75 prize money. Dave Simmonds won the 50cc race, Bill Ivy the 125. Pip Harris and Chris Vincent won the chair races and I won £18 for second in the 250. Again, Ted and I were elated with the result.

Racing in Wales

The following weekend I was down to ride at Aberdare Park on the Saturday. Ted would not come as it was his busiest trading day, but to date I could not actually recall seeing any customers in the shop. He had the bike ready by the Friday evening and I picked it up at 5.30pm, arriving at Aberdare after the long drive at 12.30am. After a short night – and having to clear away the sheep again early in the morning – I met up with Mick Manley. We agreed, after practice, that as Dan Shorey was not riding and we were both in the same heat of 15 riders (only the first five would be going into the final) it would be silly to go flat out racing in the heat and that we would circulate together for the first five laps and see what happened for the final circuit. We waited patiently for the 4.30pm start and both got away well, circulating comfortably at the head of the field. On the fourth lap, rounding the left-hander by the paddock entrance, we came across a fallen rider and his bike spreadeagled across the very narrow track. We both took immediate evasive action, me to the left and he to the right, both ending up firmly embedded in the rhododendron bushes. Panic ensued as we extricated ourselves, dragging our bikes out backwards and onto the track, and not wanting to miss the final we blasted round having no idea what positions we were in. Only afterwards in the paddock did we find out that we had still qualified, myself and Mick in second and third respectively, for the final. It was some race! The final would be much more competitive so no thought of any type of 'arrangement' could be contemplated, the heat was the first and last time I ever did anything other than race 100 per cent. I got a good start for the final and was in fifth place when the strain on the bike, caused by having to change down to first gear on several occasions, wound the clutch off the end of the crankshaft again. That was it, the end of the race, DNF.

This was the last time I rode at Aberdare, Ted deciding it was not practical or worthwhile to go there. Driving back I was so tired, after I had called Ted from Brinmawr to let him know what had happened, that at 1am somewhere near Oxford I stopped and parked in a field and slept until mid-morning. I then carried on to Chigwell where the local police were having their Gymkhana. Ted had graciously agreed to display his race-winning Yamaha for a bit of local publicity. We debriefed and afterwards took the bike back to the shop.

What could be done about the crankshaft problem?

The following Tuesday I went to the shop and had lunch with Ted in the local café, afterwards helping him to strip the bike. Something had to be done about that crankshaft problem. We examined the offending piece and brinel hardness tested it, and this showed it to be very hard through the complete cross section and not suitable for the purpose. This was more food for thought, and cost, because the whole engine had to be stripped and rebuilt, as did the complete crankshaft assembly. This was not a five-minute job as getting the crank very accurately aligned was one of the 'secrets' of this engine.

After the rebuild Ted wanted me to try it out and run all the new bits in and said he would see me at Brands the following Wednesday, 2 September. I was always ready to do this, as they say practice makes perfect, and anyway all I wanted to do was to ride racing bikes (I had long since given up riding a bike on the road, in fact it was since buying the Mini van and then the Thames van, which became my everyday transport). Imagine my surprise when I arrived at Brands and Ted not only had the 250 Yamaha but also his 350 and 500 Manx Nortons for me to ride. What a great day I was about to have!

Trying the Nortons

Running in the Yamaha was a joy as it meant one 20-minute session limiting the revs to 9,000 and not using all the power on acceleration, but the response and agility which goes with lightness was there. Duly completed, Ted said 'Try the 350

Norton, but don't go over 7,000rpm'. I trundled down the hill and bump started it. In comparison, it felt like sitting on an armchair with its wide seat and much more sit-up riding position. I took it on the track and opened it up waiting for the power, looked at the rev counter and oops, it was already nudging 7,000. Up through the gears without any feeling of real acceleration or speed; it was, in fact, very sluggish. Even with my feet scraping on all the bends I felt no sense of urgency. Yes, it handled impeccably, but somehow without feeling – it was just far too rigid. The 37bhp and 300lb weight was no match for the Yamahas 34bhp and 200lb and my lap times were two seconds slower – how disappointing.

Ted was sponsoring Dave Chester on the Nortons. He was a good rider, generally finishing in mid-field positions, and just wanted me to do a few laps to compare times. Yes, I was marginally faster than Dave but felt the 350 really lacked speed and would not be competitive to run in the top 10 of national meetings. The 500 was different, its 49bhp and 300lbs giving a similar power-to-weight ratio to the Yamaha. The acceleration was good, lively in fact, and on a couple of occasions lifted the front wheel slightly coming out of Clearways. I enjoyed the experience and would have loved to have ridden in all three classes, but Ted was finding that the time and expense required to run all three was too great. He had campaigned the Nortons for the previous three years and now they were five years old and not competitive against the serious 350 and 500cc runners with their Beart and Lacey tuned machines. Also, the new Matchless G50s were performing well in the hands of Tom Kirby's riders. Dave would continue on Ted's Nortons for the remainder of the season but thereafter Ted would only retain the competitive Yamaha, the marque which he was selling in his shop.

'So near and yet so far'

The following Saturday I collected the Yamaha for the race at Snetterton, 6 September. It was, as usual, the last race of the day but practice had gone well with no mishaps and the weather was great. This time only three Yamahas were in the field: Tony Godfrey, myself and V.D. Chatterton from Boston. There were 10 Greeves, seven Aermacchis and now three Cottons, a trio of Minter, Rex Butcher and Peter Darvil, out of the 40 starters. Somehow I did not get a good grid position on the string draw and was back in the third row, but after making a fair start I was in the top 10 going into Riches. During my six laps I went past the others, having some little tussles on the way, but without too much trouble until I was in second position to, you guessed it, Derek Minter on that Cotton. I could see him in front but, try as I might, just could not make any impression on him. Boy, that Cotton was fast and very well ridden. At the chequered flag all were beaten except Minter, and I was surely at the top of the profession. Well, nearly – King Derek was still unbeaten! So near and yet so far. Ted was really thrilled with the performance, my very fastest lap up at

Snetterton averaged 87.11mph, and our bond was cemented. We were a team, we knew our places and our boundaries, and our lifelong friendship had been started.

We had three more meetings that year, two at Brands on 20 September and 11 October and one at Mallory Park on 27 September. These, I must report, were not very successful and the season ended without the euphoria of the mid-season results. In fact, during practice on the Saturday before the first Brands meeting the clutch dropped off the end of the broken crankshaft again. We took the bike back to the shop and it was again a complete rebuild, working late into the night before driving straight back to Brands for the Sunday race. This did not go well either. It started OK but it just was not running well and misfired irregularly, until finally only one cylinder was running and I finished seventh. The acknowledged stars did not finish either so the regulars had a field day, with Pladdys winning, from Gordon Keith, the new Southern Rhodesian Greeves star sponsored by Orpin/Stevens. Then came Degens, Grotefeld and Roddar, and they all enjoyed it.

Mallory was even worse for me as after I was progressing well, in only my third meeting there and lying fifth, the engine seized solid going into Gerrards Bend. This was very exciting for a second, but somehow I had a 'sixth sense' when it came to knowing if an engine was about to seize, and I whipped in the clutch and coasted to a standstill – another DNF!

The following day Ted had the misfortune to have a crash in his beautiful metallic gold 3.8 Mk II Jaguar. It was not too bad and we got it back in his workshop for repair. I had grown to like this car as Ted had lent it to me on a few occasions, its grace and pace had entered my sight and I hankered after one.

More problems

Practising at Brands the following Saturday the gearbox locked up on the Yamaha but I had another good run on the 350 Norton, as Ted had entered me for the last meeting. On Sunday Ted came with me to Southend to look for a 2.4 Jaguar but we did not find a good one. However, that evening I found one in Chelmsford, it was a private sale of British Racing Green, a 2.4 Mark I saloon. It really looked the business but I wanted Ted to see it before I committed myself. On Wednesday evening we met and Ted gave the Jag his blessing. The following day, at lunch time, I went to see the bank manager and he loaned me the £150 I needed for a 'family saloon'.

On Saturday 10 October we took the Yamaha to practise at Brands and the bike went well. On Sunday the 350cc race was first and Ted had decided to see how competitive the Norton was with me aboard in a real race. My start position was on the inside of row four and I did not think it would be a good start. Sure enough, even at the end of the first lap I was only 20th. On the second lap Minter, who had also made an awful start, came past me on the back straight like I was going backwards. Scratching as hard as I could on about lap five, when I was 18th, I

At Brands Hatch for the final meeting of 1964 Reg not only rode Ted Broad's Yamaha...

At Brands Hatch for the final meeting of 1964 Reg not only rode Ted Broad's Yamaha...

finally caught up with my good friend Joe Iszard on his AJS 7R. This spurred us both into life and we had a good scrap, passing and repassing in fun until finally I beat him to the flag for 17th position. We had a great laugh about it afterwards, about riding like loonies to finish 17th and 18th. Ted also decided not to race his 350 Norton any more and Joe decided that a competitive 125 Bultaco would be much better for his future racing career.

For the 250 race I was, again, at the back of the grid. Ted and I wondered about this, on the third and last row behind 28 other riders every one of which (except Minter) I had beaten. The line up was impressive, all being well-known riders: Minter, Ivy, Simmonds, Robb, Tait, Duff, Vincent, Beale, Smith, O'Rourke, Pladdys, Keith, Grotefeld and Degens were the first two rows! Tommy Robb was on the Works RD56 (1963) Yamaha, as was Duff, but his bike seized in practice. I had the worst start ever from the back row and was almost last into the first corner and so had to go through the field. I really enjoyed it, however, finally passing Gordon Keith on his Greeves to finish fifth. Robb, of course, won easily with Ivy (Cotton) just beating Degens. Minter's Cotton, which slowed towards the end, was fourth and I was fifth – he beat me again!

...but also for the first time Ted's 350 Norton.

The green light for next season

The following day I went to see the man with the Jag and bought it; I then went over to see Ted at his house. He was happy and we confirmed our intention to continue for next season – but that was six long months away. He promised me a Yamaha for the 350 class as well so I was delighted. The 1964 season had been a strange one with great highs and lows. The

Reg (47) chases Derek Minter (Norton, 11) during the 350cc race at Brands Hatch, 11 October 1964.

lowest was not having a bike to race until 10 May, Ted's Yamaha, and the first two rides ending in failure. But then came the TT, my last race on a Greeves, finishing in eighth place. This obviously helped my confidence and honed my technique after the eight month layoff, because my first finish on a short-circuit race was in first position, my first national win, followed by two second-places to that man Minter. A year of only 12 races, one first, three seconds, four other placings and four DNF. What a roller-coaster but what success – I really had it in my sights now, so what would next year bring?

The closed season

As the winter drifted by, I was still very involved with ESSA; including club nights, committee meetings and dinners. Joe and Joyce Iszard were with us on many occasions and we had become firm friends. I also still went to gymnastics once a week at Thundersley with Bob Mills. That, plus swimming at the indoor pool in Hornchurch with Joe, Bunny and others, kept me fit and active. After swimming one Thursday, two girls remarked as I surfaced in the pool 'Oh, look, there's a bloody walrus!' This was enough incentive – and the facial fungus that grew in profusion since my 18th birthday (and only being removed very briefly for my wedding when I was 21) was ceremoniously shaved off on Saturday 21 November – I was 24 years old and a bit!

Ted had a big change and moved to a super new house, which was still in Perry Street, so eveidently the shop and Yamaha sales were not doing too badly. I was still doing jobs in the van and on Christmas Eve had to deliver a big crate to Southampton docks for some people who were emigrating. All in all, I was very busy but what would happen in 1965? Only time would tell.

Chapter 8

1965 – My Sixth Season

Today, at the beginning of the 21st century, very large machines predominate and 1000cc racing is normal. In the period I am describing 500s were generally the largest engines and this was certainly the limit in the Grand Prix events (now equivalent to Moto GP), even more so in my era, but although the 500s were the largest, the 250cc class was by far the most competitive and had the biggest following. This was generally because in the 500cc class there was virtually no factory involvement, it was mainly private Nortons and Matchless machines with one or two others – namely MV Agusta, Gilera and Paton with just one or two machines – which won easily and often those had a 'Private' label. Whereas the 250 events were hotly contested by many factories including Yamaha, Honda, Suzuki, Montesa, Bridgstone, Kawasaki, Aermacchi, Bultaco, Ossa, Morini, MZ, Benelli, Ducati and Derbi, some of the Grand Prix meetings had, in fact, only 50, 125, 250 and sidecar races, totally leaving out the 350 and 500 classes.

A very high profile

So the 250cc category had very high profile at all meetings. It was in this class where fame and fortune were being made and a factory ride for Honda, Yamaha or Suzuki was the highest prize of all. It was in this environment that I was about to begin my sixth season of racing. Albeit not at GPs but at British Championship level, which at that time was being contested by those very men who were winning the Grand Prix events. This was a daunting task!

Because the previous year I rode and competed with the best, I was really looking forward to the start of the season. Ted had purchased another TDI so we had two machines. He converted it for me to ride in the 350cc races by machining one millimetre offset crankpins. He thus increased the stroke by this amount and the capacity to just over 250cc. This meant it was eligible in the larger class; although the 250 was still to be our prime target and the number-one machine and class. The 350 would be an aid for testing, practising and trying to augment available prize money.

Freezing at the Mallory season opener

The first meeting was at Mallory Park on 3 March, but it was still very cold and winterlike – it was freezing! The first three meetings just were not good for me, it was a start to the season that we did not want. Although I was third in my heat behind Minter and Cooper, the other heat was won by Ivy and Degens, I just could not really get in the groove for the final. Cooper's Greeves lost its clutch at the hairpin when leading, and so Minter won with Degens second, Dave Simmonds on his Honda Twin third, then Bill Ivy on the Cotton and yours truly in fifth place. Cooper won both the 350 and 500 races and Bill Ivy the 125. While lying fifth in the 350 heat on the second lap my rear chain broke – so another DNF there.

Brands on 21 March was worse as I did not start in the 250 and did not finish in the 350. Minter again won on the Cotton from Degens, Blanchard and Ivy, while Cooper dropped the Orpin Greeves at Clearways.

We hoped our luck would change for Snetterton on 28 March, to which we took only the 250. Again I did not finish but this time Bill Ivy won on his Cotton from Simmonds, and Tom Phillips (now recovered from his very bad Isle of Man crash) did well to finish third on his Aermacchi. Minter had retired on the second lap when his engine seized. These early-season results showed how dominant Minter and Ivy were on the factory Cottons.

Good Friday at Brands

Easter came and the 'King of Brands' meeting was on Good Friday. The 16 April event was the real curtain-raiser and the 250cc race was hugely contested. Number one was Mike Duff on the Works Yamaha, a machine that was so fast that production racers did not stand a chance. Our Yamaha was the only other one in the race. Minter and Ivy were on the Works Cottons, Cooper on Greeves, Gordon Keith (Royal Enfield) with Geoff Duke as team manager, Derek Woodman (MZ), Simmonds (Honda), Robb (Bultaco), Degens (Aermacchi), Inchley (Villers) and Joe Dunphy (Aermacchi) were just the first 11 in the front two rows on the grid, what a field! I was put on the third row, in the middle, so I just had to get a good start. This I duly did and at the end of the first of eight laps on the long circuit I was third behind Duff (who had cleared off) and Ivy on the Cotton.

Here I would like to repeat what *Motor Cycle News* said on the following Wednesday: 'Everett – Great! Mike Duff won on the 250 Yamaha with ease. The great surprise, however, was the Yamaha bid for second place! Reg Everett on Ted Broad's production racer was terrific, he passed and steamed away from Bill Ivy (Cotton) and Dave Simmonds (Honda) and looked all set to make it a Yamaha benefit, only to fall off on the last lap at Druids Hill hairpin. He remounted and finished eighth. The oil patch which claimed Everett also took out Bill Ivy in the big race'.

Needless to say I was both gutted and elated in equal measures, so was Ted, as the Yamaha Works' people were there and watched my progress (and Bill Ivy's). The final race result was Duff, Ivy, Simmonds, Minter, Robb, Inchley and Degens, with me next, still beating many of my old rivals even after crashing and

remounting (I may have done better but the gear lever was bent and stuck in second gear so the remainder of the lap was slow). Who knows where my career would have led if that oil had not brought me down?

Smiling at the Palace

Ted now had to prepare both the 250 and 350 for Crystal Palace on the Easter Monday (for some strange reason we had not got an entry for Snetterton on Sunday, which was probably just as well as I was still sore from the crash). The

*Crystal Palace, Easter
Monday, 19 April 1965.
Reg won the 250cc race
and was runner-up in the
350cc event on an
overbored Yamaha.*

competition was not so great at the Palace as many of the top men refused to race there as they deemed it to be too dangerous. Again *Motor Cycle News*'s headlines on 21 April 1965 said 'Yamaha Challenge at Crystal Palace' and went on to say 'Reg Everett and his entrant Ted Broad just couldn't stop smiling at Crystal Palace on Monday. Riding much "breathed upon" Yamahas in the 250 and 350cc classes, Reg finished first and second respectively'. I had won my 250 heat and was second in my 350 heat so two wins and two seconds for the day, giving us a total of £45 in prize money – a great day out. It was also very significant in that it was the highest placing for a non-works two-stroke in a 350 national race in recent times, and in retrospect can be seen as the beginning of the end for four-strokes in this class. I also set the fastest lap in the 250 at 1 min 07.6 secs, 74.02mph. My racing was back on track and the weekend was a great success. If only I had not crashed at Brands!

A 350 setback

Three weeks later at another Brands long-circuit national meeting we suffered another setback in the 350 race, where I was in fourth position on the first lap and going well, when at Westfield bend I again lost the back end in a big way and slid off at high speed into the mud banking on the outside of the circuit. Luckily the mud was soft as I hit my head, my face and mouth were full and covered with it and the marshalls had to pull me out and clean me up quickly, but they did a great job. The bike, though, suffered more – the forks and frame were bent, the fairing was destroyed and there was a vital piece missing. Ted had been spending time and effort on the 350 and had hand-made a beautiful new alloy petrol tank for it that he was very proud of. When I came to my senses I had been cleaned up, and while examining the bike I asked the marshalls where the tank was. Without hesitation they pointed to the sky, which puzzled me. I looked up and there, lodged in the uppermost branches of an old oak tree, was Ted's beautiful tank – except it was not beautiful any more, but very flattened. We had no way of retrieving it and when I returned with the bike in the breakdown truck to the paddock after the race Ted said 'are you OK?', to which I answered 'yes', then he asked 'where is my tank?' – 'flattened and up a tree' I answered. Ted's language was colourful in adversity and for the rest of the day he spoke to no one and no one dared to speak to him! Minter won the 250cc race on his Cotton – I could not race because of injury.

Victory at Snetterton

We did not take the 350 to Snetterton the following weekend (16 May 1965) and the 250 only needed a gearing change, so preparation was not stressful. There were 13 Greeves in my race and one other Yamaha (ridden by Derek Chatterton) plus all the other regulars. At 5.35pm (last race again) we started and I was soon in a race-long dice, which was great fun, with Peter Inchley on his Works Villiers special. He was in charge of development at the Wolverhampton factory, and his bike was really flying. I had to use his slipstream down the long straights just to stay with him. I did just beat him to the line to have a great victory but he got the fastest lap, together with Bill Ivy on the Cotton at 88.21mph, 1 min 50.6 secs, a very fast speed. Third on this occasion was Derek Chatterton, but he was just coming into sight around Coram Curve when I crossed the line. Ted was again elated and in a very good mood but was still sore about his tank, once again the highs and lows of racing were present.

Mallory Park, so far, had not been one of my best circuits, and a third in the heat and fifth in final at the first meeting this year had yet to be bettered. So, on 23 May 1965 we hoped we could change this. My 250 heat was a ding-dong affair, with me beating Bill Ivy and Dave Degens. The final was nearly a repeat, but this time it was Ivy who beat me to the flag. Minter tried to get by us all race long, but could not get the better of us and had to be satisfied with third in front of Degens and Pladdys. I managed an eighth place in the 350 heat but the bike was not running well so I did not start in the final. First in the heat and second in the final was a great improvement and beating the top men yet again (including Minter!) was a fabulous feeling. Bill Ivy also won the 125 and 500cc events.

Other things were going along as I was thinking of leaving Marconi for a different challenge, one that did not interfere with the racing. I was also working on my Jaguar as I had lent it to a 'friend' at work who drove it a long way and did not check the oil, so when he returned it to me the big-ends were gone. My old school chum Stan Vanhinsburgh helped me again in his father's garage (which was now in Rettendon) and I took the crankshaft over to Ted, who got it reground. I got up early (3.15am) on the Tuesday after Mallory to watch Cassius Clay fight Sonny Liston for the Heavyweight Boxing World Championship. Much to everyone's surprise, Clay beat Liston who failed to get off his stool!

Stuart Hull

Swimming and gymnastics were keeping me very fit and Stuart Hull, with whom I had found Ted, became my right-hand man and came with me in the van to all the meetings. We had a bit of a lull in the racing for one month as it was TT time and Ted would not enter due to cost and the fact that he doubted that the bikes were reliable enough to finish races of such length, which were well over 200 miles.

Joe and Joyce Iszard were my ever-present friends and we went out or stayed in socially on many occasions. I often visited Ted's shop to help in whatever way I could and he assisted in the Jaguar engine rebuild. He was a great character.

With him and Gerry Honeyman (who was Ted's friend, helper and gopher) there was never a dull moment – life was very full.

We returned to Mallory for the Post TT International but this was a total failure as the crank oil seals went in practice and I did not race.

Stuart and I collected the bikes for Brands Hatch the following weekend from Ted's shop, drove there and stayed over in the van for the meeting on Sunday 27 June.

A unique day

This day was unique, being the first-ever motorcycle relay race consisting of four riders in four teams made up of 125, 250, 350 and 500cc. Each rider had to complete five laps. This race was at the end of proceedings and to my, and Ted's, credit we had already won the 250cc race from Dave Simmonds (Honda) and Peter Williams (Orpin Greeves), which made our day.

The four teams for the relay consisted of:

BLUE	Degens	Dunphy	Everett	Simmonds
WHITE	Minter	Chandler	Lawton	Scivyer
RED	Driver, D.	Williams	Carney	Pladdys
YELLOW	Ivy	Croxford	Robb	Curry

Machines:	500	350	250	125

This relay was a terrific spectacle ending in a close finish and went like this:

The 125s were first away, Scivyer went in front until he was caught by Simmonds who had been left on the line, third was Pladdys who was ahead of Curry. As each rider came around Clearways at the end of their five laps, the next rider in each class was flagged away from the pit area. As Simmonds came first, closely followed by Scivyer, I set off with Lawton alongside followed by Carney and Robb. In my five laps I pulled away easily to give our team a 15-sec advantage, while poor Tommy Robb had to scratch like mad to make up for Curry's deficit, overtaking Carney and then Lawton.

A press cutting from the Brands Hatch Match Races, 27 June 1965, with Reg (14) alongside Barry Lawton (Aermacchi) as the two riders race out of the pit area.

An unusual shot of Reg Everett (Yamaha) and Barry Lawton (Aer Macchi) storming out of the pit area in the relay race at Brands Hatch on Sunday

So, when Robb handed over to Croxford, the Yellow team was second with Dunphy (Blue) trying to maintain our lead. Croxford diced with Chandler (White) and Dave Williams (Red) way behind with slim prospects.

Dunphy's lead was 11 seconds when Degens took over for the final stint but he had not reckoned on the out-and-out battle behind. Minter was only two and a half seconds behind Ivy and this pair were catching up fast, and Paddy Driver, a lonely fourth, could do nothing. With two laps to go, the Minter–Ivy struggle had Degens in sight, and Degens knew this as on his last lap at Bottom Bend he had a bad moment but stayed on – he was really trying hard to keep in front. This last lap was a cracker with the bikes disappearing round the back. When they reappeared they were all together side by side, the crowd was going mad waving their programmes. The three bikes stormed in to the finish. It was Ivy! In a tremendous spurt he had 'done' Degens on the line, so it was Yellow, Blue, White and Red at the finish – a terrific spectacle.

Would it ever be repeated? Great times, great racing, great people – it was just perfect. I had a win in the race and was second in the relay, what a way to live!

A holiday abroad

For some reason it was a month before the next race – so what to do? What about a holiday for a change? A few days after the relay, I said to Stuart and Brian (another friend and helper) 'What about a holiday in the South of France on the Mediterranean?' I had been abroad twice – once with school to Switzerland by train in 1955 and once to Jersey in 1961 on my honeymoon! Neither Stuart or Brian had ever been abroad before – 'How? When?' they asked. 'Next Monday,' I said, '5 July. We'll drive down in the van and stay at a camp site for two weeks then come home'. There was lots of mumbling and reasoning and details, then eventually they both said 'Yes, great! Let's do it!' – and so it was planned.

We were to get the ferry from Tilbury at 9am Monday morning. They stayed over on Sunday night and we duly caught the ferry. Both had hired tents for their accommodation, but I would stay in the van. It took until 3pm before we arrived in Calais and we got to Paris by 8pm that evening. After Paris at about 11.30pm I decided to have a kip in the back and Brian took over the driving. Then, at 2am Tuesday I was woken by a huge bang! On investigation, it was found that the fan belt had broken and as this drove the water pump and dynamo, the water had boiled and the top radiator hose had burst. So much for red lights on the dashboard! I fitted a new fan belt and taped up the rad hose at a place called Sens and we got on our way and were in Lyon by about 4am. Continuing, we finally found a Ford garage and had a new piece of hose fitted, arriving in Aix-en-

Provence by noon. It was now hot and we were hungry and tired so we ate and rested awhile until 3pm. We found a nice campsite by the sea, at a place called St Maxime, at 6pm that evening and swam in the Mediterranean. It was, in all, an almost non-stop journey time of 36 hours, as there were no motorways.

We had a great time in the sea, it was hot and sunny and we made friends with some people from Manchester who had a speedboat and I learnt to waterski – just how good could life get?

Starting our return we left St Maxime at 2pm on Friday 16 July and visited St Tropez and Toulon, then stopped at 11pm south of Lyon where we camped for the night. We then went from Lyon to Paris, getting there at 5.30pm. We saw the Eiffel Tower, had a meal and left at 9pm. We got to Calais by 1.30am, where we camped for the night again – this was certainly a very much easier and casual return as we had a good look around Calais and sailed at 3.30pm, getting home at 10.30pm on Sunday 18 July. According to my speedo reading we had covered some 1,959 miles!

On the following morning, going to work was an anti-climax. I phoned Ted to tell him all was OK and that I would pick up the bike on Saturday for Snetterton on Sunday 25 July.

In the meantime I went swimming at Ipswich, did a removal job, went swimming at Hornchurch, took my mother and father to Southend to catch a boat for their holiday in Belgium and then went to pick up the bike. As forecast, it was just non-stop doing and going.

The meeting at Snetterton was a disaster as, in practice, the big ends went and the day was over so we packed up before the racing even began and took the bike back directly to Ted's shop that evening. Peter Inchley won the 250 and Minter crashed in practice and was walking round the paddock with a stick. He started on the back of the grid with a pusher and got into the lead, finally finishing third behind Martin Watson.

Hutchinson 100

The next race was the Hutchinson 100 at Silverstone – always a great international meeting – but was not until Saturday 14 August, another three-week wait. Strangely, we were not accepted in the 250 race but did get an entry in the 350. I also had a chance for another ride, this time in the Road Production Class race on the Works Cotton, where I had the opportunity of getting to know that great character Pat Onions, who was the engineering director of Cottons and a true enthusiast. Obviously, Inchley, Minter and Ivy (Cottons regular riders) were too engrossed in the main races to ride in the production 250 class. The 350 Yamaha failed early in practice so my only race that day would be on the Cotton. It was good to get a comparison even though this bike had lights and a form of silencing,

At the Hutchinson 100 meeting at Silverstone on Saturday 14 August 1965 Reg rode a works Cotton for the first time in the production race. After leading by a considerable margin near the end of the event, the coil lead came off and the bike was out of the running.

otherwise it was their road racer. I soon found out it was amazingly fast and handled beautifully. I enjoyed the experience and certainly realised now how Minter and Ivy had been so successful on it.

Practice went well but the race was very wet. I had a fair start but was soon circulating very quickly, leading the 250s by a large margin and was 11th overall. Unfortunately, when I was nearing the end of race, a lead came off the coil and it stopped. My race was over. Mike Hailwood won the production race on a 650 BSA Spitfire and the best 250 was Sammy Miller (Bultaco) who was 13th. Interestingly, they had a speed trap at this meeting at the end of Hanger Straight. Hailwood on his MV was fastest at 135.9mph but the second and third bikes were a surprise, being the 250 Works Yamahas of Duff and Read at 129.9 and 127.7mph respectively. The fastest non-works 250 was Terry Grotefeld on a Yamaha TDIB entered by Padgetts, at 114.3mph – a huge 15mph slower than the GP machines!

The following day we went to race at Brands, and this time on the short circuit we managed a 12th place in the 350cc race; although the bike was off song and I could not really compete.

Derek Minter winning at Brands Hatch on the 15 August 1965. His factory Cotton Telstar featured a specially tuned engine and 6-speed gearbox.

As for the 250 event, I did just one shaky lap before the rear chain came off! That was that. Minter won the 250 and 350 but Bill Ivy won the 500 from Minter and Cooper. So now it was three meetings without a 250 finish. Perhaps our luck would change at Mallory Park the following weekend (2 August), where we just had the 250. Sadly it was not to be, as the plugs oiled up at the start so again I recorded no result. This time the 250 was won by Simmonds, followed by Inchley, Martin Watson, Minter and Cooper (now on a DMW), then Degens.

Breaking race and lap records at Crystal Palace

Ted now had to really look at and repair the 250 for Crystal Palace on 30 August – Bank Holiday Monday. He was always anxious to do well here as most of his bike sales were from the London area and the Palace was his showcase. Easter Monday here had been a great success, being first in the 250 heat and final and second in the 350 heat and final. This time the race was organised by BMCRC (Bemsee) and had a different format, not having heats and finals but 'Experts' and 'Non-Experts' races, your status being deemed by the club officials. I was number one in the 350 class and number three in the 250. Although the 350 race was after the 250, I was to be a non-starter in that class as the bike caught fire when it was being warmed up, so that race was over before it had begun! The 250 was a different story, however. I had a great start from the second row and was in the lead going into the first corner ahead of the 26 starters. I had my chin on the tank and was really going for it, with a clear track allowing me to take the best lines. My new line up for the

GREATER LONDON COUNCIL
PARKS DEPARTMENT

CRYSTAL PALACE
OFFICIAL PROGRAMME 1/-

National Motor Cycle Race Meeting
Monday, August 30, 1965
Organised by the British Motor Cycle Racing Club

Motor Cycle

THE COMPLETE MAGAZINE · THURSDAY 1s.

Programme cover for the national race meeting at Crystal Palace on Monday, 30 August 1965. It was a memorable one for Reg as he broke the race and lap records for the South London circuit.

Annerly Ramps left-right flick allowed a flat-out passage, albeit a very bumpy one, but providing you let the bike shake and did not try to control it, it gained precious time. I quickly increased my lead and even lapped up to ninth place riders, finishing 11 seconds in the lead over an eight-lap race. It was just a perfect ride. On my return, Ted, Stuart and the others were elated, with all justification, as they told me I had smashed Joe Dunphy's 250-lap record by nearly two seconds and John Surtees' race record, which he established in August 1957 on the fully faired Works NSU Sportsmax, by some 4mph. What a day! We sang all the way home with the £18 prize money in our pockets ready to celebrate. The press was full of it and *Motor Cycle News* had a great picture and caption: 'Everett Record. Reg Everett on his way to breaking the race and lap records on the Yamaha'.

My first race at Castle Combe

We did not have long to prepare and repair the bikes because I had to collect them the next Friday night for the long drive to my first race at Castle Combe in Wiltshire – another fast and open old airfield circuit. I was looking forward to a new challenge but Stuart and I would be there alone as Ted just could not make it on the Saturday, which was race day. I enjoyed practice and learning the circuit as it was very fast with some very quick bends, flat out in fifth gear for some, and having two bikes to practise on helped the learning curve no end.

Getting away well on the 250, in the race the good feeling was short-lived as the clutch cable broke (you can change gear without a clutch, of course, but with the Yamaha's fragile crankshaft I did not want to break the engine). You may have

Reg during his victorious ride in the 250cc race at Crystal Palace on 30 August 1965, breaking lap and race records in the process.

noticed that we had not broken a crank lately by the clutch wringing itself off, as Ted had made his own by using steel from a Jaguar half shaft and case-hardening it. This gave the component the torsional strength it required.

The 350 lasted a little longer and I finished fifth in my heat, but try as we might it just would not start to go out in the final; however, despite the problems with the bike, I liked the track and was happy to return.

Snetterton the following day

A very long drive was in front of us as we were at Snetterton the following day, so the long trek from Wiltshire to Norfolk began. I phoned Ted to let him know what had happened and he said he would be there at 8am in time to look at the 250, but he doubted that he could get the 350 going as he thought it was the oil seals and that required a complete engine rebuild. So after a 200-mile cross-country drive in the middle of the night, a very short sleep in the van and fry-up for breakfast, we started the 250 repair in time for the 9.30am practice. This went well and the bike seemed OK but again it would have a very long wait for the 250 race scheduled for

5.20pm. Whether it was because I was so tired or because the bike was not quite on song I will never know, but I finally finished fifth behind Dave Simmonds who won easily on his 250 Honda twin ahead of Inchley, Ivy and Minter. 'Just how long will it be,' Ted and I kept asking ourselves, 'before we can beat that man Minter fair and square and win the race?' It was an aim I had for a long time, as he was a real star and the man to beat at short-circuit racing, the acknowledged King of Brands Hatch and most other circuits. This had been a dream years ago – I had got closer and closer, even with wins and seconds, but often he had retired or not been racing. This last mountain still had to be climbed before I could truly say that I had finally made it. Nobody else may have cared but we did, it was my final real challenge. In my mind I knew I could do it and that it still had to be done, it was just a case of when.

Dunlop triangular tyres

When the middle of September comes, the racing season is reaching its end and all the season's expectations have either come or gone. Mine certainly was full of highs and lows, not at all predictable or consistent. I knew I was riding well but still had one or two finishes where I should have done better, but really it was still my first full season where I had been truly competitive on a machine that was also capable of winning, with a great sponsor who tried everything he could to make it happen. This year was also, for everyone, a new tyre year, as Avons had stopped providing racing tyres and most of us were using Dunlop Triangulars, which some riders did not like and would never get used to. I personally did not mind, maybe they suited my style of riding.

Thinking about the racing and different circuits and bends became very important, and whenever I could I would walk the tracks to really look at the surfaces, the peel off and braking areas, to see where it was good and where the sight lines were. I also watched the big names in the other races on each bend to see what and where they were doing things. I studied maps of the tracks to see where straight lines were possible, as this is the shortest distance between two points and to save yards in a lap means you can be yards in front. So to me, every time, every practice lap was a learning curve and a new venture, and it was with this attitude that I approached every race. I also could not say I was ever nervous as I really enjoyed what I was doing; of course, I was quiet before a race but the adrenaline was pumping! I just wanted the flag to drop so I could get on and do the thing I loved best.

A beautiful autumn day

19 September 1965 was one of those beautiful autumn days: dry, sunny and warm, and Brands Hatch looked spectacular. The crowd started rolling in early and so a

good few were there for practice. I felt good and the bike was responsive and easy to ride. The track was in perfect condition and I put in some quick practice laps without trying too hard, but I was really concentrating on smooth, straight lines with an accent on late braking. I was second quickest to Dave Simmonds on that quick Honda twin that only he seemed to have access to, except for Tommy Robb on occasions.

I really felt relaxed. Ted continued to tinker with the bike after our practice debriefing. The sun still shone and we warmed the machine up in the paddock just outside the tunnel and changed to the hard racing plugs. Restart, down through the tunnel, out on the track for our sighting lap and then onto the grid, where I was on the front row by the grandstand. Stop the bike and wait. The stand was packed, the crowd huge, and we were chatting to each other on the grid. Stuart was nearby in case of plug problems but all was OK. The starter came out to his rostrum, all was quiet so I went through the routine. Check petrol on. Check in second gear. Pull back on compressions. Free clutch. Goggles down. Clutch in. Push hard as possible against bars with front brake on. Watch the starter's hands and as soon as they move release the front brake. Two steps. Side saddle bump, dropping the clutch simultaneously – the noise was deafening, full throttle, leg over, up into third, chin on tank and you are racing!

Leading From the Front

All this happens so quickly and it is a fantastic feeling. First into Paddock using the fastest line, hard as you can up the hill into Druids, brake as late as you dare but treat this slow corner with respect on the first lap especially accelerating out, do it slowly and keep tight so you are upright quicker and can accelerate upright and have the fastest line through bottom bend. Still in the lead but I could hear the others behind me. Keep smooth, good lines, no one in front allows you to really use the fastest lines – great. First lap leading. Ted was signalling with thumbs up. It felt great, I was gradually pulling away building up a lead, what a feeling. This continued the whole race. Ted gave me the last lap sign and I must say I worried a bit listening for noise, etc. 'Keep your concentration' I said to myself and got stuck in again, just not using full acceleration or top end to the limit. Coming out of Clearways on that last lap I knew the win was mine and as the chequered flag dropped and I crossed the line the tears started to flow, I had done it. My dream of beating Minter fair and square, and at the same time winning the race, had come true. I completed the running down lap and pulled in to the pits. Ted and Stuart were ecstatic jumping up and down. 'We did it! You did it!' they said. The result: Everett first, Minter second, Simmonds third. *The Motor Cycle* said 'Reg Everett was complete master of the 250 race'. The scrap behind me apparently was fantastic and also involved Curry, Watson and Inchley. In the paddock afterwards the crowds thronged around us and even Minter came over, all he said to me was 'why didn't you wait for us?' I replied 'it was up to you to catch me!' and we continued to celebrate.

Realising an ambition

What a race – I had realised an ambition that I really thought was impossible. I was now at the top of my chosen profession.

To say the rest of the season was just as successful would be a dream, as outside factors beyond my control again played a significant part. At my next meeting at Mallory Park on 26 September, bringing Ted and I down to earth with a bump, the plugs again oiled up on warming-up for the race and the bike just would not re-start.

The very long journey for my first-ever outing at Oulton Park was next on 3 October, this proving a difficult drive. The last part, late at night, was in the pouring rain and found us without a spare fan belt, but we did a bodge up without the dynamo and had to use a torch out of the passenger's window to help see the way!

I thought Oulton was great and loved the swooping bends and learnt so much in a very short space of time, so I finished third in my heat and was set for a great race in the final. This was a real fight and was the best of the day as it was very close, high-speed dicing. Bill Ivy led until his exhaust fell off and at half distance Tommy Robb was in the lead with Ashworth, Burgess and myself dicing for second spot. By the end both Burgess and I passed Ashworth, I finished third at my first-ever Oulton outing and we went home pleased. Much more so than Dunphy and Cooper, who collided and crashed at Knicker Brook on their 500s, Cooper breaking his collar bone.

The Works Yamaha

Returning the bikes to Ted on the Monday, he said that I must be at Brands for practice on Wednesday to try them for the big international meeting, the *Evening News*-sponsored 'Race of the South' for the Brands finale that year on Sunday 10 October. In itself this was not unusual, but it certainly turned out to be. When I arrived I was also surprised to see Bill Ivy there and with him a Works 250 RD 56 Yamaha. Ted's van was parked alongside and Ted was talking to Bill. I parked up and went over to Ted and Bill and we got chatting. Ted seemed to be advising Bill on the bike situation, which I thought strange as Bill had been with the Yamaha works team on a regular basis already. It turned out that Ted had been put in custody of the works bikes for this meeting and you cannot imagine my surprise when he stated that a second machine was to be ridden by me! I had often looked lovingly and longingly at these fantastic red-and-white liveried disc-valved twins. They were Grand Prix winners and the best 250 two-strokes in the world with over 50bhp (more than Minter's 500

Norton) and very light. Real high-speed projectiles built by the best, for the best. It was an honour just to be able to sit on one let alone have the chance to ride one. I kept saying to Ted 'Are you sure? Is this a joke?' but he just said 'get your leathers on and go and practice. Enjoy it but take it steady as we don't have any spares and I don't know if the small ends have many hours left in them. Just get to know the bike so you can handle it'.

I did not need a second invitation to try out the seven gears and the 12,500 rev limit (with its 3,000rpm powerband) and a power output which was at least a third more than Ted's production TD1A. I was given one 10-lap session to get to know the bike as Ted did not want to chance it any longer.

What an experience

I cannot really describe how great it felt to be riding this machine, it fitted perfectly, the gearbox worked like clockwork – very positive minimum movement just tick, tick, tick, through the gears up and down – and those dual brakes, twin leading shoe 10in front, I just was in awe at the stopping power. The handling was

By now Reg Everett's name was being seen as a future star, and he was loaned this 250cc works RD56 Yamaha with disc valve induction at Brands Hatch on 12 October 1965. Unfortunately, after storming through the field after a poor start the small-end seized.

perfect. Yes, I was truly on a world-class racing machine. On the Brands short circuit it was exhilarating, and if we start from rounding the hairpin in first gear it was up to second and third for Bottom Bend, fourth, fifth, sixth, Bottom straight, down to fifth, fourth, third for Clearways, up to fourth again, fifth, sixth, seventh, top straight, down sixth, fifth, fourth for Paddock, up fifth, then sixth to Druids hairpin then down to fifth, fourth, third, second, and first for the hairpin. It was some ride, and I did it in 58 seconds, my quickest ever time on Ted's watch. Just fantastic, another dream come true. The acceleration was unbelievable! I just could not stop talking about it and went home a very happy man.

Race day came quickly, and I really could not wait. When I went out in practice everyone was looking and staring. Derek Minter came over, pointed and went 'wow', or some such sound, 'what are you doing on that? Watch out, though, they are prone to seizure.' By now these remarks went over my head – I had a job to do and I would do it to the best of my ability. Practice went well and the bike continued to impress me, its handling on the faster corners of the long circuit was impeccable. How could you not win on such a machine?

A 'who's who' of 250 racing

The 250 field was a 'who's who' of 250 racing and had 12 different makes of machine on the grid. Bill Ivy on the other Works Yamaha, Dave Simmonds and Bruce Beale on those special Honda twins, Derek Woodman Works MZ, Tommy Robb, Peter Williams, Ralph Bryans, Percy Tait, Drixl, Lawton, Inchley, the list goes on and on, all pedigree riders. Both Ted and Bill told me it was easy to oil the plugs at the start if it did not fire cleanly and I took note of this. When the starter dropped the flag I took extra steps to make sure the engine was turning well and pulled in the clutch when it fired, giving it two or three hefty tweaks on the throttle to make sure it was running cleanly. With such a class field by the time I had done this and got away I was at the back going into Paddock Bend. From then on I just got stuck in, easily passing all my rivals until at the end of lap two, when I was third behind Woodman MZ and Ivy who was well away. Coming out of Clearway on the third lap I went past the MZ as if he was going backwards and set about trying to catch Bill. This did not happen and, as Ted had prophesied, the small-end seized during the next lap and I pulled off most dejected. The thrill had gone and I felt empty and drained, my dream ride over. Bill's bike stopped with a broken crank during the next lap and Derek Woodman went on to win comfortably. Again I had experienced the highs and lows of motorcycle road racing.

A cold and wet Mallory finale

Mallory Park hosted the last race of the year on 3 October, and what a horrible day it was, very cold and very wet. *Motor Cycle News* said in its headline 'Only the pace was hot. The strong cutting wind made the conditions more difficult'. I finished second in my heat being caught and passed by Martin Watson. Tom Phillips had a fantastic ride on Vic Camp's Ducati to beat Dave Simmonds into second place and win the other heat (Tom was always fantastic in the wet – remember he stayed with Jim Redman on his Works Honda four at Silverstone two years earlier). Any of the seven on the front row could have won. Woodman on the MZ was favourite but water in the ignition put him out.

Dave Simmonds got away well and at the end of the first lap he was in front of Degens and myself. Tommy Robb was sixth but by the end of the third lap he was with us and seemingly enjoying the ride. We all diced nose to tail and even sideways. Tommy got by us all to lead and Gordon Keith on the Orpin Greeves relegated me to fifth (I cannot say I was enjoying it!).

Poor old Tom Phillips, who was sixth, lost it at Gerrards and retired muddy and shaken, while Martin Watson (Bultaco) passed me again and I finished sixth.

What I did not know was that if I had won I would have been the 250 British Champion (ACU STAR). Even after my year of great results and many failures it finished as follows:

1 – Dave Simmonds	58 points	– Honda
2 – Reg Everett	**52 points**	**– Yamaha**
3 – Derek Minter	50 points	– Cotton
4 – Bill Ivy	47 points	– Cotton
5 – Peter Inchley	40 points	– Villiers
6 – Dave Degens	39 points	– Aermacchi

And so 1965 came to a close. Certainly, it was a year when I had finally mixed it with the best riders and, even though I had narrowly missed out on the national title, I had at last achieved a major ambition of beating the acknowledged king of the British short circuits, Derek Minter, fair and square.

Chapter 9

1966 – Racing with the Stars

1966 was a big year for Reg – the year he really made the top rung of the ladder in British short circuit racing circles. He is seen here in the Brands Hatch paddock with Ted Broad's 250cc Yamaha at a practice day prior to the start of the season.

Nineteen-sixty-five had been my busiest year to date, competing in no less than 38 races. I achieved my ambition of racing at a very high level and beating the current stars, experiencing both the highs and the lows in the process.

I had 16 Podiums (as they are now known – although neither the word nor the physical stand had even been thought of then) which equates to 42 per cent of the races. Equally I had 15 DNF or DNS due to mechanical reasons (including one crash) which was 39 per cent, so about half and half.

I had also changed my job and now was at English Electric but this was to be a real failure as the position they employed me for just did not exist! This was to be a bonus too, however, as I was left alone and came and went as I pleased, which fitted in with racing perfectly.

Unfortunately, my marriage to Pearl had fallen apart and I was living in 'digs' but this allowed me to have complete freedom of movement to concentrate 100 per cent on the racing. 1965 had started poorly and had a great middle but not such a good end, so what would 1966 bring?

A Winter of Development for Ted

Ted had not been idle all winter and the 350 was developed more (it was now 310cc), so hopefully we could have more consistent rides in that class. So it certainly proved, as during the 1966 season we competed in 32 250cc races and 28 350cc races, 60 in all – a really busy year.

The early season opened at Mallory on 6 March 1966 – I came fourth in the 250 heat but the front brake torque arm broke in the final. I had a great scrap with John Cooper in the 350 heat and finished runner-up, but the engine seized in the final. Peter Inchley won the 250.

Reg practising on the Boad Yamaha at Brands Hatch, February 1966.

Leading Derek Minter (Seeley AJS, 2) during the 350cc race at Mallory Park on 5 March 1966. The other rider is John Cooper (Norton).

Brands Hatch on 13 March was a disaster when the larger Yamaha's engine seized in practice and I made a beginner's mistake! When I was in the lead, while riding the 250, on the first lap I accelerated too hard coming out of the hairpin, lost the back end, corrected it, only to highside and land on my head in the middle of the track. How everyone missed me I do not know. I was carted off by ambulance to the medical centre on the circuit. They looked at me and said I was OK but badly concussed (my crash helmet had split apart). I drove back home but the next thing I remember was waking up in hospital three days later after being unconscious, with bones broken in my hand and foot.

I was in no condition to ride at Snetterton on 20 March but did go to Brands on 8 April. I still did not feel too good and had a poor start from the second row.

The pair of Broad Yamahas at Brands Hatch on 13 March 1966. Unfortunately, Reg crashed in the 250cc and was unable to come out for the 350cc event.

I did not feel 100 per cent and managed six slow laps before retiring – in truth I was still nursing a foot injury. Perhaps our old favourite, Crystal Palace, three days later on Easter Monday would prove better. I elected to have a push start from the back of the grid and carved my way through to win my 250 heat. The final was not as good as it was very wet and a persistent misfire set in – I finished third. For the 350 heat I was a good second until the engine seized and I coasted over the line to finish seventh.

Reg at Brands Hatch, 8 April 1966. The unpainted helmet was due to having to buy a new helmet after his crash at the Kent circuit on 13 March.

Reg (16) on the 310cc Broad Yamaha during his heat at Crystal Palace on Easter Monday, 11 April 1966. Unfortunately, when lying second the engine seized and Reg had to coast over the line to finish seventh. This ruled him out of the final.

This was not the start to the season I had hoped for. Peter Inchley had won at Snetterton (the meeting I did not race at), also at Mallory (we did not enter), so he already had three wins and two third places against my one third place. He was riding very well and his Works Villiers Special was really flying and was exceedingly reliable – a great asset.

Peter Inchley with the very fast Villiers Special (essentially a works Starmaker engine with 6-speeds and mounted in a Bultaco chassis), seen at Snetterton on Easter Monday, 11 April 1966.

A great dice ensued at Brands Hatch on Bank Holiday Monday, 1 May 1966, between Peter Inchley (Villiers Special, 78), Reg (Broad Yamaha, 46) and Peter Williams (Orpin Greeves, 16).

Bank Holiday Monday at Brands

The short circuit at Brands would be our next challenge on 1 May – Bank Holiday Monday – and a great crowd was there. The 15-lap 350 race was the second race in the programme. It was hot (75-degrees F) and dry with the track oily and slippery, and there were many crashes during the day. I made a bad start from the third row and was a very poor 30th at the end of the first lap. I fought and scratched my way up to 12th at the end, having a great dice with Martin Watson and Rodney Gould, which proved to be good training for the 250cc race to come. The race was won by Dave Degens, ahead of Peter Williams, John Cooper, Rex Butcher and Dave Simmonds, with Minter a lowly sixth. Tom Phillips, Alan Barnett, Griff Jenkins and Martin Watson finished seventh to 10th respectively – what a field, what a race. I felt that finishing 12th in that company after being 30th in the first lap was really not bad!

What a dice

My 250cc start was not much better. It seems that I was still worrying about my foot and was just not putting the effort into it, and I was 14th at the end of the 12-lap race. Enjoying the overtaking, I was soon up to fourth where it was more difficult, and it took two laps to get past Dave Degens and set my sights on catching Inchley and Peter Williams on the very fast, watercooled Reg Orpin Greeves. By laps seven and eight I was with them and a great three-way race ensued as I led on the ninth, 10th and 11th, but only by a wheel or so – what a dice! It was fantastic and the crowd loved it. Peter Williams pulled a little in front of me on the last lap out of Druids and Bottom bend but we were still side-by-side. Approaching the Clearways complex a back marker was ahead, and Williams went on the outside as I went up the inside. The back marker saw Williams first and reacted by moving over to the inside too, and how we did not collide I will never know (there were no blue or overtaking warning flags in those days). This, however, was enough to make me shut off and my line in the corner was poor and slow as a result. Inchley then saw his chance as well and came past me. Try as I might, I just could not get past them again and Williams won from Inchley and I was third – just. It was a great race, though, and we often talked it. There was a great colour photograph in the *Motorcylist Illustrated* (the centrefold) and it showed us all going round Druids side-by-side. It was something really special.

Inchley – the man in form

Peter Inchley and I had a great dice again at the next Mallory meeting on 22 May 1966. My heat was very wet but I won easily. It was only damp, although patchy, for the final and after a race-long scrap Peter won. He was riding well and that bike was really quick (this was his fourth win already that year with one second and two thirds as well, against my only finishing in three finals – one second and two thirds), he really was the 250 rider/machine combination of the year! In my 350 ride I was seventh in a damp heat. The final was in torrential rain and I got up to second but water in the works started a misfire and I dropped back to finish seventh.

The next weekend at Snetterton was fine and dry but, with a strong headwind down the Norwich Straight, in my 350 heat I had a great dice with John Cooper and Rex Butcher and beat them both, but I still only finished fifth. Again a very bad start in the 350 final saw me 30th at the end of the first lap, but I fought through and finished 10th.

In the 250 it was a very different story as Peter Inchley, Derek Minter and I had a race-long fight for the lead. There was nothing between us, bikes and riders being equal, and a great deal of overtaking occurred. On the last lap I was in front past the Start/Finish and going into Sears on the absolute limit. There was a bump on Sears which we usually missed, Minter was right on my back wheel but just inside pushing

Mallory Park, 22 May 1966. Here Reg leads Peter Inchley.

Reg on full bore around Devil's Elbow, Mallory Park, 22 May 1966.

me slightly wide, my rear wheel hit the bump, jumped and lost adhesion – I immediately corrected the slide but overdid it and went into a highside crash at about 85mph, so my race was over. So was Peter Inchley's, and although he was about 10 yards behind he also crashed and Derek went on to win! I landed up on the outside of the circuit near the spectators, against the bank and fence, and someone asked 'Reg, are you OK?' It was a good friend Bobby Hoare and his dad who had, up until then, been cheering for me, but they were happily surprised that I had survived this horrendous crash relatively unscathed. Poor old Ted was distraught, he really thought we were going to win that day – so did I! Again, *Motorcyclist Illustrated* had a fabulous picture of the moment just as I was about to be thrown over the bars, someone really

In 1966 (and 1967) one of Reg's main rivals for 250cc honours was Peter Inchley (seen here on 8 April 1966 at Brands Hatch).

The big incident at Snetterton on 29 May 1966 which was captured by Motorcyclist Illustrated *– the very moment Reg was just about to be thrown over the handlebars of Ted Broad's 250 Yamaha. Also in the picture are Derek Minter (11) and Peter Inchley (16) who also crashed.*

knew their job well! Very recently I was to learn from Mick Walker that the photographer was Vic Barnes, who was then stationed at a local RAF base.

Brands Hatch the following day (an international on 30 May 1966 Bank Holiday) was not a good day; the 250 did not start, I felt really beaten up from the crash the day before and in the 350 the union on the bottom of the left-hand carburettor came undone and lubricated my boots and the new tyre with petrol. Not only that, I also finished 11th – what a weekend!

Post TT at Mallory Park

After the TT, which was actually a break for me, came the Post TT International at Mallory on 19 June. In one respect it was one of the best days of my racing career – the 250 heat was fantastic, despite being only five laps. I led from a good start but Jim Redman on the Honda Four got by me. I re-passed to lead on the next lap but in the end finished third to Redman and Akiyasu Motohashi on the Works Yamaha. This was a great thrill to ride against World Champions on such exotic machines, and passing Redman in the dry round the Esses made my day, but better was still to come. Unfortunately the 250 final was a disaster against so much expectation as my bike failed to start with oiled plugs – from hero to zero!

Mike Hailwood on the larger four-cylinder Honda was in my heat of the 350s and by now there was torrential rain (but now I was very happy and confident in the wet and actually enjoyed it), which helped against faster machines as rain was a leveller. Hailwood got his usual flying start but I was not far behind and was able to follow him, even though totally outpaced down the straights, but I could live with him going round Gerrards. On the second lap I decided I could go round Gerrards quicker but at first hesitated in passing the great man. The racing instinct quickly took over and the will to win was there, so I drove round the outside of him going round the last half of Gerrards. Down the Stebb straight – the wail of the Honda Four as he came alongside haunted me – I expected him to come flying past, but no, I outbraked him into the Esses, led round the hairpin and past the start/finish.

I gradually pulled out a 100-yard lead in the next two laps, but again disaster struck! My engine started misfiring, I had water in the electrics, running on one cylinder only. Everybody passed me and I finished a lowly 14th. After the race Ted and I were discussing events by the van and Mike walked over to us. 'What happened, Reg?' he asked and I told him about the water. He really was interested and went on to say that, in all his experience, he had never seen anyone ride in the wet as well as I did, and he just could not keep up with me. Well, for once in my life I was speechless! What an accolade from, in my opinion, the greatest rider of all time! This, indeed, was a day to remember whatever else I may achieve. In history it is only the result that counts and that day I had, in the finals, just two DNF – but for me it was a great, momentous and memorable occasion.

Brands 500–Miler

Peter Inchley and I were real rivals but for the 500-mile Production race at Brands on 26 June 1966 we were brought together as teammates to ride the Works Cotton Conquest. In 1965 Peter had been paired with Derek Minter, the regular Cotton rider, and they won the 250 class convincingly. So we had our work cut out. The Cotton was great to ride and handled like a dream even with a full five-gallon tank. The speedo showed 110mph down the back straight towards Hawthorn Hill bend. It was a great day, warm and sunny, and I had my new girlfriend (Ronnie) with me. The Cotton behaved impeccably, did not miss a beat and Peter and I enjoyed the whole experience. We won the 250cc class easily from Tommy Robb and Chris Vincent (Suzuki Super Six) and were second in the 500cc class, just a lap behind the winners, Tom Phillips and Dave

Reg (250 Cotton Conquest) leading Joe Dunphy (650cc Triumph Bonneville) in the Brands Hatch 500-mile production race on 26 June 1966. Reg and Peter Inchley finished first in class.

Cotton advertisement proclaiming the Peter Inchley/Reg Everett victory.

Reg holding the pit board for Peter Inchley during the 1966 500-miler at Brands Hatch.

Croxford on Geoff Dodkin's Velocette, and seventh overall at a speed of over 75mph. Some achievement from a 250cc two-stroke single cylinder engine.

Cotton retained the Veedol trophy with Peter and I receiving replicas and laurel wreaths, plus £50 each for our effort. Pat Onions of Cotton was really happy with the publicity we received in the press. Finishing first in a 500-miler did my confidence the world of good and Peter and I had recorded identical fastest laps on the same machine, so we were both happy rivals again.

What would happen when we raced against each other? We would have to wait and see, but nevertheless our friendship was sealed.

Castle Combe

The fast bumpy circuit of Castle Combe on 9 July was my next test. In practice it was drizzly and cloudy, but the track was virtually dry for the races. I suffered a poor start in the 350 heat and just managed 13th place to qualify for the final over 10 laps. Again I had a poor start but finished a good fourth behind Minter, Williams and Barry Randle. It was still a little damp in my 250 heat and I got a bad start but got up to second by the end, behind Peter Williams on that fast Orpin Greeves. Peter also won the 500 that day, beating Minter by just 0.4 secs. My dear friend, Joe Iszard, finished a great fourth on his 125 Bultaco.

The 250 final was fantastic, as this time I got a reasonable start away with the leaders (except Peter Inchley who was not entered) – Minter, Williams, Tait and Gould. Derek and I were leading but all five of us were in a great race for the first few laps of the 10-lap race distance. Williams' Greeves broke its rear chain and Gould's Bultaco cried enough, leaving Derek, Percy and myself to race for the lead, but Derek and I pulled away and had a race-long dual, no quarter asked for or given – it was side-by-side racing at its toughest. Those watching likened it to the tragic race in which poor Dave Downer was killed in its competitiveness – real hard, winner-takes-all racing. I must say I enjoyed every second of it, this is what races were meant to be like. Down the Dean Straight going into Camp Corner on the penultimate lap I was just in front, thinking of my strategy for the last lap knowing that Derek would try anything to pass me here to win the sprint to the flag. I led into Camp, outbraking him, and then we got to the apex of Camp Corner – 'bang' – he hit my rear wheel. How I did not crash is not known, but he did crash; although fortunately he was unhurt but had really messed up his new dark green leathers. This left me with an easy last lap and I won ahead of Percy Tait (who was riding the Geoff Duke-entered Works Royal Enfield GP5) by 3.8 secs. It was really a great win in a terrific race, Ted arriving just to see me cross the line and win – he had left the shop early that Saturday to see the race. He missed the drama but was ecstatic with the result. Things were looking up, the fastest lap was 86.70mph, 1 min 16.2 secs, and I averaged 83.85mph for the 10-lap, 18.4-mile race.

Cadwell Park

On 7 August we went to our first meeting at Cadwell Park. It was a strange restricted meeting and had, for us, an unlimited 1000cc race and a handicap. It was a horrible day, cloudy and drizzling all the time. Not knowing this track, and it being wet, was not the best situation to be in, and in the unlimited race (on my 250) I tried as best as I could, despite not being able to see too well in the drizzle, and finished ninth. The handicap race was not much better as I had a bad handicap and a poor start. Peter Williams passed me on his 500 and I finished fifth, winning a total of £6 for my endeavours. It was a long way to go for such a meeting and left me wondering why we had entered.

Backwards at Brands

That year, 1966, the Hutchinson 100 was not at Silverstone but at Brands Hatch on 14 October, and to make it fair for everyone it was to be run anti-clockwise – that is, the bikes would go up Paddock Bend instead of down so everyone was on a 'new' circuit. We all had a good practice on the Saturday before the Sunday racing. This was probably just as well as the circuit was so different going the other way round. Clearways just got tighter and tighter before heading out the back (instead of opening up for the dash to the finish). Dingle Dell was fantastic and going down Hawthorn Hill bend was a great feeling, and the uphill Paddock Bend opening up to the finish line was just all so different. Grid positions were on practice times and I had second row slots in both races. The 350cc Championship race was first at midday. Thirty-six starters in the race were a 'who's who' of racing, Hailwood, Read, Ivy, Minter, etc. I had a good start and held fifth position for three laps until a small-end broke up and the engine seized! Hailwood won from Minter.

I watched the other races as the 250 did not start until 2.50pm. The 125 was a Suzuki benefit. World Champion Hugh Anderson took the win from his teammate Frank Perris. John Cooper won the Production race on his 650 BSA Spitfire II from Percy Tait (650 Triumph T120) and dear Charlie Sanby won the unlimited non-experts race. Read, Duff and Ivy were the favourites for the 250 on their Works Yamahas, with Duff beating Read on this occasion. I had a fantastic start and led through Clearways, Stirlings, Dingle Dell and Westfield, but then going along the Portobello Straight the engine started to miss, then it stopped. I pulled over to the left and the field came streaming by, the noise from all the different machines running flat out was deafening. Coasting round Hawthorn Hill bend I pulled off the circuit at the bottom of the hill onto the grass and applied the front brake to finally bring me to a standstill. Unbelievably, the front brake cable immediately broke! I was totally gobsmacked and the 'what ifs' started in my mind! Well, if the engine had not stopped I would have been on the brake hard to go into the terrifically fast downhill Hawthorn Hill bend and to do that without the front brake would have spelt disaster. It was another unbelievable occurrence and, in hindsight, a great piece of luck. So why had the bike stopped? Ted and Stuart, and of course myself, had not filled the bike with petroil or checked that it had been done. How all this happened, and why, we will never know, but in the records it was just another DNF. What a finish it might have been!

Croft

My first-ever visit to Croft and the long trek north to Darlingtonn that this entailed, was our next venture for Saturday 20 August 1966. We did not arrive until the early hours and had to park outside the circuit. Feeling really bleary eyed, in the early morning we gained access and had a drive round the circuit before going to the pits. It was sparse, open and flat, the surface was of dubious quality and had a lot of straw bales to delineate the circuit. I had to learn fast as the local competition was severe, but I had a lot of problems with the straw bales and they seemed to be everywhere.

When I went out for my 250 heat I arrived at the grid to be confronted with two or three packed rows across the track. It seemed like 'first come first served'. So I stayed back and started my engine on the flag drop, pulled off the track onto the grass and led into the first corner – great – and pulled away to win. In the first 350cc race Trevor Burgess and I had a great dice and he beat me, but only just. He was then disqualified as he only had one bike, a 246cc Greeves, and the race officially was 251–350cc, so I was given the win on our larger Yamaha.

The 250 race was again a great dice. This time I was beaten after a terrific scrap with Burgess and Derek Chatterton, who won with me coming third after colliding with a straw bale in the Chicane – it was really great racing.

I had another great ride in the 350 final, in which I lead all the way and became Yorkshire 350 Champion. I was presented with a huge silver trophy previously won by Mike Hailwood among others. The day was rounded off by a second place on the 350 in the unlimited handicap race. Not bad for my first-ever visit to the circuit – three wins, a second and a third. Going home in a happy and jubilant mood, but with two worn-out bikes to be raced the following day at Mallory Park!

Ted came to Mallory and set to work on the bikes. He was not happy with the 350 as basically it was worn out (three hard races and practising at Croft had taken its toll) and kept oiling the plugs, so we did not race. The weather was awful –

Reg outside Ted Broad's Ilford, Essex, dealership holding the 350cc Yorkshire Champion trophy, after winning both 350cc events at Croft on 20 August 1966.

raining and cold, in fact it was so bad that the last sidecar race was abandoned. Pip Harris refused to start. Our 250 race was good but the bike was a little off song; although I had a great race-long dice with Burgess and Gould and we crossed the line within 0.2 seconds of each other. Martin Watson was the master of the conditions and won with me coming fourth. What a weekend. We felt tired, wet and happy as, after the race, we cleaned up and had a celebratory fry-up in the van before making for home.

In the money at the Palace

Bank Holiday Monday, 29 August, brought our traditional trip to Crystal Palace and we had been able to practice there on the Saturday to make sure the bikes were going well after their rebuilds. It was dry and warm and on the 250 I lapped within one second of my own lap record, so all looked good for the race on Monday. The weather was OK early in the day for the 350 where I started off in sixth place and had a good ride to finish fourth. For the 250, though, it changed and the rain came down. I really did not mind, in fact I had a great ride and won easily from John Blanchard. With my £20 appearance money and the £7 for the 350 and £18 for my 250 win, I went home with £45 in my pocket, giving our team a total of £260 for the year so far.

It was September and the year was drawing to an end. The season was getting better as it went on, after an indifferent start and some great, close racing. It had given me plenty of thrills, continued confidence and high expectations. At Castle Combe on 10 September, I won my 350 heat easily with Dave Simmonds on his fast Honda winning the other. Barry Scully and I had a dice in the 350 final but his

Castle Combe, 10 September 1966. During the 250cc final Reg (55) and Rod Gould (Bultaco, 5) battled for second place – eventually Reg clinched it, Rod eventually finishing fourth.

Scott ran out of steam and I led but was soon passed by Dave Simmonds – his Honda being just too fast for me. Rod Gould caught me up and we had a great scrap until I pulled away as he was worried by Charlie Sanby. I finished a good second.

The 250 was a little different as I got a third in my heat behind Peter Inchley and Percy Tait, while Rod Gould won the other. In the final I led for two laps until Peter Inchley passed me and this time I just could not keep up and he went on to win, having to break the lap record to stay in front at 1 min 16 secs, 87.16mph. I had a great scrap with Tait and Gould with Burgess, Browning and Tom Phillips in close company – great racing. Poor Tom came off after fuel sprayed on his rear tyre, the race finishing as follows: Inchley (Villers Starmaker), Everett (Yamaha), Tait (Royal Enfield), Gould (Bultaco) and Burgess (Greeves). Five different makes in the first five places, three English, one Japanese, one Spanish and all two-strokes. What a difference from when I first rode my original Greeves. I also noticed still how few Japanese bikes were being successful at national level. As, in the 250 class out of the 80 entries here, there were only six Yamahas and one Honda, and with 20 Greeves and 11 Cottons and nine Bultacos, Japanese machines very much in the minority (the exception being at Grand Prix level where the 125, 250 and 350 classes were dominated by the Oriental machines).

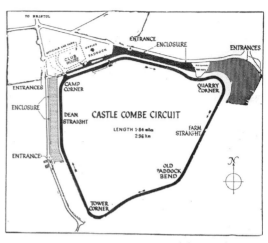

A map of the Castle Combe circuit from the programme of the 10 September 1966 meeting.

Programme cover for the Castle Combe meeting on 10 September 1966.

Back to Croft

On 17 September we returned to Croft, where at least now I knew the situation. *Motor Cycle News* of 21 September stated 'The blaze of publicity which surrounded Phil Read's first appearance at Croft on Saturday was well and truly extinguished by the end of the meeting', 'Phil's blown off by the North's top stars!' and 'This was the race of the day!' remarking on the 250 final. I had won my heat and Trevor Burgess won the other. Derek Chatterton crashed in his heat.

MCN stated 'What a fabulous final it was, both Burgess and Everett took to the fields on occasions in their efforts to get past each other and with a tremendous last lap effort Burgess just snatched the verdict!' He was a true course specialist and a great rider – and who tuned the Burgess Greeves? Well, it was my old sponsor, Brian Woolley.

I had the honour of the fastest lap in 1 min 23.6 secs, 75.36mph – race time and speed 17 mins 3.6 secs, 73.85mph. The 350 race was won by the Scot, Denis Gallagher from Tony Rutter with Read coming third, only just scraping past me at the end of the race as I had no clutch, the race being timed at 17 mins 11.6 secs, 73.28mph, which was slower than our 250 time! Rob Fitton beat Read, who was on a Dearden Norton in the 500 race. What a day, just fantastic, it just goes to show that many riders had great talent but were not in the right place at the right time or did not drink in the right bars to get to the levels they were capable of.

Race of the Year

We went to the Race of the Year at Mallory Park next, it was a real foggy morning and practice was delayed. Here my luck was out again, though I had a good 250cc heat, finishing fourth behind the works bikes of Hailwood, Duff and Robb. Early on in the final the fairing came loose and I had to retire. My 350, for some reason, would just not go. I raced but could only make 10th in my heat and 18th in the final. It was a real disappointment.

Some interesting facts came to light as here they had an electronic speed trap at the end of the main straight. Hailwood's six-cylinder Honda 250 was the fastest at 118.42, over three miles-per-hour quicker than Ago's 500 MV whose speed was equalled by Peter Williams' Matchless and Ivy and Duff's 250 Yamahas. Cooper, Shorey, Dunphy, Degens and Croxford were all equal next at 112.50mph. Martin Watson's 250 Bultaco was next at 107.14, the same as Ago, Shorey and Dunphy's 350s (no wonder he was doing so well in our 250 races) and my Yamaha was the same as Peter Inchley's Villiers at 104.65, 14mph slower than Hailwood's 250 Honda!

Hailwood won the 250, but the Race of the Year went to Ago (MV) who finished ahead of Ivy and Duff on those Yamahas and Peter Williams in fourth – it just shows that speed really helps, especially over a long distance of 40 laps.

I was due to ride Brands International on 9 October 1966 but did not ride due to some kind of sickness. This was really unusual for me as some would say that I was 'as fit as a Butcher's dog' and it must have been something quite serious to stop me racing!

The penultimate meeting

So, Snetterton 23 October was 1966's penultimate meeting. I was a non-starter in the 350 but the 250 went well. Peter Williams crashed his Greeves in practice and broke his

Programme cover for the Brands Hatch Evening News *International Race of the South, 9 October 1966.*

BRANDS HATCH

Evening News International
Motor Cycle Race of the South

Sunday October 9 1966 Programme 2s 6d

Organised by the
Brands Racing Committee
for Brands Hatch Circuit Ltd.

Motor Cycle

THE COMPLETE MAGAZINE

THURSDAY 1s. 3d.

collarbone and Peter Inchley did the same, but this time his legs were hurt because Martin Watson ran over them. They were unfortunate accidents but at least it meant that two of my big rivals were out of the way. In the race I had a great start and I led all the way without any trouble, beating Dave Simmonds and Martin Watson, recording a race average speed of 86.75mph.

The last race at Mallory (on 30 October) really was not so good but I won my 250 heat, beating Inchley, who was sufficiently recovered after his accident, and Chatterton, but a bad misfire and no first gear put me out of the running and down to 10th in the final. Also, the 350 was playing up and was down on steam, achieving a lowly eighth in the heat and a poor 18th in the final for a second time – something was way off here as it was almost a repeat performance of my previous Mallory 350cc effort.

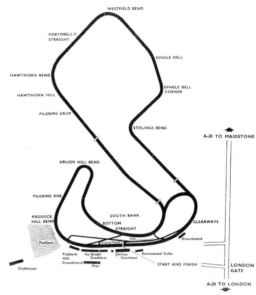

The circuit plan of Brands Hatch from the Race of the South programme.

Summarising the season

Well, what a season 1966 was – certainly my most prolific and productive. Let us just have a quick look at the statistics:

Twenty-one race meetings with 60 races and two crashes, and for combined 250 and 350 racing – 11 wins, seven seconds and five thirds (23 podiums), six fourth places and 16 others, that is 45 finishes plus 11 DNF and four DNS.

We travelled nearly 15,000 miles going to and from meetings, practising and picking up and delivering bikes.

Mallory Park, 30 October 1966, the final meeting of the British season. Reg on the 310cc Broad Yamaha tails a pair of British singles.

What about rewards? Well, in total, I received £70 in appearance money after begging/writing/asking for it and a total of £270 in prize money – a grand total of £340. Plus I got back from BP the actual money I had spent on petrol and oil to race with and get me to and from meetings. This was paid at the end of the year by submitting all the receipts to BP.

Ted Broad, being my sponsor, took the starting money to help with expenses plus half of the prize money, so at the final reckoning I had £135 for my efforts and he had £205. Taking into account that the price of a new TDIB Yamaha in 1965 was £520, and we had two, we can honestly say we did it for the love of the sport!

In the British Championship we again finished in second place to, this time, Peter Inchley, who amassed 62 points to my 50 (best eight results), his early-season wins making the difference. Trevor Burgess was third in front of Derek Chatterton, Derek Minter, Billie Nelson, Dave Degens and Rod Gould. Although, to be fair to Minter, he did not appear (for whatever reason) in the last half of the season on a 250.

Where to from here?

Where to go from here? Well, no one had offered me a works or an alternative ride and I was very happy with Ted, who was always totally committed, and I thought that maybe it would be third time lucky with the British Championships! We just did not promote ourselves at all. When the meeting was over we cleaned the bikes, packed up and left the circuit. Many riders stayed behind and entertained the press and the circuit management, doing what they could to enhance their prospects or to just party and get drunk! Did it help? Who knows. Maybe we were just naïve and hoped fame and fortune would come to us. We had raced all comers and beaten most of the top men. The only thing we lacked was consistency of results through mainly mechanical problems – but one thing for sure was it was not for lack of effort!

Ted needed some financial assistance to help subsidise his racing but he did it out of his own pocket and without sponsorship of any kind. At the end of the year I bought one of the bikes from him to help the situation a little, but one or two new Yamaha TDICs were out of the question. These machines were being developed and had the clutch moved to the gearbox shaft with new five-port cylinders and much better tuned expansion chambers, so we would have our work cut out competing against the new models. Ted, I knew, would do what he could to remain competitive – maybe a new lighter frame which would improve the handling?

So ended my seventh full year of motorcycle racing – but what would 1967 bring?

Chapter 10

1967 – The Year of Reckoning

Money was short at the beginning of this year. The bike I bought I actually sold on to Clyde Cardy, who took delivery at the end of the year as per our agreement. I managed to obtain our prize money from the 500-miler and this went into the coffers.

My job at English Electric 'expired' midday on Wednesday 1 March, but I managed to get a freelance draughting job working on Concorde wiring diagrams in Reading, which started the following Monday.

I had no van now for the start of the season on 5 March at Mallory, but Geoff Monty said he had one for sale so I got on my moped (a 50cc Suzuki loaned to me by Ted) to have a look at it. Unfortunately it was a 'dog' so I had to hire a van for the meeting.

At least we finished third in the 250 heat at Mallory and (according to my records) sixth in the final behind Pickrell on Geoff Monty's very fast Bultaco, who was followed by Inchley, Chatterton, Burgess and Rod Gould, on a DMW. I also claimed the £10 start money I had graciously received from Jack Walton after I had written to him requesting something earlier in the year.

Reg in full flight at Mallory Park on 5 March 1967.

Easter weekend

Easter soon came and Brands on Good Friday and Crystal Palace on the Monday were our normal meetings. We had tried for Snetterton but were told it was over-subscribed and there were no cancellations.

I had bought a van (a 15 cwt Ford Thames of course!) the weekend after Mallory. It was a really good one and was painted black, and it meant that our transport was secure.

I picked up the bikes on Thursday evening and went to the King of Brands Motorcycle Races where the 'Kings' were crowned for the year. I was a non-starter for the 350 but the 250 race was great. I shot into the lead early on and the only person to catch me was Ray Pickrell on Monty's Bultaco. It came past me sounding like a twin at some unbelievable revs and, I thought, sounded like it would not last long. Sure enough it did not, and before the end of that lap it had seized. Ray said afterwards that it just kept revving and riding it like that it either 'won or broke' – and it certainly broke more times than it won!

This left me to win from Simmonds, now on a Kawasaki (disc-valve, two-stroke twin), Kevin Cass (Bultaco) and Jim Curry, whose 182cc Honda was flying and with his talent and experience since 1961 on the Cotton twin (Villiers 2T engine) really made it competitive, and he was followed

The season opener at Mallory Park on 5 March 1967. Reg leads Peter Inchley (Villiers, 15) and Ray Pickrell (Bultaco, 28). Other riders include Rod Gould and Trevor Burgess.

Brands Hatch, Easter Friday, 24 March 1967. Reg leading Ray Pickrell (Bultaco) on this way to winning the 250cc King of Brands race.

King of Brands programme, 24 March 1967.

by Peter Williams and Ginger Malloy. I got my laurel wreath and did a parade lap for the crowd in a pickup as 250cc King of Brands.

Easter Monday at the Palace completed a great double when I won both the 250 heat and final from an up-and-coming Paul Smart, Martin Carney and Grant Gibson, and I took the fastest lap as well. Finishing third in the 350 final behind Ron Chandler and Alan Peck completed a fantastic weekend and netted us £75 in start and prize money to help our efforts. What a start to the season! It was just what we wanted – bikes going well and reliably, and me on top of my form and in great spirits.

Testing at Snetterton

On 13 April we went for a test day at Snetterton. Ted had made up a 305cc Yamaha engine with improved porting. It seemed to go OK but the day was very wet and my best lap was 2 min 5 secs, but until we tried it in the dry it was difficult to judge its true potential.

The Dodkin Velocette

15 April saw me testing at Brands. This time on something very different, the Geoff Dodkin 500

At Crystal Palace on Easter Monday, 27 March 1967. Reg completed a magnificent double by winning his heat and final on the 250cc Broad Yamaha.

The 15 April 1967 saw Reg testing Geoff Dodkin's Velocette Thruxton – and he was very happy to be partnering his old friend Tom Phillips at Brands Hatch in the 500-mile Grand Prix D'Endurance on Sunday 23 April.

Velocette Thruxton which Tom Phillips (who was always Geoff's main rider) had asked me if I would ride at the 500-mile Grand Prix D'Endurance at Brands on Sunday 23 April, to which I readily agreed, providing both were happy with the test. While we were there Bill Ivy was practising on the Works Yamaha and it seized going into Paddock bend. The resulting crash shook Bill but he was OK.

The test went well and I took to the Velocette readily; although riding it was so different from the Yamaha. I lapped consistently at about the same time as Tom could, so I was happy and so was Geoff (Tom and I had remained great friends ever since our Greeves days and I considered him an exceptionally fine rider).

Race day was cold and dry and practice went well. Geoff's Velo was well prepared and had won this event previously so Tom and I were very optimistic. At

23 April 1967, Reg piloting the Dodkin Velocette Thruxton. Partnered by Tom Phillips, the pairing were five laps in the lead after six hours when the magneto broke. They still finished fourth.

the end of the first hour with Tom aboard we were second to the Butler/Dixon Triumph Daytona and catching it up – they retired when a nut came off the alternator and broke the primary chain casing.

By the end of the fouth hour we were well in the lead of the 500s and lying fifth overall, the British single handling and running like a dream. This improved to fourth overall at the fifth hour, and at five and a half hours we were third overall behind the eventual winners Tait and Gould on the 650 Triumph and the similiarly mounted Dunphy and Pickrell, who came second. We were eight laps in front of the next 500 when disaster struck and the engine just stopped with me on board. I coasted back into the pits where Geoff diagnosed a non-functioning magneto (which had been especially overhauled by the manufacturer prior to the event).

The Dodkin pit during the 1967 500-miler. Geoff Dodkin is in the centre (with white coat and beret).

Tom Phillips (26) on the inside of Ken Watson (250cc Vic Camp Ducati Mach 1) at Brands during the 1967 500-miler.

Our race was run, the time ticked by and the runners' time of six hours 19 mins approached. I said 'If I was to push it back to where I pulled off to go into the pits and then push it over the line we could finish'. Duly when the flag dropped I did, pushing the bike through the straw bale chicane to the chequered flag to finish fourth in our class and 14th overall from 31 finishers! Still a result. Geoff Dodkin was disappointed but really appreciative of both Tom and my efforts on his behalf, he was a really super gentleman.

Tom Phillips, Ken Inwood and Geoff Dodkin share words.

During the winter break Ted Broad had been working on a new machine for the 250cc class – essentially the same TD1A engine, but housed in a new frame, which featured an eliptical-tube swinging arm.

A long and fruitful weekend

The following weekend we had two meetings – Castle Combe followed by Mallory Park on the Sunday. We arrived at the Combe at 11pm Friday evening after collecting the bikes from Ted's shop. Camping in the van was the start of this long and fruitful weekend, but we only had the 250 to race. There were three 250cc heats of 40 riders in each, with the first 13 to go to the finals – what a field. The organisers had split the best riders up and as I won my heat, Peter Inchley won his, and Derek Chatterton his, the final was well set.

Reg and Ted Broad with the newly contructed Yamaha Special at Snetterton.

We all got away well but Peter and I soon took the lead and were pulling away. We passed each other several times and I felt comfortable and let Peter lead for a few laps, staying right with him and pushing him all the way. Ted (who was putting in a rare appearance on Saturday at the Combe) was getting excited and trying to wave me on. I just kept giving him the 'thumbs up' as I felt this was 'my' race – and so it was. On the last lap and on the last bend I passed Peter and won by 0.2 seconds. This was a great race but Peter, I must say, was really not pleased! Chatterton was third, Cass fourth, Page fifth and my mate Tom Phillips a good sixth. Ted was ecstatic and treated us all to dinner that evening. Afterwards we stopped at Tom's house in Newbury for a while on our drive up to Mallory Park, where we arrived at 11pm.

There followed another great day, but the tables were really turned. I managed third in my heat. The final was led at first by Burgess and Ball, and Chatterton tried hard to catch them but overdid it and fell at the hairpin (he did, however, get the fastest lap). Peter and I overhauled the Burgess/Ball battle and fought long and hard for the win. This time it was Peter getting his revenge. I just could not keep with him and he beat me to the line. Ball on another Yamaha (a TDIC) was third, followed by Martin Carney and that man Tom Phillips on his Vic Camp Ducati.

Reg with the 250cc special at Mallory Park. The frame was a total duplex loop (like a Featherbed Norton).

Another Mallory Park photograph of the Broad Yamaha Special.

Let us just recap. It was just 30 April, just two months into the 1967 season and we had been to six meetings and competed in 12 races. This had resulted in five wins, one second, three thirds, one fourth and two sixth places (or, as they say now, nine podiums) from 12 races. What a fantastic start to the season – with big wins at Brands, Crystal Palace and Castle Combe we were really on a high and looking forward to the rest of the meetings.

Grand Prix entries

For two years now I had been trying to get entries in at least the European rounds of the Grand Prix, and this year we finally were accepted for the French Grand Prix at Clermont-Ferrand. The big problem was the various organisers said 'no previous Grand Prix history' but that they had to take 'the regular riders'. Something of a chicken and egg situation…

This race on 21 May 1967 came with the offer of 450 FF starting money (about £50 in those days) and went some way to cover the entry and travelling costs. With all the insurances, bike, engine, van, travel, etc. plus the cost of the cross-channel ferry (£25), it would just about do it.

It certainly was a long drive. We left at 6am on Thursday 18 May and caught the 9am boat from Dover, arriving in Calais at about 11am. We arrived in Paris at 3pm and were out of it by 4pm. Arriving in Clermont-Ferrand at 9.30pm we thought we were there but it took us another one and a half hours, following arrows, to get to the circuit at the top of a hill in the Massif Central. It was a great road circuit of nearly five miles length which had 51 bends and a lot of up and down hills, sheer drops to the left and cliff face to the right. Nearly 500ft of height difference. It would certainly be a challenge!

We changed the engine over to the practice one for Friday practice and managed four laps, which I enjoyed but decided to learn slowly, before the crankshaft broke. We put the race engine in for the Saturday practice and I did

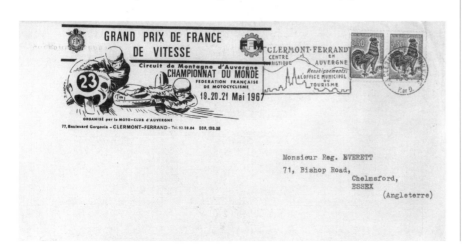

During 1967 Reg entered a couple of Continental Grand Prix races and was accepted for the French round at Clermont-Ferrand. Here is the original envelope carrying the pre-race regulations.

The Clermont-Ferrand paddock, with Ted's Yamaha in the foreground.

three more laps before the gearbox broke. I found out that because of these troubles the organisers deemed that I had not qualified with enough high-speed laps and therefore could not race.

We watched the 250 race on Sunday. Hailwood was fantastic on the Honda but problems slowed him and he was third behind Ivy and Read on the Works Yamahas, and then Woodman and Rosner next on the MZs. It was a fabulous race to watch. We all went into the town that night and had a great time, ending up in Ralph Bryans' caravan sampling the local wine!

Grand Prix de France programme cover.

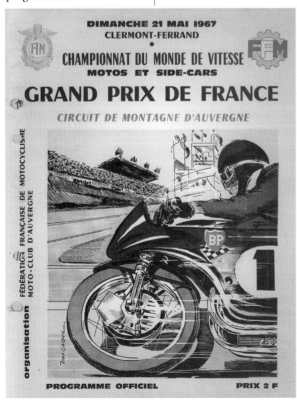

Doing Hailwood a favour

Mike Hailwood was surprised to see me there and commiserated with me about the problems. We had become well acquainted and he gave us the new 500 four-cylinder Honda works engine to deliver back to the UK where he was having a frame made.

The drive home was a sombre affair, although we stopped in Paris and did the touristy bit of going up the Eiffel Tower.

Ted, of course, was not happy with the outcome (he did not go as he had the shop to attend to and could not afford to be away for five days) and we did not get our 450FF, so it was a really expensive test of our Grand Prix skills and one which Ted was not anxious to repeat!

N°	PILOTES	MARQUES	PAYS
1	Mike HAILWOOD	Honda	Angleterre
2	Ralph BRYANS	Honda	Ireland
3	Phil READ	Yamaha	Angleterre
8	Bill IVY	Yamaha	Angleterre
9	Akiyasu MOTOHASHI	Yamaha	Japon
14	Derek WOODMAN	M. Z.	Angleterre
15	Heinz ROSNER	M. Z.	Allemagne
16	Renzo PASOLINI	Benelli	Italie
17	Silvio GRASSETTI	Benelli	Italie
18	Ginger MOLLOY	Bultaco	N^{lle}-Zélande
19	David-Alan SIMMONDS	Kawasaki	Angleterre
20	José-Maria BUSQUETS	Montesa	Espagne
22	Rég. EVERETT	Yamaha	Angleterre
23	Francesco VILLA	Montesa	Italie
24	Walter VILLA	Montesa	Italie
25	Giuseppe VISENZI	Bultaco	Italie
27	Gyula MARSOVSZKY	Bultaco	Suisse
28	Eric HINTON	Kawasaki	Australie
29	Rudolf THALHAMMER	Aermacchi	Autriche
30	Jan HUBERTS	Bultaco	Hollande
33	Horst SEIDL	Honda	Allemagne
34	Barry SMITH	Suzuki	Australie
36	Jack FINDLAY	Bultaco	Australie
38	Angel NIETO	Derbi	Espagne
39	Salvador CANELLAS	Derbi	Espagne
40	Daniel LHERAUD	Yamaha	France
41	Jacques ROCA	Bultaco	France
42	Alain BARBAROUX	Bultaco	France
43	Philippe CANOUI	Yamaha	France
44	Jean-François CHAFFIN	Bultaco	France
45	Jean AUREAL	Aermacchi	France
46	Jean-Claude COSTEUX	Aermacchi	France
47	André FARGEIX	Ducati	France
48	Alain MOSNIER	Ducati	France
50	Maurice MARTINE	Aermacchi	France
51	Marcel MOREL	Bultaco	France
52	Pierre VIURA	Ducati	France

CHAMPIONNAT DU MONDE   **GRAND PRIX DE FRANCE DE VITESSE**

250 cm3   19 - 20 - 21 MAI 1967   **18 TOURS**

LISTE DES ENGAGES : CATEGORIE 250 cm³   144 km 990

Grille de pointage permettant aux spectateurs de noter les passages des 10 premiers coureurs.

A page from the programme with an entry list including the names of Hailwood, Bryans, Read and Ivy, etc. Reg is number 22.

Freddy 'Oily' Wells

During our early break from racing in June, while the TT fortnight was in process, Ted and I were in his workshop one afternoon with Gerry Honeyman discussing the bikes, when in walked Freddy 'Oily' Wells. He was a local motorcycle dealer, rider and ex-RAF serviceman with a very large moustache – he was a real character.

We chatted generally about bikes, then without warning he said 'Well, tomorrow's Wednesday, the shops are closed and it's the Sidecar and 250cc race in the Isle of Man so why don't we go to watch it?'

Reg looking happy and relaxed before the flight in Freddy 'Oily' Wells' Piper Cherokee aircraft to the Isle of Man TT in June 1967. The flight itself, as the text reveals, proved something of a nightmare.

Well, at first we were joking but Fred was serious. He said 'I can fly, so I'll rent a plane and we'll all go!'

After some ums and ahs we all agreed, and without any further discussion we arranged to meet at Stapleford Tawney grass airfield (near Ongar) at 5am on the following day.

It was a bright, cold and dewy morning when we all blearily congregated at Stapleford. Fred had obviously been there for a while and he quickly ushered us into a blue-and-white Piper Cherokee low wing 2+2 seater aircraft (which he assured us he could fly), which was fully fuelled for the non-stop journey to Ronaldsway airport.

The flight

He taxied slowly to the end of the grass strip with some difficulty as the perspex cockpit windshield was thick with dew, which, he assured us, would go. On the rush down the strip Fred initially had his head outside the cockpit until it cleared, which it did eventually. Needless to say, a slight apprehension crept over the passengers!

Fred could obviously fly the plane. We went up steadily to a reasonable height and then he started circling the airfield. Ted was in front next to Fred in the right-hand seat and Gerry was behind Fred, with me next to him in the back. I remarked: 'Fred, why are we going round and round?' Fred replied 'I'm looking for the road! If I can find the Chigwell Road I can follow that to Woodford, then follow the North Circular round to Finchley, then Boreham Wood, and pick up the bottom end of the M1!'

We fell silent and gazed at each other thoughtfully, wondering if this was what flying was all about. We each thought of compasses and radios and things, but Fred wanted to 'follow the roads', and so our apprehension grew with the thought of things to come. Well, when we found the M1 it felt a little like 'hedgehopping' as we were flying so low it seemed that we had to go up every time we came to a bridge!

We began to feel more apprehensive when the M1 stopped just south of Birmingham. Fred then said 'The A5 has to be our guide'. It was not so easy to follow as the M1, and we lost it somewhere near Wrexham. Fred said 'Not to worry. If we keep going sort of west we will get to the coast then turn right and follow it to Liverpool. When we get there we can circle over the port and see which way the boats are going, then cross the sea to the Isle of Man.'

Well, this really made us nervous as now we were lost! Finally, we saw some water and Fred said 'It must be the Mersey'. So we flew up and down a bit, and for sure we were at Liverpool.

During our circuits Fred spotted an airfield and, to our relief, announced he would land and ask the way to the Isle of Man. We skimmed low across the Mersey and up a bit to land at Speke Airport Liverpool (now known as John Lennon Airport). While taxiing to the control tower we suddenly had cars with flashing lights escorting us. When we stopped and got out, it appeared that the people in the cars were very angry with us – they took Fred away! Later on we found out that we had landed in the wrong direction and other aircraft on approach had to be diverted. We also had not informed anyone we were landing!

Fred somehow talked his way out of the situation – as it appeared at one time that they were not going to allow us to continue. They were very helpful though and gave us a compass heading to follow once we had taken off, and instructions on how to use the radio, tuning us in to the Ronaldsway frequency. The control tower said they would contact Ronaldsway to ask them to look out for us on their radar and call us on the radio to guide us in when we approached. Ted decided that I should change places with him and sit in the front to assist Fred with the radio and compass, as he felt safer in the back!

Eventually we took off again and climbed to the 2,000ft level that Liverpool indicated we should fly at. I checked the compass, we attained the correct altitude, and I directed Fred on to the right heading.

It had become very hot in the cockpit and flying over the sea for some way got the nerves really jangling. It finally got to Gerry, who was then violently sick. The vomit went all over Fred in the front, on his head and down his back, with the rest on the floor where Gerry and Ted's feet were paddling in it. I fortunately escaped this, but the stench in the hot cockpit was awful!

The radio then crackled into life and focused our minds. 'This is Ronaldsway Airport.' it said. 'Are you the crazy B******s who have just left Liverpool? – Over.' I took the hand and headset, clicked the switch and meekly said 'Yes – Over.' The voice said 'Keep your radio on this frequency, keep at the same height and heading, we have you on radar. When I give instructions, please follow them accurately'.

We flew for a few more minutes. 'Ronaldsway,' said the radio, 'bear left until I tell you'. Fred made a gentle left turn. 'OK' said the voice. 'Continue on this new heading'. Fred and I checked the compass. 'OK' I replied and we continued for a few more minutes. To our surprise and relief, in front of us we could see an island! To say we were relieved was an understatement.

The radio continued to give us implicit instructions which we followed exactly, adjusting our heading and height as demanded. Fred actually handled the aircraft very well and, in this respect, the flight was smooth. Unbelievably, they talked us in right to the end of the runway and when we were taxiing in the radio said 'Welcome to Ronaldsway'. We all cheered and clapped and sheer relief overcame us when we finally climbed out.

Diamond Jubilee TT

Of course, this saga was far from over, but suffice it to say, we all (except for Fred who stayed behind for a while doing jobs on the aircraft) jumped into a taxi and went to Braddon Bridge spectators' area to watch the racing. Fred joined us soon after. We had a great day and the racing did not disappoint us as both the sidecar and the 250 races were well worth watching. This was the Diamond Jubilee year and they were celebrating the 60th anniversary of the first TT race.

The sidecar race was in the morning and was won by Siegfried Schauzu, from Klause Enders, Colin Seeley and Pip Harris, all on BMWs. My great local friend Derek Yorke was still going strong and was a fine 13th on his Triton at 76.65mph.

Mike Hailwood on his Honda sounded great as he went through Braddon Bridge's left-right curves and up the gearbox, accelerating out and away. He won easily at 103.07mph followed by Read, Bryans and Dave Simmonds on the Kawasaki. Bill Ivy retired.

We returned to the aircraft with some trepidation, but it was certain that Fred had learnt a lot on the outward trip and, to our relief, the radio was in full operation when we took off.

This time Speke Airport Liverpool helped us and when we were over the airfield they gave us a compass heading to follow to return to London.

We took off from Ronaldsway at 5.15pm precisely, and all went without any mishap. It was a day out none of us will ever forget for, oh, so many reasons!

But now back to our racing – little did we know that this was the start of our most depressing period of racing. I will not detail every misfortune, but will instead give more of a summary.

Reg with Mike Hailwood riding up to the start line for the 250cc event at the Brands Hatch 35th International Hutchinson 100, on 13 August 1967.

A most depressing period

During the period May to October – that is the remainder of the 1967 season including the French GP – we competed in 14 more race meetings, 29 races, but out of these we only had 10 finishes. We did win at Crystal Palace again on the 250 and a heat victory at Castle Combe, while two meetings at Mallory produced a third in the heat and fourth in the final, and the very last race of 1967 I managed a third in the heat and second in the final again of the 250 class. I had a great race at Snetterton, finally finishing fourth. Another fifth in a heat at Mallory and sixth at Crystal Palace on the 350 and a trip to Oulton Park achieved a fourth in a heat. The remaining results were from four meetings at Brands, obtaining five non-finishes and two non-starts. The remaining six races were also non-starters or non-finishers. Comparing these last 29 races to the first 12 of the year, I had only two wins, one second, two thirds, three fourths, one fifth, one sixth and 10 non-finish, plus nine non-starts!

It was a real disaster. Absolutely nothing would go right and, as much as Ted and I tried, literally two-thirds of our attempts came to nothing. He made a new frame for the

The Hutchinson 100 programme cover.

Following Martin Carney (Bultaco) in the 250cc race, Snetterton, on 15 October 1967. Reg finished fourth.

Reg, pictured in September 1967.

250, it was lighter and stronger with a new fairing. The fairing, we found to our cost, did not have enough cooling access (not to the cylinders but to the crankcase), and was a significant contributing factor in the unreliability, as it cooked the electrics.

We had all kinds of failures, many you could possibly attribute to the fact that the components were just getting old; although the parts looked OK they had reached the end of their useful life span.

In every race I was trying harder and harder, usually with little or no rewards. I was experiencing something that was beyond my control and I did not like it. Others were winning – their bikes getting quicker and quicker in some instances. I just could not keep up any more and became more and more disillusioned. By now

During the 250cc race at Snetterton on 15 October 1967, Reg (22) is seen here being chased by Martin Cavney (Bultaco, 9), Rex Butcher (Greeves, 40) and Dave Degens (Aermacchi, 12).

I knew any hope of a works ride had passed me by, but I had still achieved more in my career than I had every dreamt of.

What to do next?

What to do next? I still loved the sport but realised that I could not go on.

Many things were showing me it was the time I should start working for my living as the racing was costing a lot more than it was making and was keeping me poor. I could not afford new machinery and Ted had no intention of buying them, but he was willing to continue to try and improve the existing bikes. He had the idea of a full aluminium monocoque frame. I was just not convinced, so at the end of the racing season I informed him that I would not be riding for him or anyone else the following season. It was a huge decision and we were both very sad as we had been a team for four years and together had got to the top of our tree. We had shared terrific successes and abject failure and disappointment, but still had a common goal and a lot of camaraderie.

The press soon got hold of the news and the front-page headlines read 'Smart favourite to replace Everett', and rumours abounded. That, in fact, did not happen and Paul, though he tried out the bikes, decided not to go along the Team Broad path. But I had made up my mind. This was still not the end of my racing exploits, and would you believe because of my great early results I still finished runner-up in the British 250cc Championships for the third time in a row? Not that it had any rewards or accolades, as the ACU gave nothing for this. In fact, they did not even advise me of the results! No money, no presentation, no dinner, except for the winner who had a very small gold star (less than half-an-inch across) tie pin. Some reward from our governing body.

Chapter 11

The Final Stint

The winter of 1967–68 was much the same as the previous compulsory racing breaks as I busied myself with earning money and looked for a suitable long-term job. I was still freelance draughting but knew this would not be my final profession.

The problem began in February 1968 when regulations for races in March (Brands, Mallory, Snetterton) started dropping through my door, as well having the possibility of riding the Velocette for Geoff Dodkin with Tom Phillips in the 500-miler.

Now I really had begun to miss the racing, what was I going to do at weekends? I just had not realised the void it would leave, not just the racing, but the travelling, action, camaraderie and friendship now being sorely missed. Ronnie, my girlfriend, also experienced a different person in me and one who was not so easy to deal with – something just had to be done.

Vic Camp

Vic Camp (latterly Tom Phillip's sponsor) had a dealership near Ted's and had purchased all of Ted's remaining stock of Ducati bikes and parts. Vic contacted me one day saying: 'Reg, I know you have retired from normal short-circuit racing, but how about a couple of long-distance events, starting with the 500-miler at Brands on 12 May?' He also made me a monetary offer that sounded even more attractive. We met for further discussions and Vic, and his mechanic Bert Furness, were professional and very keen. Bert especially revelled in the task. Vic announced that my partner on the bike would be none other than Derek Minter, whom he had also lured out of retirement for this occasion! Wow, this would be something to look forward to and it certainly cured the blues for a while.

The bike we were due to ride was a 340cc Ducati Mark III (actually a converted Sebring tourer), even this appealed as we were to compete in the 500cc class, so we had our work cut out. Derek and I went to Brands one Wednesday for a try-out practice and agreed that it handled nicely, was easy to ride but was generally very slow! We were still happy to give it a go.

It was a two-day meeting and we practised on Saturday from 3pm to 5pm. All was fine and our lap times were as good as we could hope for. Bert was very optimistic and happy and declared that our times were virtually identical on his stopwatch, and as fast as most of the 500s – except the Nixon/Butler Triumph

Daytona, which was running very well. We also had a run around the track for final checks between 10 and 11am before the Le Mans-style start at midday and an estimated finishing time of 6.20pm.

Racing the Ducati in the 500-Miler

Derek did the running start and got away OK, circulating well in fourth place of the 500cc class, then rushing through the field relegating Tommy Robb on the 492cc Suzuki Cobra into third place. He went on to lead the class for about half an hour. Then a mysterious misfire set in and he came in. Bert was perplexed, he checked the sparks and fuel and I went out. It seemed OK for a while and then the misfire set in again. Pulling in, we drained the petrol and the carb to find there was water in the fuel. This was replaced after washing the tank and carb with clean fuel, and I continued to finish my stint. Changing again, Derek set to in his own inimitable aggressive style to try and catch up but suffered a nasty crash at Westfield corner after tangling with the Douglas Cash/Adrian Cooper, Suzuki Super Six.

Although billed as a '350 Mark III Ducati', the machine which Reg shared with Derek Minter in the Brands Hatch 500 Grand Prix endurance race on 12 May 1968 was, in fact, a converted Sebring touring model.

The 340cc Ducati was completing against full 500cc machines, and although it handled superbly, it was well down on power compared to the larger-engined bikes.

The programme cover for the 500-mile Grand Prix d'Endurance at Brands Hatch on Sunday 12 May 1968.

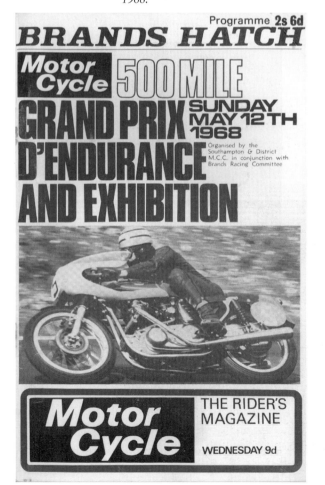

Managing to return to the pits on the bike, Derek decided he could not go on as he had hurt his leg. Bert and I got to it, straightened the superficial damage and, with about two hours of the race to go, I got back on it again. Our little bike was OK but it was the slowest of the 500s, going through the electronic timer down the back straight towards Hawthorn Hill Bend at only 94.7mph. Robb's Suzuki recorded 102.9mph and the fastest 500 was a Triumph at 104.7mph. This compared with the quickest bike – a 750 BSA of 114.7mph – and the quickest 250 at 97.3mph.

We hoped the race would finish within the remaining two hours as this was the longest I could stay on the bike and not get disqualified. We just made it and the race finished at 6.37pm after the winner – the Nixon/Butler 500 Triumph – had completed the 189 laps, winning the £500 prize money. In spite of all our problems, we managed 175 laps and were still fourth in the 500 class – I had ridden for four of our six and a half hours!

Our winnings included a £25 bonus for completing the most laps in the 500 class between the third and fourth hour and £10 for our fourth place. Derek and I split the £35 between us. This was definitely to be Derek Minter's last race.

The Ford Thames van used for transport down to Spain for the Barcelona 24-Hour Race on 6–7 July 1968.

Barcelona

It was not my last race, however, as Bert had talked Vic Camp into entering the Barcelona 24 Hour Race on 6 and 7 July at Monjuich Park – the most prestigious round of the European Coupe d'Endurance for motorcycling's governing body, the FIM. I enjoyed this type of racing and the 24-hour event had a huge following and reputation. Again, Vic made me a good offer but I was eager to compete. This time Charlie Sandby was to be my co-pilot, but as it happened he had a crash just before we were due to leave. Luckily we found a great replacement in Paul Smart. Paul and

Co-rider Paul Smart pictured upon the team's arrival in Barcelona. Paul stepped in as a last-minute replacement for Charlie Sanby.

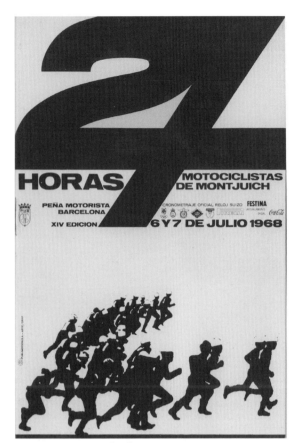

*Programme cover for the
1968 24 Horas.*

*A map of the Montjuich
Park, Barcelona, circuit.*

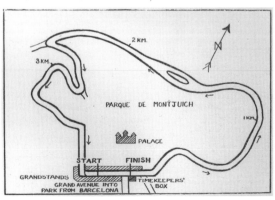

I had raced against each other on several occasions so we already knew our comparative skills. Paul was younger and up-and-coming – if he continued he would have a good chance of reaching the top. This was his first international and his first ride on a Ducati.

Bert and Paul travelled in Vic's Thames van with the bike, and Ronnie and I went in the other as we began our long journey ('race') to Barcelona. We just drove and drove and drove, taking 24 hours to the border where we were stopped because of paperwork for the bike – the Customs were very officious. After two hours they took our two cartons of 200 cigarettes and said 'OK you can go'!

Just the other side of Barcelona we found the camp site where we were staying until the circuit opened. Vic did not come to this race, much to his subsequent regret. His wife Rose did and she was in charge and organised many things but stayed in the centre of town in the Hotel Barcelona, which was a very different accommodation to ours.

Paul was not accustomed to foreign food, nor was he very good at Spanish. Mind you, neither we were for that matter! One evening in town, while having dinner, he ordered something that turned out to be a plate of fish bones! What a laugh we had. This was cut short as, on our return to my parked van, we found it had been broken into. It was ransacked but nothing except some loose change was missing – we assumed they were just looking for money. We told the police (Guarda Civil) but they just shrugged their shoulders and went on their way.

Arriving at the circuit

We actually went to the circuit early on Saturday morning, 6 July 1968, and were shown to our pit counter where we would spend the next 38 hours. We were number 38 to race, although we were shown as number 36 on the programme. This put our pit near to the rear of the 42 starters, out of which 24 were 250s, two were 750s, eight were 650s, two were 600s, four were 500s, one was a 360 and one a 350.

Practice in the morning and afternoon went well but the circuit was hard to learn and torturous with some punishing hairpin bends, so brakes and transmission (clutch) played an important part. We were soon lapping consistently at about 60mph average, without using full revs, in 2 mins 18 secs. We could, then, do 180 miles in three hours, which was consistent with a very full tank of petrol.

Our strategy was born. We did three hours on and three hours off (this three hours was the longest period in which one rider could stay on the bike, the minimum rest period was 30 minutes). Bert had rigged up a front number plate, which during the day covered the front lamp but at night could be moved back so the headlight could operate – at least it shone!

The Le Mans start

The Le Mans-type start was not until 8pm so we had already been up for 14 hours when the race was due to start. A huge crowd lined the 2.3-mile park road circuit and in the pit area and stands opposite were simply thousands of people – what an atmosphere! Spain, and Barcelona especially, celebrated this as their biggest sporting spectacle of the year and a true carnival mood engulfed us all.

As I was going to do the first stint I lined up with the other riders about 35 yards across the track from our machines. The crowd was cheering us all, what a noise – the riders were jittery waiting for the big Spanish national flag to get into position.

Riders line up for the Le Mans start; Reg is third from right.

The crowd hushed, the flag dropped and the dash began. There were riders everywhere! I ran as fast as I could and there was Bert behind the bike with the kickstarter poised. I jumped on, kicked and the engine immediately fired. I put it in gear and charged away.

There was pandemonium, bikes and riders so thick you could hardly move. Most people, it seemed, were intent on winning the race on the first lap, and there were many crashes especially at the first hairpin. Bodies and bikes were all over the track. I am certain I hit one poor guy as he went down. I had never seen anything like it. Fortunately, I survived and things calmed down and I was able to get into my rhythm. Paul and I did not think (a) the bike would finish or (b) that we had much of a chance against the full works teams of Spanish bikes like OSSA and Bultaco, who were the favourites and determined to win at all costs. We decided to go as quickly as we could, and if we were there at the end so be it! If not we would have an early shower and good dinner and enjoy the beach the following day!

In the first hour I covered 25 laps in 18th position, so I was roughly on schedule and the bike was going like clockwork. In the second hour I made 26 laps and was in 12th position. Then after 10pm it started getting dark. The circuit was unlit, the front number plate device kept pushing back during the daylight because of the small screen above it, but would you believe in the dark at night it kept suddenly dropping over the front light – something had to be done about it. My third hour was nearing its close and I kept looking for my pit board with 'In' on it – then I knew they would be ready and waiting to refuel and change. Not being able to see it in the dark I just had to go in, and as the clock ticked to 11pm I pulled up by my pit, much to the relief of all who had been going mad and waving in vain.

Reg during the early stages of the 24-hour marathon.

The change-over

The change-over went well, and I said to Paul as he headed off 'good luck, go for it!' My first three hours were over and I could have a well-earned rest. We had done 75 laps, were in 12th place overall and second in the 250 against the flying Roy Bisby/Harry Rayner Suzuki Super Six and just in front of the three Works OSSAs. Who was leading? Well, the 360cc Works Bultaco (a thinly disguised GP racer) was already three laps in front having completed 86 laps – 11 more than us!

Just 21 hours left to go – I had something to eat and drink, the atmosphere was electric – there was no chance to sleep, I just tried to relax, but I found this hard as mentally I was out there with my teammate!

Paul was going really well and in his first hour did 26 laps, pulling up to 11th place. Hour five – 25 laps, as was hour six, so 76 laps in the second stint and 11th place overall, a total of 151 laps. But we were now the third-placed 250 behind one of the Works OSSAs whom Paul had been scrapping with.

The Suzuki had done 155 laps and was still going well but that 360 Bultaco was now 12 laps in the lead and on 172 laps. At 1am I took over again with still 19 hours left. It is hard to describe just how long a 24-hour race is, but we had virtually completed a Brands 500-miler and still had three-quarters of the race to go!

Night riding

My night hours went well, 2am and 26 more laps, 3am and 27 more laps, time up at 4am and another 24 laps (coming in well on time this time), 75 again in all, 228 in total. Nine hours gone and we were now in eighth place overall – still the third

Paul on the Vic Camp Ducati 250cc Mark III during the night in Barcelona.

250, Rayner/Bisby having completed 231 laps. That Bultaco 360 was now 19 laps in the lead on 259 laps.

At 5am Paul took over again for our last session in the dark. I sat down and had another well-earned rest. I also made use of a free facility provided by the organisers of seeing the doctor and having a massage. You tend to get fixed in position after three hours in a racing crouch. Hands had to be looked after too as many competitors were suffering from blisters.

Little did we know (until he came in after his three-hour session, completing the most laps in that three hours for our whole race – 28, 27, 27 i.e. a total of 82) that Paul had actually crashed in the dark. He slid off on one of the hairpins, braking to avoid another fallen rider. There was little damage to show for this apart from a missing piece of front mudguard, so we refuelled and were on our way.

Now it was 8am on Sunday with just 12 hours gone. We were only halfway through the race, but it seemed like forever.

Other things had happened during Paul's ride – the Bisbey/Rayner Suzuki had struck gearbox trouble and was dropping back fast. We were second in the 250s now on the same circuit as the OSSA at 310 laps and Bisby/Rayner one behind. It was still very close after 12 hours of racing and we had moved up to sixth overall as the Goddard/Butcher 650 Dresda Triton and the Green/Guy 500 Triumph had struck trouble and dropped down the field to ninth and 10th respectively. That Canellas/Rocamora 360 Bultaco was still flying in front on 345 laps from Peck/Andrew (321 laps) on their 441cc BSA Victor, who were also doing a great job.

My three-hour ride was enjoyable and the laps were just being reeled off. I completed 80 laps in my session which finished at 11am. During this time disaster struck the Bultaco when it crashed heavily and broke its frame. Somehow (possibly across country) it got back to the pits and was welded up and sent on its way again. It had lost its 24-lap lead and the Peck/Andrew BSA in front was in the lead but on the same lap.

Moving up the field

We moved up and were leading the OSSA by one lap at 390 laps and into fifth place overall, just 12 behind the leaders. This was just beyond our wildest dreams, but still with nine hours to go it was far too early to be thinking of a result, though our little bike was just running perfectly.

Back into the fray with Paul aboard for our last scheduled three-hour ride. We had decided that if we were still going at 18 hours we would go down to two-hour sessions as obviously rider fatigue would be setting in and concentration was at a premium (still remembering that in the British 500-mile race, two hours is the maximum a rider can do).

Paul had one hell of a scrap with that OSSA during this time and we dropped from fifth to sixth, then back up to fourth by the end of the session. The Squalo Nestor/Sala OSSA was now five laps behind due to a tangling together with Paul, who came off best and the OSSA went to ground (but somehow soon reappeared). The Julia/Maner OSSA now was the second 250 and was four laps behind. The Bisby/Rayner Suzuki was still going in seventh overall. Also, the Peck/Andrew BSA was dropped by Andrew on a slow corner and he had to push it back to the pits as it would not restart. There they had to replace a capacitor, coil and a bent pushrod. The delay cost them 65 minutes and dropped them down to ninth place. The Bultaco still led by seven laps on 485 laps from the Juanjo/Fargas 750cc Norton, the Buckmaster/Kinsella 650cc Triumph on 477 laps and ourselves at 468.

The 18-hour distance

I can tell you, that after 18 hours everyone was nervous. Bert was starting to fret. It had gone so well up to now, would it continue? His reputation as a fantastic and serious machine preparer was on the line!

Rose Camp had been a brick, truly supporting us. Ronnie was just great too and pandered to the riders' needs. Paul and I were now thinking that we could do this, and again were eager to get going. The track was dry and it was warm – it was going to be us and the OSSAs, who seemed to have so many bikes and riders that when a mishap befell them they were instantly on the case again.

You could cut the atmosphere with a knife – the tension was so great. No sleep; little food. It is difficult to explain how we felt – we were all on autopilot.

In the 19th hour the Bultaco finally expired – it crashed again. The front wheel was changed and they got back in the lead – then the crankpin sheared. Their race

Heading towards victory in the 250cc class and third overall, Reg pushes the little Ducati on to a magnificent result.

was over, there was no going back. This promoted us up to third overall but after my two hours were up the OSSA was only a lap behind and going strong. In fact, now we were at 518 laps and the three other OSSAs were on 517, 514 and 504 laps, with the Suzuki just astern on 499. The OSSA camp had plenty of bikes and riders to just keep going.

Paul was young, eager for the scrap and in a fighting mood, so with just four hours to go he remounted to get back to the fray. His point was not lost and he did 27 laps in the next hour and 24 to finish off his ride, our lead went up to three laps on hour 21 but back down to one lap at the end on 569 and 568 respectively – and now with only two, yes two, hours to run. The crowd were jumping. Still the three OSSAs were chasing the lone Ducati with 'English' aboard – it would be do or die!

A change of tactics

For the last two hours we changed tactics. I rode next and the final hour was Paul's. During the changeover Paul shouted to me 'Watch the front brake, it doesn't work!' Bert heard and immediately got to work only to find that all the adjustment had gone and the shoes were just plain worn out. No time to change the wheel – we just had to live with it; although the hairpin bends were a challenge. Paul had been using the gearbox and back brake and I had to do the same. We just wanted to get on with it!

The engine and the rest of the bike were still behaving but it was exciting, racing the OSSAs and going into those bends without a front brake.

At the end of my hour I had completed 27 laps – only one below the very best of 28 both of us had achieved for the whole race – and still leading the OSSA, but we were on the same lap and only led the other by four laps. We were third overall with 596 laps, and the Norton was leading with 610 over the Triumph's 606. No chance of catching them!

Our race was on and Paul was up for it. He was so determined and aggressive, and with no front brake we feared disaster at any moment. That last hour was certainly the longest, most nail-biting hour in our lives and the tension was electric.

On every lap we cranked our necks out to see him appear and then looked for the OSSA Number 29 to appear. It closed on Paul, we could see he then threw caution to the wind and slowly pulled away. Thirty minutes to go, then 20, then 10! The countdown had begun and the crowd was in a frenzy, we were all wrecks! Shouting, jibbering, crying, ifs, buts, and maybes – there was every emotion under the sun!

The chequered flag drops at last

The chequered flag dropped at exactly 8pm. We had won the 250 battle and finished third overall in the world's most gruelling, demanding motorcycle race.

Reg with the trophies which were awarded by the organisers of the Barcelona 24 Horas.

We were ecstatic – crying, laughing, hugging, patting each other, this was such an achievement for Bert, Rose, Vic, Ronnie, Paul and I. We had all done our share and together reaped the rewards. The crowds, the photos, the accolades were all soaked up! Suddenly we were not tired any more, we just wanted to celebrate and dance and sing.

All thought of going back to the campsite was abandoned and after phoning Vic, who was just over the moon, Rose booked us all into the Hotel Barcelona – where sunken marble baths and champagne awaited us riders (still in our leathers) when we arrived.

What a celebration

What a celebration! What a night! It was a culmination for me of nine years of racing. This was truly a fitting end to my career and I was never to race in anger again.

The Prize Giving, in a sort of 'Palace', was a truly magnificent, grand affair and we each were given two fantastic trophies, one for the first 250 and one for third overall. One of each of these was presented to Bert, which was our thanks for a magnificent job well done. We won thousands and thousands of pesetas – how much I do not know, but adding that to our start money and bonuses at the 12-18-24-hour marks of £85 from Vic it all amounted to a nice little earner in those far off days.

We stayed in the hotel for two nights before Rose, Bert and Paul had to leave to return to the UK.

Ronnie and I decided it was holiday time and spent two glorious weeks in the sun, just eating, drinking, relaxing and enjoying ourselves. I even learnt to scuba dive before reality set in (and we had spent all the prize money!) and we had to go home to continue the rest of our lives together.

Paul Smart back in Britain with the 650cc Curtis Domiracer, just one of the many machines he rode in a career which took in the 1960s and 1970s.

Chapter 12

After Racing

Immediately after my retirement from racing it was difficult and, as I have commented earlier, I just did not know what to do with myself. I actually rejoined Marconi in a specialist drawing office as a mechanical designer. I even went to Cyprus on a job for them.

I liked travelling – it had got into my bones, so going every day to the same office did not suit me one little bit. One day I bumped into an old friend, Keith Lodge, who had worked on a milling machine in Marconi Baddow workshop. We were good friends and he had followed my racing.

A new career

Keith had left and joined a Swedish company called Atlas Copco, who sold compressors. He was successful there but went on to become a sales manager of a distributor of pneumatic equipment in Hornchurch. While looking for a salesman for this venture, he approached me, saying 'You like travelling, you know engines, you are an engineer and can talk to anyone – you'll be ideal! I can also give you a car to travel in [a new Ford Escort] and match your existing salary.'

I discussed it with Ronnie and we both agreed that I had nothing to lose. So off I went selling compressors, air tools, full installations and automating machinery by use of compressed air.

On 26 January 1970 Ronnie (Scott) and I got married in Chelmsford and moved into a small house we had purchased.

One day Vic Camp phoned me and said 'Reg, how about becoming an instructor at my new racing school at Brands Hatch?' This only entailed Wednesday afternoons so I readily agreed, and in the summer I took my work's Ford Escort to Brands and helped Vic. This entailed showing the pupils the lines round Brands with a few laps in the car.

Then – on the 250 Ducatis that Bert had prepared – the six or so pupils would follow me (on another Ducati) around for a few laps to get the hang of things before I pulled off to let them go it alone. It was really good for them and, with the classroom instruction, in one afternoon they achieved and learnt the rudiments of road racing. It was a far cry from how I had begun a decade earlier!

Left to right: Charles Mortimer Senior, Tom Kirby and Vic Camp. Charles Mortimer had begun the racing school in the mid-1960s (using Greeves Silverstones). It was later taken over by Vic, who was subsequently joined by Tom.

Above: A Kirby/Camp Racing School advertisement from 1970.

Far left: Kirby/Camp Racing School machines (Ducati 250 Mark IIIs); Brands Hatch, spring 1970.

I really enjoyed this but the few laps I did in my company's Ford Escort was certainly not good for the tyres and after four short sessions at Brands they were worn out!

We had sales meetings on Friday afternoons and for the next one I arrived early, as had another salesman in a similar car. What an opportunity! Without hesitation I set about changing my wheels for his unworn tyres, and my problem went away!

A great laugh

Four weeks later the same problem occurred and this time I decided to go to the works director – a very miserly man who counted the coffee money in piles on his desk – and tell him about my tyres! I said I was sorry but after only 5,000 miles in the new car the tyres had worn out. I just did not understand it. To my utter amazement he said it did not surprise him and that I was lucky, as one of the other salesman's tyres had lasted only 3,500 miles! The tyre company said that we must have had a faulty batch so we were to go and change them. Vic and I laughed and laughed over this and I really enjoyed the experience of the Vic Camp Racing School.

Although I was doing well at sales, I thought I really should work with a manufacturer of compressors. An advertisement appeared in the local paper with the UK arm of a large American compressor company, Joy Sullivan, who also made coal -mining machinery. I applied and attended an interview in Chesterfield, Derbyshire, where a grand elderly gentleman interviewed me. One of his statements was: 'If you get this job you will travel the world!' Of course, I took this statement as a 'come-on', but it intrigued me nonettheless.

In due course I had a letter informing me that the company wanted to employ me at a salary of £2,000 p.a., which was £500 p.a. more than I was getting – plus I would get a company Ford Cortina!

Scott arrives

At the same time dear Ronnie had given birth to our son Scott (15 August 1970) who was our pride and joy, and the extra income came in useful. Ronnie was great

Reg's second wife Ronnie and baby Scott in Spain, 1972.

and continued working from home in her chosen profession as a technical handbook illustrator – a job she loved and was exceedingly good at.

I started with Joy as sales engineer, south-east England. Driving around all day, visiting factories and talking to engineers really appealed to me and I did it with enjoyment.

As the years went by I gained promotion to area manager, then on to the major engineering consultants in London. Finally I became UK sales manager with seven area managers to look after, and obviously I had to travel nationwide.

Then, things took a turn. The American parent company invited their worldwide sales managers to a huge training seminar in Bruge, Belgium. Going there made me realise how large our company was as it employed 14,000 people in

Reg pictured at Brands Hatch in 1975, as an instructor for the racing school. The machine is a 350cc Desmo Ducati.

American International Sales, Joy Manufacturing Corporation, Pittsburgh, 1976. Reg is pictured far left, front row.

total and had a turnover of approximately 900 million US dollars. Some organisation! The people I met were mainly Europeans, Americans or Canadians, plus others from the Far East and Middle East. I had already travelled many times to Europe on jobs for the engineering consultants in London and even to Japan on compressor projects, so I fitted in readily.

Imagine my surprise, though, when after this meeting in 1976 I had a letter from the Joy Pittsburgh head office offering me the European sales manager's position, which I readily accepted. This entailed a lot of travelling and I was soon jetting all over Europe – what had that gentleman said?!

As the years passed I was given more and more responsibility and travelled more and more – to the Middle East, Far East, Africa and the Eastern Bloc countries – my feet rarely touched the ground.

Rebuilding a Gold Star

Obviously this was my 'business time', but I had not lost touch completely with motorcycling. When at home I was rebuilding a 1957 BSA 500 Clubman Gold Star which I had purchased as a 'Bitsa' and by 1984 it was up and running. That same year I bought (with some pension money that Joy had released) a 1970 series II fixed-head E-Type Coupe for my wife's 40th birthday – a present she never used! I wonder why?

Another big change came about in 1986 and rumours abounded within the Joy empire about a takeover. I started thinking about my position. With my worldwide experience and knowledge I deemed I could become an independent consultant offering my services to all compressor companies. A guy called Gerd Cromm, with

Back with motorcycles. A 1986 photograph of the 1957 BSA DBD34 Gold Star, with Reg, Barry Flegg and Len Dixon.

whom I had done business in Germany before, was now shareholder in a company and immediately asked me to build up his export business. I agreed and parted company with Joy, whom I had been with for 17 years but was still on very good terms with. Not long afterwards Joy was taken over and virtually disbanded through asset stripping and, apart from some divisions, the company disappeared from existence.

At first my new job took a lot of effort and travel, I was averaging 150 flights per year worldwide, but I still found time to 'play with motorcycles'.

Next I obtained a 1963 31CSR AJS to rebuild, then a 1954 G3LS Matchless.

The Greeves Prototype resurfaces

Then, unbelievably, when I returned from a trip Ronnie told me that a guy had turned up on the doorstep in motorcycle gear and said 'I am looking for Reg Everett'.

He told Ronnie that he thought he had my Greeves Prototype racer and he wanted me to authenticate it. Without hesitation I called him – his name was Geoff Deakes from Romford and he said he bought the machine from Lawrence Casey before stripping it and giving it away in the late 1960s.

The man whom he had given it to had contacted him quite recently and said 'You know those bike bits you gave me? Do you want them back?' He eagerly accepted them, started a rebuild and came looking for me. I arranged a date and visited him at his home in Romford. As soon as I saw the bike I knew it truly was my old Greeves. The bracket holding the float chamber was the one I had made all those years ago and the Gold Star carburettor was still in place – a miracle. Of course I wanted to buy

Reunited with his 1962 Greeves Special (but now with a RAS Silverstone tank), circa early 1990s.

it there and then, but he said 'no, he wanted to ride it', but I was determined to have it. I found a genuine Silverstone RBS which was all there but needed a bit of TLC and was more suitable for him to ride. I approached him and he readily agreed to a swap! I had my Greeves back, which was a super feeling and one I could not believe.

Eric Miller, a well-known local motorcycle sidecar trials rider and restorer, was a good friend and helped significantly in the rebuild too – back to the total original from my front room in Basildon in 1961. This was most mind boggling and when we started it – well, all the years were blown away and the emotion came rushing back. The compressor business had been good, but the racing was a total way of life and the thrill was still there!

Before I paraded the Greeves I had been invited to go to Mallory Park for the VMCC Easter meeting. This was in 1995 and I was offered the chance to parade the 250cc Villiers that Peter Inchley had ridden to win the Championship all those years ago and which was now owned by Andy Molnar (of reproduction Manx Norton fame). I had not been on a racing bike since 1968 except for the Vic Camp school so I hesitated for a while then said 'yes' and jumped at the chance. I was still very busy with work and was now helping a Belgian company to re-establish itself (after going downhill) back into a worldwide force.

Going back to Mallory

Going back to Mallory was a trip back in time, when I got there little seemed to have changed. The bike looked fine and I got into my leathers – the years were going away, it was like being in a time warp.

Old friends reappeared: Derek Minter, Terry Grotefeld, Harry Rayner, Dick Standing, it was just marvellous. I am home, I thought.

At Mallory Park for the Post TT meeting 1995, Reg meets up with some old friends, including Harry Rayner (Norton, 17).

Andy said 'Are you OK?' as he stood with the bike in the warming-up area. I got on and said 'I don't know. It's 27 years since I sat on a racing bike at a race meeting – I just don't know what will happen or even if I can do it!' It was pouring with rain – just how would I feel?

They flagged us onto the circuit and I did a steady lap, but I felt great – no – fantastic, and I got my head down. Going round Gerrards in the wet was just like it felt before, and I found I could crank it over still – these new tyres were perfect! Three laps gone and it was just like I had never been away. Then Minter on a 500 Norton came past! No way! I said to myself 'Get stuck in!' and the race was on…

The crowd and, especially, Andy Molnar, loved it – but too soon it was all over back to the pits. Andy was waiting and smiling. I also had a grin all over my face. Dear Ronnie was beside herself and hit me on the head. 'You B******!' she said 'you are mad!'

Taking the leathers off and then going to have a sandwich with the other lads was like all our yesterdays at once and the whole experience was unforgettable.

Another miracle

I paraded the Greeves a couple of times with just as much fun, then my friend Joe Iszard phoned and said he had found a Yamaha TD1A in a shed. We went and looked at it, and another miracle occurred, it was Ted's machine! We were aghast – it had lain there since 1969 and was in a sorry state. Needless to say I bought this as well, and again Eric helped rebuild it. We got it running and it sounded just like it did before – again tears were in my eyes.

Shortly after this things started going wrong as I did not feel too good and Ronnie insisted I went to the doctor. After tests it was found I had a blood problem

Parading the Greeves Special at a very wet Brands Hatch, 1999.

The original Broad Yamaha TD1 in Reg's Gallywood, Chelmsford, workshop, 26 May 2005. The machine had been rebuilt by Eric 'Dusty' Miller.

Reg photographed in 2004, at the 50th anniversary of Snetterton in September that year. Left to right are Joe Iszard, Reg and sidecar racer Derek Yorke.

Above: Another 'old boys' picture, this time with former sponsor Geoff Dodkins, of Velocette fame.

Above right: With the restored Yamaha at Mallory Park are Reg, Peter Williams and Yamaha enthusiast Richard Tracey.

The 1957 Gilera 175 purchased by Reg from Cheffins auction, July 2007. News of this machine had come via Mick Walker.

Another gathering of old racing pals, left to right: Rob Foster, Reg, Joe Iszard and Dick Standing.

which fortunately was treatable, but after having the treatment things really went wrong. A subsequent later test revealed an entirely different problem.

During the following months and years things really deteriorated and did not look good, some of the times were very serious. This led me to the decision to get rid of the bikes and the E-type. The road bikes went to local lads but the Greeves was sold to the National Motorcycle Museum owned by Roy Richards in Birmingham, adjacent to the NEC, so its future is secure and all can see it. What I did keep was my Yamaha as I just could not part with it.

Now, after four years of further treatment, I am beginning to live again.

A picture taken in August 2008 during the 'Four Stroke' meeting in Kent. Rear row, left to right: Trevor Barnes, Joe Dunphy, Grant Gibson, Paul Smart. Front row: Reg and Rex Butcher, old adversaries and great friends.

A happy Reg – probably after getting news that From Rocker to Racer was to be published.

My illness prompted this book and gave me an aim with something to do as I could do little else. Doctors, nurses and friends have been fantastic and for sure I would not have survived without their encouragement and expertise.

Now I feel honoured to have survived, not only the racing (where so many of my friends did not, whether on or off the track) but my illness, where again other close friends did not.

So this book is to all of them with my heartfelt thanks of having had the honour to share my life with you. Many thanks also go to my family and friends, who have had to put up with so much from me over my lifetime. Thanks for everything.

Reg Everett – Road Racing Results

Date	Circuit	Machine	Result
1960			
17 April	Snetterton	500 Gold Star	22nd
6 June	Brands Hatch	500 Gold Star	9th
24 July	Snetterton	500 Gold Star	18th
1 August	Crystal Palace	500 Gold Star	?
20 August	Silverstone	500 Gold Star	5th
21 August	Brands Hatch	500 Gold Star	7th
4 September	Snetterton	500 Gold Star	Crashed
8 October	Silverstone	500 Gold Star	23rd
1961			
2 April	Snetterton	500 Gold Star	15th
2 April	Snetterton	500 Gold Star	DNF
20 May	Silverstone (1000km)	250 Greeves (Twin)	DNF
22 May	Brands Hatch	500 Gold Star	11th
25 June	Brands Hatch	250 Greeves (Twin)	5th
25 June	Brands Hatch	250 Greeves (Twin)	8th
9 July	Brands Hatch	500 Gold Star	6th
30 July	Snetterton	250 Greeves (Twin)	16th
30 July	Snetterton	500 Gold Star	18th
7 August	Crystal Palace	500 Gold Star	7th
3 September	Snetterton	500 Gold Star	Crashed
17 September	Brands Hatch	500 Gold Star	6th
30 September	Silverstone	500 Gold Star	?
1962			
1 April	Brands Hatch	250 Greeves (P)	1st
1 April	Brands Hatch	250 Greeves (P)	2nd
22 April	Snetterton	250 Honda (Twin)	6th
23 April	Crystal Palace	250 Greeves (P)	4th

23 April	Crystal Palace	250 Greeves (P)	9th
28 April	Snetterton	250 Greeves (P)	2nd
11 June	Thruxton	250 Greeves (P)	1st
11 June	Thruxton	250 Greeves (P)	12th
17 June	Snetterton	250 Greeves (P)	3rd
23 June	Thruxton (500M)	250 Greeves (Twin)	DNF
8 July	Brands Hatch	250 Greeves (P)	7th
21 July	Snetterton	250 Greeves (P)	6th
21 July	Snetterton	250 Greeves (P)	3rd
29 July	Snetterton	250 Honda	7th
6 August	Crystal Palace	250 Greeves (P)	10th
19 August	Brands Hatch	250 Greeves (P)	6th
25 August	Snetterton	250 Greeves (P)	1st
25 August	Snetterton	250 Greeves (P)	1st
10 October	Snetterton	250 Greeves (P)	4th
14 October	Brands Hatch	250 Greeves (P)	?

1963

23 March	Snetterton	250 Greeves (SB)	DNF
30 March	Mallory Park	250 Greeves (SB)	DNF
6 April	Silverstone	250 Greeves (SB)	11th
12 April	Brands Hatch	250 Greeves (SB)	2nd
14 April	Snetterton	250 Greeves (SB)	DNF
15 April	Crystal Palace	250 Greeves (SB)	4th
15 April	Crystal Palace	250 Greeves (SB)	6th
27 April	Mallory Park	250 Greeves (SB)	6th
27 April	Mallory Park	250 Greeves (SB)	Crashed
11 May	Aberdare Park	250 Greeves (W)	4th
11 May	Aberdare Park	250 Greeves (W)	12th
12 May	Brands Hatch	250 Greeves (W)	9th
3 June	Brands Hatch	250 Greeves (W)	4th
10 June	Isle of Man TT	250 Greeves (W)	DNF
14 July	Brands Hatch	250 Greeves (W)	5th
28 July	Snetterton	350 Gold Star	24th
17 August	Silverstone	250 Greeves (W)	1st

24 August	Aberdare Park	250 Greeves (W)	3rd
24 August	Aberdare Park	250 Greeves (W)	DNF
25 August	Brands Hatch	250 Greeves (W)	DNF
8 September	Snetterton	250 Greeves (W)	DNS
22 September	Brands Hatch	250 Greeves (W)	5th
22 September	Brands Hatch	50 Kreidler (W)	DNF
6 October	Snetterton	250 Greeves (W)	2nd
12 October	Snetterton (250M Enduro)	50 Kreidler (W)	DNF
13 October	Brands Hatch	250 Greeves (W)	Crashed
13 October	Brands Hatch	50 Kreidler (W)	DNS
20 October	Duxford Sprint	250 Greeves (W)	3rd

1964

10 May	Snetterton	250 Yamaha	DNF
18 May	Brands Hatch	250 Yamaha	DNF
8 June	Isle of Man TT	250 Greeves	8th
26 July	Snetterton	250 Yamaha	1st
16 August	Brands Hatch	250 Yamaha	2nd
22 August	Aberdare Park	250 Yamaha	2nd crashed
22 August	Aberdare Park	250 Yamaha	DNF
6 September	Snetterton	250 Yamaha	2nd
20 September	Brands Hatch	250 Yamaha	7th
27 September	Mallory Park	250 Yamaha	DNF
11 October	Brands Hatch	250 Yamaha	5th
11 October	Brands Hatch	350 Norton	17th

1965

7 March	Mallory Park	250 Yamaha	3rd
7 March	Mallory Park	250 Yamaha	5th
7 March	Mallory Park	350 Yamaha	DNF
21 March	Brands Hatch	250 Yamaha	DNS
21 March	Brands Hatch	350 Yamaha	DNF
28 March	Snetterton	250 Yamaha	DNF
16 April	Brands Hatch	250 Yamaha	8th crashed
19 April	Crystal Palace	250 Yamaha	1st

19 April	Crystal Palace	250 Yamaha	1st
19 April	Crystal Palace	350 Yamaha	2nd
19 April	Crystal Palace	350 Yamaha	2nd
9 May	Brands Hatch	250 Yamaha	DNS
9 May	Brands Hatch	350 Yamaha	Crashed
16 May	Snetterton	250 Yamaha	1st
23 May	Mallory Park	250 Yamaha	1st
23 May	Mallory Park	250 Yamaha	2nd
23 May	Mallory Park	350 Yamaha	8th
23 May	Mallory Park	350 Yamaha	DNS
20 June	Mallory Park	250 Yamaha	DNS
27 June	Brands Hatch	250 Yamaha	1st
27 June	Brands Hatch	250 Yamaha	2nd relay
25 July	Snetterton	250 Yamaha	DNS
14 August	Silverstone	250 Cotton	DNF
15 August	Brands Hatch	250 Yamaha	DNF
15 August	Brands Hatch	350 Yamaha	12th
22 August	Mallory Park	250 Yamaha	DNS
30 August	Crystal Palace	250 Yamaha	1st
4 September	Castle Combe	250 Yamaha	DNF
4 September	Castle Combe	350 Yamaha	5th
4 September	Castle Combe	350 Yamaha	DNS
5 September	Snetterton	250 Yamaha	5th
19 September	Brands Hatch	250 Yamaha	1st
26 September	Mallory Park	250 Yamaha	DNS
3 October	Oulton Park	250 Yamaha	3rd
3 October	Oulton Park	250 Yamaha	3rd
10 October	Brands Hatch	250 Yamaha (wks)	DNF
31 October	Mallory Park	250 Yamaha	2nd
31 October	Mallory Park	250 Yamaha	6th

1966

6 March	Mallory Park	250 Yamaha	4th
6 March	Mallory Park	250 Yamaha	DNF
6 March	Mallory Park	350 Yamaha	2nd

6 March	Mallory Park	350 Yamaha	DNF
13 March	Brands Hatch	250 Yamaha	Crashed
13 March	Brands Hatch	350 Yamaha	DNS
20 March	Snetterton	250 Yamaha	DNS
8 April	Brands Hatch	250 Yamaha	DNF
11 April	Crystal Palace	250 Yamaha	1st
11 April	Crystal Palace	250 Yamaha	3rd
11 April	Crystal Palace	350 Yamaha	7th
11 April	Crystal Palace	350 Yamaha	DNS
1 May	Brands Hatch	250 Yamaha	3rd
1 May	Brands Hatch	350 Yamaha	12th
22 May	Mallory Park	250 Yamaha	1st
22 May	Mallory Park	250 Yamaha	2nd
22 May	Mallory Park	350 Yamaha	7th
22 May	Mallory Park	350 Yamaha	7th
29 May	Snetterton	250 Yamaha	Crashed
29 May	Snetterton	350 Yamaha	5th
29 May	Snetterton	350 Yamaha	10th
30 May	Brands Hatch	250 Yamaha	DNF
30 May	Brands Hatch	350 Yamaha	11th
19 June	Mallory Park	250 Yamaha	3rd
19 June	Mallory Park	250 Yamaha	DNF
19 June	Mallory Park	350 Yamaha	14th
19 June	Mallory Park	250 Yamaha	DNS
26 June	Brands Hatch (500M)	250 Cotton	1st
9 July	Castle Combe	250 Yamaha	2nd
9 July	Castle Combe	250 Yamaha	1st
9 July	Castle Combe	350 Yamaha	13th
9 July	Castle Combe	350 Yamaha	4th
7 August	Cadwell Park	250 Yamaha	9th
7 August	Cadwell Park	250 Yamaha	5th
14 August	Brands Hatch	250 Yamaha	DNF
14 August	Brands Hatch	350 Yamaha	DNF
20 August	Croft	250 Yamaha	1st
20 August	Croft	250 Yamaha	3rd

20 August	Croft	250 Yamaha	2nd
20 August	Croft	350 Yamaha	1st
20 August	Croft	350 Yamaha	1st
21 August	Mallory Park	250 Yamaha	4th
21 August	Mallory Park	350 Yamaha	DNF
29 August	Crystal Palace	250 Yamaha	1st
29 August	Crystal Palace	350 Yamaha	4th
10 September	Castle Combe	250 Yamaha	3rd
10 September	Castle Combe	250 Yamaha	2nd
10 September	Castle Combe	350 Yamaha	1st
10 September	Castle Combe	350 Yamaha	2nd
17 September	Croft	250 Yamaha	1st
17 September	Croft	250 Yamaha	2nd
17 September	Croft	350 Yamaha	4th
25 September	Mallory Park	250 Yamaha	4th
25 September	Mallory Park	250 Yamaha	DNF
25 September	Mallory Park	350 Yamaha	10th
25 September	Mallory Park	350 Yamaha	18th
9 October	Brands Hatch	250 Yamaha	DNS
23 October	Snetterton	250 Yamaha	1st
23 October	Snetterton	350 Yamaha	DNS
30 October	Mallory Park	250 Yamaha	1st
30 October	Mallory Park	250 Yamaha	10th
30 October	Mallory Park	350 Yamaha	8th
30 October	Mallory Park	350 Yamaha	18th

1967

5 March	Mallory Park	250 Yamaha	3rd
5 March	Mallory Park	250 Yamaha	6th
24 March	Brands Hatch	250 Yamaha	1st
27 March	Crystal Palace	250 Yamaha	1st
27 March	Crystal Palace	250 Yamaha	1st
27 March	Crystal Palace	350 Yamaha	6th
27 March	Crystal Palace	350 Yamaha	3rd
23 April	Brands Hatch (500M)	500 Velocette	4th

29 April	Castle Combe	250 Yamaha	1st
29 April	Castle Combe	250 Yamaha	1st
30 April	Mallory Park	250 Yamaha	3rd
30 April	Mallory Park	250 Yamaha	2nd
21 May	Clermont Ferrand	250 Yamaha	DNS
29 May	Brands Hatch	250 Yamaha	DNF
29 May	Brands Hatch	350 Yamaha	DNS
18 June	Mallory Park	250 Yamaha	3rd
18 June	Mallory Park	250 Yamaha	4th
18 June	Mallory Park	350 Yamaha	DNS
24 June	Oulton Park	250 Yamaha	4th
24 June	Oulton Park	250 Yamaha	DNF
24 June	Oulton Park	350 Yamaha	DNS
1 July	Castle Combe	250 Yamaha	1st
1 July	Castle Combe	250 Yamaha	DNF
30 July	Snetterton	250 Yamaha	DNS
30 July	Snetterton	350 Yamaha	DNF
20 August	Mallory Park	250 Yamaha	5th
20 August	Mallory Park	250 Yamaha	DNF
20 August	Mallory Park	350 Yamaha	DNF
28 August	Crystal Palace	250 Yamaha	1st
28 August	Crystal Palace	350 Yamaha	6th
3 September	Brands Hatch	250 Yamaha	DNF
3 September	Brands Hatch	350 Yamaha	DNF
17 September	Mallory Park	250 Yamaha	DNS
17 September	Mallory Park	350 Yamaha	DNF
1 October	Brands Hatch	250 Yamaha	DNF
1 October	Brands Hatch	350 Yamaha	DNF
15 October	Snetterton	250 Yamaha	4th
15 October	Snetterton	350 Yamaha	DNS
22 October	Brands Hatch	250 Yamaha	DNS
29 October	Mallory Park	250 Yamaha	2nd
29 October	Mallory Park	250 Yamaha	3rd

1968

| 12 May | Brands Hatch (500M) | 340 Ducati | 4th |
| 6–7 July | Barcelona (24Hr) | 250 Ducati | 1st |

Abbreviations

Twin   –   Twin cylinder road bike

P   –   Prototype – my home-built racer

SB   –   Show Bike – RAS 101 from Earls Court

W   –   Woolley's – Brian Woolley sponsored

Wks   –   Works – Yamaha Grand Prix machine

1000Km–   Bemsee 1000Km Production Bike Race

500M   –   500 mile Production Bike Race

250M   –   Endurance Race for 50cc machines

DNF   –   Started but Did Not Finish the race

DNS   –   Did Not Start in the race

Overall Summary

Career Races   223

Finished in   151 or 67.7% of races

Podiums   71 or 47% of finishes

Of which:

     Wins   33 or 21.8% of finishes

     Seconds 21 or 13.9% of finishes

     Thirds   17 or 11.3% of finishes

     Crashes 9 or 0.6% of finishes